Cement, Earthworms, and Cheese Factories

CEMENT, EARTHWORMS, AND CHEESE FACTORIES

Religion and Community Development in Rural Ecuador

JILL DeTEMPLE

University of Notre Dame Press

Notre Dame, Indiana

Manufactured in the United States of America

Library of Congress Cataloging-in-Publication Data

DeTemple, Jill Michelle.
    Cement, earthworms, and cheese factories : religion and community
development in rural Ecuador / by Jill DeTemple.
        p.   cm.
    Includes bibliographical references (p.   ) and index.
    ISBN 978-0-268-02611-0 (pbk.) — ISBN 978-0-268-07777-8 (e-book)
    1. Ecuador—Church history.   2. Church work with the poor—Ecuador.
3. Community development—Religious aspects—Christianity.   4. Community
development—Ecuador.   I. Title.
    BR690.D48   2012
    278.66'083—dc23

                                                            2012024894

In memory of

Eve Carson, Marcos Lucio, and Ramiro Martinez.

Luchando, luchando.

CONTENTS

Acknowledgments   ix

Introduction   1

ONE   "Things Both Good and Bad": Religion and   19
Development in Latin American Contexts

TWO   *La Lucha*: Negotiating Desire, Community, Religion,   37
and Progress in San Marcos

THREE   Pedagogies of Power: Alternative Developments   67

FOUR   Good Housekeeping: Negotiating Religion   103
and Development at Home

FIVE   Cement Things: Imagining Infrastructure,   137
Community, and Progress

SIX   Spiritual Cardiology: Wholeness, Becoming,   169
and (Dis)Integration

Conclusion: Truman's Earthworms   197

Notes   205
Bibliography   221
Index   241

ACKNOWLEDGMENTS

Many people and organizations in many places have made this book possible. In Ecuador, I am grateful to *familia* Martinez-Pacheco, who hosted me in my early days in the country, taught me Spanish, and became family. I also thank Carmen Bauz, who has given me shelter, warm tortillas, and unbounded enthusiasm for almost two decades, and the Lucio family, who have opened up their homes and lives in ways that have improved this work and made its existence feasible. I also thank Peace Corps–Ecuador, especially the headquarters and training staff, for allowing me to conduct research with a very fresh group of trainees. In the town I call San Marcos, I would like to extend special gratitude to the extensionists of the municipio, Santa Anita women's cooperative members, and the missionaries I call Joyce Davis and Ruth Bauer. All of them were more than generous with their time and resources, enriching this work with their comments and suggestions, and my life with the stories of theirs.

In North Carolina I owe a tremendous debt of gratitude to my adviser, Ruel Tyson, Jr., and to Laurie Maffly-Kipp, Charlie Thompson, Orin Starn, and Randall Styers, who read the earliest versions of this work with humor, skill, and critical eyes, and who epitomize a truly helpful dissertation committee. Arturo Escobar acted as mentor and cheerleader, and I thank him for his support. I am also grateful to the Tinker Foundation, which funded initial research for this project, and to the Graduate School at the University of North Carolina at Chapel Hill, which awarded me a dissertation completion fellowship when I needed it most. Maryellen Davis-Collett, Phil Hassett, Kathryn Lofton, Tom Pearson, Nora Rubel, and David Shefferman made graduate life enriching and enjoyable. The Danger Girls—Celeste Gagnon, Miranda Hassett, Marsha Michie, and Quincy Newell—improved my writing, my thinking, and my sense of humor in ways various and deep. Eve Carson and Anna Lassiter gave me new eyes with which to see San Marcos. Hope Toscher and Myra Covington Quick held my hand, loved on my newborn, fed me chocolate, and pushed through paperwork in ways I still deem heroic. You truly are the pillars of the earth.

At Southern Methodist University I am grateful for a University Research Council grant that allowed me to do fieldwork in Ecuador. Thanks too to my remarkable set of colleagues in the Religious Studies Department. Bill Barnard, Rick Cogley, Mark Chancey, Johan Elverskog, Serge Frolov, John Lamoreaux, and Steven Lindquist have all read pieces of this manuscript and contributed to a uniquely collegial and supportive environment in which to see it through to its completion. Peggy Varghese and Kenitra Brown proved that the title "department assistant" is an understatement of epic proportions. Thanks to both of them for support ranging from the mundane to the extraordinary. Thanks also to my students, especially Katye Dunn, Erin Eidenshink, Katie Josephson, Wesleigh Ogle, Robert Perales, Lindsey Geist, and Luke Friedman, all of whom took a special interest in this project and made some real contributions to it in conversations both in and out of the classroom. At the University of Notre Dame Press, special thanks to Chuck Van Hof, who gave this book a chance; Robyn Karkiewicz, who handled more details than I can imagine; and to the anonymous reviewers who took extraordinary care in reading the manuscript. Rebecca DeBoer and Margo Shearman provided keen editorial eyes and ears as they made the text sing. This work is better because of all of you.

Finally, this book would not be possible without the continual support and sacrifice of my husband, Brian Bunge—partner in Ecuador, partner for life. My sister, Rachel, has been a constant cheerleader. My parents, Janet and Duane DeTemple, not only gave me wings but exhibited unusual courage in letting me use them. I hope to do the same for Molly and John, who have already discovered the joys and the magic of running with scissors.

INTRODUCTION

"So, are you an evangelical, or what?" It was a misty afternoon in 1996 in a small community high in the Ecuadorian mountains. Vicente,[1] a middle-aged Catholic farmer, had paused as we worked together on a composting project, squinting at me over shovels and small creatures wriggling in our hands. He was "just checking," he explained after I assured him that I had no desire to change his religion. He had heard of other communities that had converted wholesale from Catholicism to Protestant Christianity in order to receive coveted development assistance—including water systems, microenterprises, and latrines— and he wanted to be sure that I wasn't one of the suspected evangelicals, using earthworms to win his soul. My curiosity piqued, I asked other people in the community if they had heard of evangelical Christians offering aid for conversion and came to learn that Vicente was not alone in his fears. "The Protestants!" one woman exclaimed as we sorted corn seed on her front porch, "They're taking over [*conquistando*] the world!"[2]

These comments, and countless others that I would hear from *campesinos* in Ecuador's Bolívar province as a development worker and later as a researcher, reflect rural Ecuadorians' keen awareness of changes in the religious makeup of Latin America which have marked the past thirty years. Since the 1980s Protestant Christian denominations, especially evangelical and Pentecostal churches, have attracted increasing numbers of Latin Americans. Brazil, almost exclusively Roman Catholic in 1970, is now less than 90 percent Roman Catholic, and 46.6 percent of Christians identify as charismatic or Pentecostal. Ecuador, which

1

had virtually no Protestant population in 1970 (1.4 percent), is now approximately 93 percent Roman Catholic, and the church is both growing more charismatic and losing about 2 percent of its adherents per year.[3] With such rapid change under way, Viche had a reason to query the religious status of the earthworms and their potential to be linked to conversion.

But Vicente's question also points to other changes that Ecuadorians have experienced as citizens of a "developing" country that receives approximately $60 million in U.S. foreign assistance annually, and which is home to more than one hundred NGOs (nongovernmental organizations) dedicated to development work.[4] The "boom" of NGOs engaged in overseas projects came after the end of the "development decades" of the 1950s–80s, when development was primarily under the auspices of government programs that emphasized national economic strategies, programs and restructuring. The increase in NGOs also reflects a shift in development strategies to more localized and "needs based" endeavors administered by local organizations. These trends have opened the door for faith-based organizations to become primary points of contact between the recipients of development and aid programs and the government donors that regularly fund them.[5]

While Vicente's question and the remarks of the woman on the porch point to recent situations in which religion and development have become entangled in donor agencies and sites of reception, the woman's comment offhandedly invoking the Conquest of the New World by Spanish forces evokes a much longer entanglement of religion and development. I was surprised at Vicente's question because I believed myself to be in Ecuador holding earthworms and fielding questions about my religious motivations because of what I saw as a secular system of international assistance launched at the end of the Second World War. Vicente's question, however, points to a longer and more complicated history that has mixed religious change and technological innovation from times before Europeans set foot in the Americas. It also highlights religion, development, and their confluence in rural areas as spaces in which Ecuadorians and other actors in the "developing" world negotiate the contours of that world.

These negotiations, constitutive of modernity, simultaneously refute the secularization model of 1960s social scientists, embrace some aspects of "needs based," "alternative," and "capabilities" approaches to development while refusing others, and highlight the roles of desire, place, and embodiment in both religious and development practices. These are themes I returned to Bolívar to investigate during summer research trips in 2000 and 2001, for ten months in 2002–3, and again for summer season research in 2006 as I lived and worked in San Marcos, a cantonal capital of six thousand people at the intersection of the mountainous and coastal regions of the province.

San Marcos was an excellent field site because several development agencies, both secular and religiously affiliated, are active in the area and have been for more than twenty years. San Marcos is home to North American evangelical missionaries, Jehovah's Witnesses, two growing Pentecostal congregations, and an active and vital Catholic Church. In many cases, development and religion are elided in the lives of people and institutions, making their overlap, and the play of religion and development as local and global phenomena, relatively easy to see and talk about.

San Marcos's status as a cantonal capital in a rural area also made it attractive as a study site. The weekly market draws people into town from a wide area, revealing the give-and-take of development and religion as institutions that connect people over space and time, as well as a moving snapshot of local politics and people. As the regional political center, San Marcos is home to many government development programs. The agricultural extensionists from one of these programs, UMATA (Unidad Municipal de Asistencia Técnica Agropecuaria— Municipal Team for Small Farm Assistance), invited me to join them for projects in San Marcos and in Sinche, a coastal community. Every two weeks, I crowded into a municipal truck, a four-wheel-drive vehicle— or, as the funding for the program dwindled, onto a series of buses— and made the trek to the coastal region of the canton with UMATA employees to plant seedlings, talk about guinea pigs, or plan for future projects. When not with UMATA, I attended the weekly meetings of the Catholic Santa Anita women's cooperative, and also spent time with Ruth Bauer and Joyce Davis, two evangelical missionaries who had lived and worked in San Marcos for almost thirty years. All of these groups included people eager to talk, and I conducted more than sixty in-depth interviews, as well as dozens of informal interviews and discussions with group and association members, project participants, and people from San Marcos and surrounding communities.

My initial questions during the early stages of my research echoed Vicente's. I wanted to know if people were switching religious affiliation to garner development aid offered by faith-based organizations, and how they decided to make such a change. Very early on, however, I realized that this was not the most useful trajectory. Anthropological and economic studies on "social capital" had already examined religious affiliation as a determinant factor in the success of development projects, and such studies often had the effect of characterizing religion in moral functionalist terms, citing religion as something that was likely to keep communities together due to shared "values" and "understanding," which aided in collective goals and strategies to implement development projects.[6] Communities that prayed together, many scholars and faith-based development practitioners hypothesized, might be more likely to stay together and to take ownership of development processes, goals, and the daily work required for success.[7]

These moral and functional descriptions of religion, however, failed to account adequately for religious experiences, institutional structures, and points of contact with other parts of daily life evident in central Ecuador. Vicente's question points to the ways in which religion affects social constructions not just of communities but also of objects and places, and the ways in which those objects and places become involved in religious understandings of the world, a process similar to what American religious historian Robert Orsi has termed "lived religion." Orsi writes that "Workplaces, homes and streets—as well as churches, temples, shrines, class meetings and other more immediately recognizable sites of religious activity—are the places humans make something of the world they have found themselves thrown into, and, in turn, it is through these subtle, intimate, quotidian actions on the world that meanings are made, known and verified. 'Religion' is best approached . . . by meeting men and women at this daily task, in all the spaces of their experience."[8] Religious meaning and experience are sited, multivalent, and ripe for entanglement with a wide variety of actors, ideas, places, and things. Earthworms, shovels, and a foreign technical adviser may all be used to encounter, produce, and make sense of religious worlds.

Development is similarly produced and experienced in daily tasks and spaces. As I lived and worked with my husband, Brian, in San Marcos—sharing a courtyard with our landlady, her children, and a variety of domesticated animals—we were often engaged in the daily work of "progress" as we fed the "improved" guinea pigs kept in a cage with which we shared a wall, and as we installed an on-demand, electric "Frankenstein" shower in our outdoor bathroom. Lucía, the woman from whom we leased our two-room cinderblock house, used our rent money to make improvements on her property, amassing materials for a new kitchen and adding a greenhouse to her garden across the street with Brian's help. We often talked as we met in the process of doing laundry in the courtyard *lavandería,* Brian and Lucía comparing tips and tricks for making the labor-intensive work go faster. In San Marcos, this kind of work, and the language of its planning and improvement, are summed up in "*la lucha,*" the fight or struggle of everyday existence. Religion—specifically Christianity—and development are a part and parcel of the *lucha,* acting as guides for its enactment at the same time that they promise liberation from its unceasing necessity.

It is this liberatory promise that has caused some scholars to compare development to religion, dubbing both "transcendent." Arturo Escobar, Gilbert Rist, Wolfgang Sachs, and others writing as "postdevelopment" scholars in the 1990s roundly criticized international economic development (IED), arguing that it had become an idealized form of colonialism with universal westernization as its ultimate goal.[9] This view characterized development as a discourse made up of ideologies and programs that shaped global thinking about a normative "progress" based on Western and largely secular ideals. As a transcendent discourse, international economic development seemed composed of the stuff of "global faith," its ontological status as a global good unassailable even in the face of evidence that it had failed to work.[10]

Certainly, development, like religion, possesses some of this transcendent, even sacred, quality. Development and religion are discourses that supersede physical, ideological, and chronological boundaries. Religious traditions such as Christianity and Judaism, like development, exist as "things in themselves" even as they are, as J. Z. Smith warns, categories, "creation[s] of scholars' study."[11] But religion and development are not experienced or enacted in that transcendent, transnational, transhistorical realm. Rather, religion and development are "lived" and often become entangled in the quotidian world of bedrooms, kitchens, organizational meetings, and buildings. Lived development, like lived religion, is invented, contested, produced, and reproduced in the places, objects, and stuff of everyday life.

It is in these spaces, as well as in the networks spun by global forces, that religion and development become entangled, acting on one another even as they act on the experiences, perceptions, and production of meaning of those whose lives they touch. Development and religion are embedded not only within one another, but within the moving and volatile streams of neoliberal capitalism, the U.S. "plan" to rid Colombia and Ecuador of coca production, and the amorphous "war on terror" that has revived many of the early "hearts and minds" campaigns of the American anti-communist era. The long interaction among religion, development, and the global forces in which they are entangled attests to their deployment and the consequences of that deployment, as Ecuadorians, like so many people in what we have come to call the "developing world," engage in a continuing struggle for agency and identity in their courtyards, kitchens, fields, and bedrooms.

Indeed, the entanglement of religion and development in the contemporary Andes reveals, in a particularly clear light, processes of continual negotiations about the meaning of modernity, about its legitimacy and authority in daily life. Where Ecuadorians encounter religious and development ideologies and apparatuses, they often strategically respond to those ideologies and apparatuses, incorporating, changing, and rejecting them in ways frequently unintended by those with whom such discourses originate. The nature of these negotiations, especially as they play out in the creative spaces of homes and communities, points to a modernity in which people remain invested in retaining traditional cosmologies and life ways, even as they redefine and support those cosmologies and life ways using the tools and language of "progress." What remains contested is the nature of that "progress" and the right to define its parameters and end goals. A focus on the intersection of "the modern" as it is embodied in lived religious and development spaces exposes the ways in which Ecuadorians are continually reforming not only Christianity and development, but modernity itself.

In naming these processes of negotiation and contestation a *reformation* of modernity, I am consciously invoking the religious and historical overtones embedded in the Protestant Reformation of sixteenth-century Europe. Specifically, I highlight processes of contestation, change, restoration, and struggle which characterized the European Reformation. I also highlight mechanisms of production, reproduction, and pedagogy which make what Arjun Appadurai calls the "global imagination of modernity," and thus its global negotiation in local spaces, possible.[12]

Here, some clarification in terminology will be useful. By modernity, I mean the particular worldview, predominant in Europe beginning in the sixteenth century and especially prominent in Western societies during industrialization, which favors an ethos of rationality, progress, mechanization, specialization, and a distinctive break from the past. Many philosophers in the Enlightenment era sought to define an enlightened, rational modernity against tradition, and specifically its incarnation in religion, claiming, as did David Hume in his *Natural History of Religion,* that "ignorance is the mother of devotion."[13] For Max Weber, writing more than a century later, modernity, and in particular capitalist modernity in Protestant contexts, was defined by a continual de-sacralization of daily life. Weber's "iron cage" of meaningless, profane work is one ultimate expression of this divide.[14]

More recent scholarship has described the defining feature of modernity as that of a "rupture" that has reconfigured, and continues to reconfigure, social constructions of reality and possibility.[15] Characterizing modernity as "the everyday cultural practices though which the work of the imagination is transformed," Arjun Appadurai rejects a hierarchical model in which modernity is invented by Western elites and remains out of the reach of the majority of the world. Rather, Appadurai argues, processes of globalization, and specifically a global media coupled with migration, have expanded modernity beyond simple, geographically described boundaries of rationality or progress to an expanded, changing, and universal imaginative field.

My analysis begins at this point of universality, seeking to describe its deployment, and the consequences of that deployment, at a specific place and time. Such a starting point necessarily rejects a view of modernity as transcendent or invulnerable to the discourses and global forces in which it is produced and reproduced. As Bruno Latour has argued—and as the continued marriage of religious and development discourses illustrates—modernity's hallmark division of nature and culture, tradition and progress, is continually breached.

Latour's discussion of modernity, in which he outlines a "modern Constitution" that divides nature from culture and science from politics despite the proliferation of their hybrid forms, is particularly helpful as we examine the roles of religion and development in contemporary Ecuador. Beginning with the assertion that modernity is often described in human terms, as the "birth" or the "death" of a certain kind of humanism, Latour makes the argument that modernity is equally defined by the invention and separation of a nonhuman world composed of things, objects, and beasts. Like a system of government that appoints judicial authority to one branch and legislative to another, the modern constitution declares that science shall be humanity's access to nature—the world of things that has an unchanging ontological status. Politics shall be the space in which discourses concerning the social shall take place.[16] God, Latour argues, must remain "crossed out," removed to the sidelines so that God's dual status as a natural and social being does not interfere with either side of the modern divide. "No one is truly modern," writes Latour, "who does not agree to keep God from interfering with Natural Law as well as with the laws of the Republic."[17]

The problem with this constitution, and with modernity as a seemingly self-evident and self-contained state, Latour goes on to argue, is that the divide that defines modernity is impossible to maintain in practice. A hallmark of the modern state, for example, Ecuadorian road construction is often the center of social and scientific debate that ranges from indigenous land and cultural rights to the feasibility of constructing international highways on muddy jungle floors and steep mountain slopes.[18] Billboards sponsored by the Ministry of Transportation and Public Works in 2002 depicted a stylized road leading into the sunset of an equally idealized future as a caption proclaimed, "Only one way, only one road, the development of the country!"

These entangling processes have ensured that religion maintains and even strengthens its presence in the early twenty-first century despite predictions of its demise. Scholars have noted this, and many focus on religion as they seek to redefine modernity or explain the instability of its operational terms. Some have theorized, for example, that the rise of global fundamentalism, be it Christian or Islamic, indicates a resurgent resistance to modernity, usually characterized in terms of rationality and technology, and its incarnation in globalization. In this vein, David Martin and Harvey Cox described the rise of global Pentecostalism in the 1990s as an expression of resistance, both to the exploitations of capitalist systems and to a certain hegemony of the rational. In ways similar to music, Cox theorized, speaking in tongues and laying on hands allow Pentecostal practitioners to recapture something primal, a divine truth and eschatological hope that biblical exegesis and medical science leave behind.[19] By pitting jihad against McWorld, Benjamin Barber also pointed to religion as that which resists a certain form of modernity, here encapsulated in globalization.[20] All of these authors set religious practice and expression against science, or the rational, and pointed to the conflict itself as the hallmark of the times in which we live.

What I suggest here, however, is that what we are witnessing in the rise of mainline Protestant, Pentecostal, and charismatic Christianity in the Southern Hemisphere, and in fundamentalist strains of religion globally, is not so much a resistance to modernity, but, again, a significant reformation of its terms and conditions, enacted, as was the Protestant Reformation, through vehicles of negotiation. It is, in many senses, a restorationist movement, though not one that should be taken to be pure or transcendent. Religious fundamentalists, missionaries, development workers, and many rural Ecuadorians with whom they come into contact and who do their work, are not so much pitting faith against rationality, as Cox and Martin suggested, as they are arguing against ideas of rationality and progress that leave faith and religious or "traditional" ways of knowing behind. When medical missionaries distribute Bibles with bandages and sermons with surgeries, they do not reject medical science but "restore" to it sets of values and meaning they feel a compartmentalized modernity has abandoned. When rural Ecuadorians either accept or reject their medical care and/or the religious messages that accompany it, they join the missionaries in establishing meaning and agency, sometimes meeting missionaries in their vision of integration, and sometimes refusing to accept the combinatory message they offer. Missionaries and their clients are engaged in processes of negotiation that work to reform the meaning and significance of progress, its desirability and its contours, in the modern world.

The ways that people perceive and negotiate the discourses of religion and development as they have and do come together and break apart in their homes, communities, and national life are as vital and as varied as the discourses themselves. A careful attention to this negotiation displaces many of the common and disempowering tales of a hegemonic development invented, implemented, and analyzed solely by a (neo)colonial and secular West. Development, and indeed modernity, have not only never been secular, they have never been entirely Western in their invention, application, or possibility as a source of local knowledge and power.

Orientation: Three Scenes from the Road

My choice of San Marcos as a site in which to research religion as an academic came partially out of my experiences working in development as a Peace Corps volunteer. Having lived a little more than two years in Bolívar province as an agricultural extensionist, I came to this project with some idea of local concerns and with a working vocabulary for the realities of agricultural development. I knew whom to talk to at the Ministry of Agriculture office and at the feed-and-seed store. I also came into the project knowing that I had friends and family up the road. While I had not worked in San Marcos before, I knew people who had, and they paved the way for an unusually smooth entrance into the community. Much of the difficult work of orientation was done before I arrived.

What follows are three scenes from San Marcos, meant to do similar work in orientation to some of the spaces and circumstances in which religion and development interact, and to the consequences of that interaction as they manifest in the particular modes of desire, community, and a tension between what Ecuadorians call "cement things" and newer expressions of development which focus less on infrastructure and more on social and communal wholeness and becoming. These scenes are a prologue, an introduction to some of the people, places, and institutions that occupy these pages. They are the beginning of my attempt, using the tools of ethnography and historical, religious, political, and economic analyses, to answer Vicente's question about the religious status of my earthworms more thoroughly than I did that day in 1996. These scenes acknowledge that his intimations about the connections between religious and technological change were well founded, and continue to merit inquiry as he and others in his community negotiate a growing and complicated array of development and religious institutions, ideologies, and practices.

Birth

Coming into the small house in Puyupamba, Henry Palacios and a visiting medical resident moved quickly to the midwife and her patient, asking questions. They were relieved to find that the woman had been in labor for only a few hours, despite the worried words of her husband when he interrupted their supper in the evangelical Runa (indigenous) church across the street in order to summon their help. The baby, it seemed, was correctly positioned for a normal delivery, and labor was proceeding unexceptionally.

With this established, Henry, an HCJB medical missionary,[21] knelt down next to the midwife, ready to work. It was soon apparent, however, that his North American upbringing and medical school education had limited merit in the context of the Runa birthing style in which a woman squats, supported by a sister or other female relative. He couldn't see anything, the doctor complained, telling the crowd that had gathered in the room that he "[had] no training for this position." Smiling, Ruth, a fellow HCJB missionary who had lived and worked in San Marcos for almost thirty years, commented that he should look again. The baby's head was crowning.

Henry's remarks were the topic of conversation for those of us returning to San Marcos for the night in "Moses," the Chevy Suburban that houses HCJB medical caravan supplies and people. As we rode into town, dodging potholes on the dark and muddy road, Ruth told stories of her time in the field, recounting some heroic deeds in a breech delivery a few years before. A trained nurse, she had acted as midwife, negotiating a tangled umbilical cord and four gangly limbs coming into the world in reverse order. "I've seen all kinds of things," she mused as we rounded a corner and the lights of San Marcos came into view.

Party X

For the most part, the meeting had gone well. The municipal agricultural team had survived the ride to Sinche in the *alcalde*'s (regional mayor's) Chevy Vitara, dropping more than a thousand meters on the slippery dirt road to the coast with few problems. In Sinche, on the coastal plains at the southern extent of the canton, forty peasant farmers had gathered, and thus far sat attentively as the agricultural team and the *alcalde* spoke about the projects they had accomplished during their time in office. The election was only a month in the future, and the group was giving a technical talk in lieu of attending a rally for their political party, Lista X, that was taking place in Guaranda, the provincial capital.[21]

Assuring folks that the meeting in Sinche was not a political event, a municipal extensionist took the floor and explained that the municipio used to work only in infrastructure, in "*cosas de cemento*" (cement things). Now, however, they had begun to work in agriculture, directly with farmers. He then asked what the people gathered for the meeting thought they needed, commenting that it is better to respond to actual needs than merely to divine what those needs might be. "We're here," he said, "because we won't accept conditions as they are." At the same time, he continued, "we're not bringing anything new, not inventing anything. We're here to help you change and become what you want to be."

When he had finished, a middle-aged woman in indigenous dress spoke from the back of the crowd. Her voice rising in frustration, she explained that this kind of meeting and talk of agricultural progress was all well and good, but the real problem locally was the lack of a viable road. The municipio in San Marcos had promised the people of Sinche a grader and a bulldozer to make repairs. Where were they? Why didn't the people of Sinche have a route to the highway?

Blessed among Women

Leaving town, the members of the Santa Anita Catholic Women's Association were exasperated, confused, and angry, upset at the turmoil that had delayed their departure and the relaxed and happy atmosphere of the previous afternoon. The women were headed to Guayco, home to a Catholic shrine marking an apparition of the Virgin Mary, and on this day, to a celebration of International Women's Day sponsored by the Salesian priests who oversee the cooperative's parent organization, Promoción Humana (Human Promotion). The bus they had hired, however, had not arrived to pick them up, canceled by the cooperative's president when it appeared that not enough women wanted to attend the event. Only a great deal of scrambling and the aid of family connections to a bus owner restored the possibility of vehicular transport to the occasion. While the group was well organized and profitable in their knitting and cheese-making endeavors, events such as Women's Day often sent tempers flaring with additional work, time commitments, and administrative hassles.

The tension on the bus was palpable until a cooperative member broke the general silence by suggesting that the group sing a song to the Virgin. Hesitantly, the women did so, asking for the Virgin's blessing in a simple rhythm. As they neared the top of the hill on the way out of town, the song ended and the same woman began a compressed Hail Mary, her voice low over the growl of the struggling engine. "Hail Mary, blessed among women, pray for us today and in the hour of our death." She repeated the petition, quietly, until most of us on the bus joined with her, creating a delicate concordance as our voices came together: word with word, breath with breath.

All of these scenes—the birth in Puyupamba, the meeting and agricultural talk in Sinche, and the cooperative trip to the Women's Day event—are snapshots of the way development, and often religion, deploy in Marqueños' daily lives.[22] In homes, at meetings, on buses, development and religion are part of the social fabric of San Marcos, woven into events as singular as birth and as mundane as organizational meetings and bus rides. Development and religion are global forces, but they are experienced and recreated locally.

Indeed, these snapshots illustrate some of the ways religion and development interact on the ground, as Henry put it, in "positions." In particular, they highlight *desire, community,* and tensions between "cement things" and "becoming" as sites of negotiation created by the interplay of religious and development discourses; as sites where actors employ those discourses to shape social and physical manifestations of "progress."

The Runa man's desire for the presence of an American medical doctor even though it was not required and the woman's plea for a road point to desire as a foundational experience of development, one that is simultaneously facilitated and proscribed by religious institutions and beliefs. Negotiations around desire—its necessity, utility, and dangers—are central as Ecuadorians position themselves in the spaces of bedrooms, institutions, and economies. They are also negotiations that highlight "community" as an important and often troubled ideal, something demonstrated by the cooperative members' use of a religious trope to regain harmonious relations among themselves, the self-conscious denial of political community by the extensionists, and also by the indigenous woman's resistance to "community" and communal "becoming" as an idealized development goal at the meeting. Flexible, political, and often transient, idealized notions of community often drive development and religious projects, and require negotiations about the nature of community in planning sessions, applications, buildings, and the private spaces of bedrooms and kitchens as food, sex, and clothing mark group identity and affiliation. In a similar manner, the tension between the need for "cement things" such as infrastructure and roads, and social development, marked by the extensionists in Sinche as "becoming," highlights similarities between moral, participatory aspects of religion and its counterpart in more recent "alternative" and "participatory" development discourses. Negotiating in planning sessions, bedrooms, and congregational meetings, Ecuadorians work to balance physical needs with social histories and questions over definitions of a "good life" (*buena vida/vida mejorada*).

While questions about what constitutes "progress" are one theoretical axis, tensions between local spaces and global forces are another.

Desire, community, and the tension between "becoming" and "cement things" are both locally positioned and the result of globalization and modernity, imagined as universal processes. Each of the three scenes we just visited took place "on the road" not just in a physical sense, but also in the way that the possibility of their occurrence depended upon a play of ideas and actions that spread beyond national borders and strictly held notions of self-evident cultures and places. The reality of an American doctor proclaiming that he had no training for "this position" at a Runa birth is one made possible only through the advent of development as a certain kind of global practice, one that in this case depended on a particular reading of Christian mission. In a similar manner, the fact that the women's cooperative is supported by Salesian priests, many from Italy, speaks to a deployment of development that is nothing if not global, part of what Manuel Castells called a "space of flows" that links continents, people, ideologies, and desires.[23] To speak of religion or development in Ecuador is to speak of religion and development, and of their concomitant political complexities, in the United States, Japan, the European Union, and Africa. It is to recognize the fluid interplay of global forces that encompass everything from college mission trips to neoliberal capitalism in local settings.

To best reflect these kinds of combinations and fluidities, I have invented and employed my own brand of hybridity. I have closely combined my home field of religious studies with cultural anthropology, and have also pulled from political science, cultural studies, history, Andean studies, and economics in order to examine the multifaceted ways in which actors construct and experience religion and development as ideologies, discourses, and practices. This hybridity allows sufficient theoretical amplitude to examine scenes such as the agricultural talk in Sinche not only in the context of the sociopolitical realities that infused the meeting with certain tensions (or inspired the meeting as a political device), but also with an eye to the global economic forces that drive government involvement in development projects. It is a hybridity that contextualizes the woman's request for a road, as well as the reasons she was compelled to make such a request.

Necessarily, this approach is also informed by on-the-ground training and experiences from my time as a development worker. My personal and professional "routes," as James Clifford so aptly describes them, have resulted in a proliferation of networks that often link contrary or conflicting schools of thought, most notably a sharp critique of development in the poststructural vein with direct involvement in development projects, based in my experiences both as a former Peace Corps volunteer and as a researcher.[24] In my work, I have had to do what I argue rural Ecuadorians, as well as religious and development personnel, do: negotiate workable hybrids of ideologies, discourses, actions, and analytical tools. The result is a critique of both the poststructuralist position, which sometimes overemphasizes a discourse of power and underemphasizes genuine human need, and the blind faith in development that Rist and Escobar outline.

Reading Development Religiously

More than anything else, however, this book takes religion seriously. If there is something unique it is not the use of history, economics, or anthropology as disciplinary lenses appropriate for the study of development. Rather, the use of these methods in concert with the techniques of religious studies—most notably an emphasis on experience and aesthetics rather than on more sociological models favoring social status or moral functionalism—better reflects how religion and development are related in contemporary ideologies and practices. This means reading the Ministry of Transportation and Public Works billboard proclaiming there is only "one way" toward the development of the country, and development more generally, religiously. The institutions, encounters, and social structures that development produces are examined with an eye toward the religious imagery and histories that underlie their design. Without such a reading, the development depicted on the sign in words and colorful images is too easily reduced to a rhetoric of modernity and progress, too easily subsumed into a single, exclusively Western genealogy of state formation and the consequences of a colonial world. By "reading" the billboard—and development—religiously, by using an expanded genealogical gaze to include a multitude of trajectories, many of them outside formal state structures, one can begin to see the places where both development and religion are produced, disappear, change and, more than occasionally, come together. Reading development religiously, it is possible to engage the subject in every sense of that word: with care, dedication, and openness to the possibility that religions, as institutions and networks of belief and practices, remain in the picture.

In its subject and its methodology, then, this book necessarily entertains broader inquiries about the nature and study of religion in the twenty-first century. To examine religion as a part of development, and to admit that development may influence religious ideologies and practices, is to recognize the embedded nature of these discourses and also their ability to travel. Religion is not only a "global flow" that carries information and ideas in and of itself. Rather, religion is also a hitchhiker, piggybacking on other ideologies and movements as they run through new and well-worn channels of government, goods, tourism, and trade. Like these global forces, it is negotiated locally, in the spaces of cheese factories, bedrooms, parks, and community centers. This study takes such movement—and such alliances—seriously, arguing that understanding how religion moves, and paying attention to the company it keeps, is vital if we are to understand the evolving role of religion in the contemporary world.

Chapter 1 emphasizes this kind of movement as it traces the religious origins of development, working to unseat overly secular explanations of its beginnings or operations in the contemporary world. The second chapter then begins the work of positioning with an ethnographic description of a fiftieth wedding anniversary celebration. It elucidates family networks and a greater history of place as it explores modes of development, modernity, and Christianity in San Marcos. Chapter 3 examines development ideologies and practices as they relate to power, concentrating on the "participatory/alternative development" emphases on pedagogy and integration as they manifest in the training of U.S. Peace Corps volunteers. Chapter 4 continues to incorporate economic and ethnographic modes of analysis as it plays on Enrique Mayer's extensive studies of Andean household economics. It focuses on the household as a point of contact between many development projects and religious practices, and gives special attention to the role of desire and agency. Chapter 5 extends this idea by exploring the ways development networks create religious/development hybrids in projects such as the creation and dedication of the Santa Anita cheese factory. This chapter also includes a discussion of community as an idealized form of infrastructure in development discourses. Chapter 6 returns to the three scenes presented in this introduction, offering an interpretation that considers the "wholeness" rhetoric of evangelical missionaries in the light of development and modernist discourses of completion and separation, and their local incorporation and rejection in San Marcos. The conclusion returns to the theme of negotiation in the context of development, assessing agency and the possibility of a truly indigenous, localized paradigm of progress.

Finally, the interaction of religion and development is the product of a certain kind of modernity, one that has, in Latour's words, "never been [fully] modern." In examining development as a platform where hybrids are created and rejected, as a space of flows where various networks come together and break apart, I am exploring a certain perception of, reaction to, and reformation of modernity. Doing so with a particular emphasis on the ways that religion and development interact in the lived experience of Ecuadorians, and in the lives of aid personnel and of people working in the mission field, challenges Latour's assertion that the God of modernity must be "crossed out." Rather, for many Ecuadorians God has come to dwell—sometimes quietly, sometimes with great fanfare—in the cinder blocks, ledger books, bandages, and earthworms of which development is made.

"THINGS BOTH GOOD AND BAD"

Religion and Development in Latin American Contexts

October 16, 2002. The students at the public high school in San Marcos, many of whom are from outlying communities in the canton and board in local rooms in order to complete their secondary education, gathered in the school's central courtyard and athletic area to hear a speech about Columbus Day, also marked (and protested) as Día de la Raza by indigenous groups throughout the Americas. He spoke to the assembled youth through a loudspeaker that could be heard throughout the neighborhood. The principal began his talk by noting Columbus's "bravery" in his voyages to the Americas, and also the lasting legacy that the encounter between Europe and Latin America left. "He brought things," the principal noted, "both good and bad to our world." Among the good were "religion, civil society, law, and technology." The bad went unmentioned by name.

The principal's speech bookended two hallmarks of European modernity—civil society and law—with religion on one end and technology on the other. Such an encapsulation highlights both the enmeshed nature of religion and development and also their relationship with modernity, even as the context for the speech underscores colonial processes and the roles of religious and technological change in systems of oppression. This chapter explores these entanglements, offering a broad genealogy of development that reflects Latin American, and more specifically Marqueño, histories, histories that challenge accounts

19

that separate religious and development processes. Development, I suggest, has its roots in religious ideals and institutions, roots that continue to influence and mold its implementation and reception in the contemporary world.

In the Beginning: Development as Discourse

Unearthing these roots requires some genealogical work tracing the dual and often tangled histories of development and religion within Ecuador and beyond its borders. It also requires a certain clarity in terminology. "Religion" throughout this work is, following Clifford Geertz, Thomas Tweed, and Mark C. Taylor, a broadly recognized system of symbols, practices, and shared narratives that people use to explain, construct, and destabilize reality in specific times and places, a reality that both reflects and defines those times and places.[1] It is also, going beyond (or perhaps behind) Geertz and into the realm of Weber, an institutionalization of that system and behaviors related to it. In Ecuador this is a social formation most often manifested in Christianity, be it Catholic or Protestant, and as we shall see, the Western and institutional biases inherent in a simple definition of "religion," or even of "Christianity," are often troubled in local practice.

"Development" is an equally problematic term. In tracing development's genealogy vis-à-vis religion, I conceive it as a discourse that encompasses local struggles for improvements in basic living conditions, as well as national and international institutions and political actions that combine and work together. I imagine development as a cluster of entities, practices, and ideologies that are at once material and moral, and which define, enforce, and resist systems of power. Development, in Ecuador and beyond its borders, is not and has never been a single entity, but is rather best characterized as a set of ideologies and practices—a discourse—which bears what Ludwig Wittgenstein called "family resemblances." "We see," wrote Wittgenstein in *Philosophical Investigations,* "a complicated network of similarities, overlapping and criss-crossing; sometimes overall similarities, and sometimes similarities in detail. I can think of no better expression than to characterize these similarities as 'family resemblances'; for the various resemblances between members of a family: build, features, colour of eyes, gait, temperament, etc. etc. overlap and criss-cross in the same way."[2] It is these family resemblances that give development some of its particular and recognizable form, allowing it to exist in what Wittgenstein so aptly called "a complicated network of similarities, overlapping and criss-crossing" the landscapes it touches and helps to create.

While it is broad, then, and widely traveled, development is not unlimited. The new technologies the Inca and the Spanish introduced to the people living in what is now Ecuador were not part of a concerted program of progress in its modern sense. They cannot properly be termed "development." However, Inca and Spanish technological agendas may have shared many of the same attributes that came to characterize formal development programs.

By the same token, not every innovation or change that appears on the Ecuadorian landscape today can be properly classified as "development," though, again, such change may possess much of the same look and language of programs offered by development organizations. Development, like any discourse, forms lineages that gradually lose similarity to the parent model, eventually creating new, if distantly related, and recognizable ways of being in the world.[3] It is caught up in histories well outside its incarnation as an international program of advancement. Development also takes on new appearances and modes of operation, many of them tangled in other discourses, including, as indicated by the principal's speech, religion and politics. Indeed, it is in places like the speech—one of scores of points on development's genealogical periphery—that many of the hybrid forms development creates may be found. In exploring these points, it becomes possible to determine how Ecuadorian recipients of development aid, and religious and development personnel who serve them, see and experience development as an evolving discourse that has often wandered quite far from the technical side of its heritage. It becomes possible to better understand the crisscrossed, combinatory and shifting paths that development and Christianity, and the people promoting and resisting both, have created and traveled.

The beginning of one of these paths, and a place scholars often locate development's origins, is at the close of the Second World War, and specifically U.S. President Harry Truman's 1949 "Point Four" inaugural address. Speaking to an American people victorious and prosperous in the postwar boom period, the new president promised a "fair deal" in four parts to "make the benefits of our [Western] scientific advances and industrial progress available for the improvement and growth" of Third World nations.[4] Coupled with the formation of the International Monetary Fund and the World Bank five years earlier, Truman's "fair-dealing" led to the formation of a massive, international infrastructure designed to "modernize" and, less overtly, westernize the daily lives of "poor" people all over the world.[5]

This book is a direct consequence of that infrastructure. Forty-five years after Truman's speech, I arrived in Ecuador as a U.S. Peace Corps volunteer, intent on spending just over two years working on sustainable agriculture projects in a rural Ecuadorian community. At the time, I traced my lineage to U.S. President John F. Kennedy, who inaugurated the Peace Corps in 1961 as a Cold War initiative to foster international friendship and the transfer of technical skills. The basis of Kennedy's vision, and my position, however, was Truman's "fair deal." I came to Ecuador in early 1994 because of and sharing in Truman's assumptions about a worldwide need for Western assistance and "progress."

During my three months of technical, linguistic, and cultural training near Quito, I also assumed that I was involved in a secular project. Helping families acquire seeds for family gardens, planting fruit trees, and promoting integrated pest management as an alternative to chemical use were activities, in my experience, outside of any religious sphere—physical stuff, but certainly not the stuff of which metaphysics is made. I did not therefore pay much attention to repeated questions about my religious identity when I began work in the small community that had requested an agricultural extensionist. If people were asking, I thought, it was because they were interested in me as an odd, vaguely Protestant foreigner in their midst. Day after day, as we planted saplings and discussed the potential market for carrots and quinoa, I explained that I was a Unitarian, part of a remote, Protestant branch of their Roman Catholicism.

Vicente's questions about the earthworms, however, along with the woman's comment that both predicted a Protestant takeover and offhandedly evoked the *Conquista* that brought Spanish religion, technology, and bureaucratic structures to the New World, point to a long entanglement of religion and development that precedes Truman's 1949 speech by a considerable amount of time. If I was in Ecuador holding earthworms and fielding questions about my religious motivations because of Truman, Vicente was asking these questions because of a much longer and more complicated history.

Progressions: Development as Global Eschatology

While Truman's speech marks the eruption of development as a discrete discourse, development's roots reach further back to Enlightenment ideals of progress. These are ideals that postdevelopment critics, in particular, point out in their deconstruction of development ideologies and apparatuses. Writing in *The Post-Development Reader,* Teodor Shanin gives a particularly succinct definition. "Progress," he says, is the idea that ". . . all societies are advancing naturally and consistently 'up,' on a route from poverty, barbarism, despotism and ignorance to riches, civilization, democracy and rationality, the highest expectation of which is science."[6] Development, in other words, is an ideal predicated upon a belief in a common human destination based on universal human capacity for reason, the "only one way" of the Ministry of Public Works billboard by the side of the road. Founded on an eschatology of progress, development thus appears to be wholly modern in its preference for rationality, industry, and science over emotion, nature, tradition, or religion.

The imagery and phrasing of the M.O.P. billboard—evocative of evangelical signs that remind Ecuadorians that Jesus is "the way, the truth and the life," and that "only through [him] can one get to the Father" (John 14:6)—and the principal's list of the "goods and bads" of Columbus's journeys to the New World, remind us that the flip side of progress and rationality—tradition and desire—are always nearer than they seem.[7] This is certainly true in the case of development. Christian theologies of salvation preceded development as a global, hegemonic phenomenon. The assumption that two-thirds of the world is impoverished and needs to be "lifted out" of that condition by the wonders of Western technology is not so different from Spanish justifications of New World conquest for the sake of Christianizing and saving Native Americans, or late nineteenth- and early twentieth-century Protestant missions to "unreached peoples" for the sake of "saving the whole world in this generation."[8]

Indeed, the "discovery" of the New World was in many ways the beginning of the family of ideologies and actions we now call development. Even as they begin their own genealogies of development in the Enlightenment era, Shanin and fellow development scholar José María Sbert point to progress as an organizing societal principle that emerged in response to European encounters with the New World. As Europeans came into contact with the vast and undeniable diversity of humanity in the course of global exploration, they needed a way to make sense of difference.[9] The rise of progress and rationality as ordering principles was a response that allowed Europeans to classify diversity, aligning alterity along an axis of advancement. If Western technologies, societal structures, and religious systems were the natural *telos* of humanity, the conquest and conversion of American peoples were justified in order to bring them forward to the light of reason and salvation. Any attempt to understand the complete history of development, then, must depart from this age of contact and examine European encounters in the New World, working to find the overlap between conquest and mission, civilization and salvation which came to be rendered simultaneously as "things both good and bad" and "only one way."

Converting Conquest

Wednesday, October 10, 1492. The admiral sailed west-southwest.
They traveled—at ten miles an hour, and at times at twelve, and
for a while at seven—including day and night, fifty-nine leagues.
He reported forty-four leagues to the crew, no more. At this point,
the crew could stand it no longer and complained about the long trip;
but the admiral encouraged them as best he could, giving them high

hopes of the profits they would be able to realize. He added that it was useless to complain, since he was going to the Indies and must proceed this way until he found them with the help of Our Lord.

—Columbus's log

Dated on the eve of the first documented European sighting of the New World, this passage from Columbus's log is a reminder that the *Conquista* started small. Grumpy sailors wanted to know if they were "there yet," and Columbus lied to stave off rebellion as the crew began to doubt his navigational abilities and promises of imminent landfall. Forty-one days into their journey, the men described in the log were sailors packed together on small vessels, uncomfortable and increasingly unsure of their position. They were calmed by the promise of wealth, their complaints silenced by a man determined to find a new route to the Indies with the guidance of divine Providence. The dual aims of God and gold that fueled Cortés, Pizarro, and the Spaniards of the later *Conquista* were present on this eve of discovery but must have seemed ethereal to the men on Columbus's ships that October night.

Beginning with their landfall on Guanahani[10] less than forty-eight hours later, however, the material and spiritual potential of the New World began to crystallize for Columbus and his crew. Meeting with a small delegation of indigenous people, Columbus initiated a transaction that combined commercial interests with religious goals. "So that they would bear us great friendship," Columbus wrote in his log on October 11, "and because I realized that they were a people to be delivered and converted to our holy faith better by love than by force, I gave some of them red caps and glass beads that they put around their necks and many other things of little value with which they were very pleased, and remained so entirely ours that it was a wonder."[11] In exchange for the trinkets, Taino men swam out to Columbus's boats with parrots, balls of spun cotton, javelins, and bells.[12] While Columbus was little impressed with the native trade goods, he did take notice of the gold pieces the Indians wore. Here was the profit he had promised his men, and here, in the form of Caribbean peoples who Columbus famously predicted would be easily instructed in Christianity because "it seemed they had no religion,"[13] was evidence that God was indeed with the mariners, delivering them to save the souls of the island's heathen inhabitants. Christian mission and commercial interests were melded in the contact between Columbus, his crew, and the Taino, linking a religious eschatology of conversion to material gain.

This link was codified in the 1493 papal bull, *Inter Caetera,* in which Pope Alexander VI granted the gold, spices, and souls of the Indians on the islands to Spain for the glory of God and the furthering of the Catholic faith.[14] Religious ideals, here couched in a firm belief that one day all the world would be Catholic and the Spaniards glorified for having accomplished this goal, were tied to dreams of profit. Gold and spices were to be taken from their heathen uses and turned into the money of God, made useful for the crown and church in their (civilizing) missions around the world. New World resources, in other words, were to be *converted,* along with the souls of the previously doomed Native Americans.

That this conversion became a part of a greater Christian eschatology linking God's will on earth to New World wealth is particularly clear in Columbus's *Book of Prophecies.* Written in the early part of the sixteenth century, after he had returned to Spain in shackles imposed by the Spanish crown, the *Book of Prophecies* is a collection of biblical texts Columbus believed foretold his unique place in Christian history. A letter to the king and queen of Spain at the beginning of the work outlines this role, calling for the wealth garnered from New World endeavors to be used for "the restitution of the holy temple to the holy Church Militant."[15] The riches of the Conquista were to be used for a new crusade, converted from heathen places of worship to a Christian restoration of the temple in Jerusalem, something Columbus, and many Catholics of his day, believed to be a necessary condition for Christ's return and the initiation of God's kingdom on earth.

This double conversion, both material and spiritual, was the crucible in which the antecedents to modern development were forged. As they came into the coastal plains and mountain highlands of Central and South America in the course of conquest, the Spaniards conquered with technology, bringing new lands to the crown and new souls to the church with guns, wheels, writing, horses, and eventually, European agricultural practices. For the indigenous peoples of the New

World, there was never a time when a Catholic eschatology of salvation was not connected to technological change—to Spanish ideals of progress, civilization, and material gain embodied in the institutions of church and crown.

States of Reason

> Our continent has within it potentialities for every facet of development revealed in the history of nations, by reason of its physical characteristics and because of the hazards of war and the uncertainties of politics.
> —Simón Bolívar, "Letter from Jamaica," 1815

As the Conquista ended and colonization began, development, as a program of European technological introduction and instruction, remained a dual project of church and state. The Spanish crown formed the Council on the Indies to oversee its colonies and the wealth it hoped to extract from them, a mandate that also included the protection and "civilizing" of the Indians. The council, in turn, handed the bulk of this "civilizing" work to religious orders in the form of missions and church-run estates, which combined wealth extraction with proselytization and more general education and technological transfer. Jesuits, Franciscans, Augustinians, and Dominicans tended to the task of converting natives to Christianity, and to the spiritual and educational needs of the growing numbers of European colonists. It was through these educational endeavors that the missionaries aided a shift in ideologies that replicated these early forms of development, expanding them from the realm of religion into the more secular sphere of the state. In the time of colonization and later in the formation of nation-states, development was reproduced into the space of the "modern," complete with a new eschatology of progress seemingly removed from the Christian triumphalism from which it sprang.

The Jesuits, especially, helped to form development as a rational project. The order built a combination of farms, factories, and educational facilities which placed them in a unique position in colonial Latin America. Alan Figueroa Deck, along with historian Nicholas Cushner, credits the Jesuit emphasis on education and early capitalist agriculture with the expansion of Western-style modernity, particularly an emphasis on rational or scientific understandings of "every sphere of existence" in the New World.[16] By the time the order was expelled from Spanish colonies in 1767, they had left their mark: a fusion of technological innovation and societal progress supported by a large, visible infrastructure. Spiritual salvation was still important to the Jesuits, but it became a salvation entwined with material advancement. Progress in its broadest sense—spiritual, cultural, and technological—became the optimal way to achieve salvation's ends.

The Jesuits of course did not function in isolation, and many of the ideologies that fueled their projects in Europe and the New World were reflected and expanded in the burgeoning ideologies of the European Enlightenment. Encompassing a secularized eschatology in which salvation rested less on the establishment of the church in the world and more on the shoulders of a perfectible rationality, Enlightenment thinking shifted European goals away from the reconquest of Jerusalem and toward progress as a salvific end unto itself. Immanuel Kant, writing in his seminal 1784 essay "What Is Enlightenment?" defined enlightenment as "mankind's exit from his self-incurred immaturity."[17] Indeed, the exit Kant described was necessary for the continuation of civilization as he implored men to become enlightened lest they "doom" future generations to live in ignorance and tradition, a circumstance many Europeans associated *a priori* with New World peoples.

The details of Kant's essay are useful here in tracing an eschatology of progress, and also the specific emergence of a concept of advancement that became linked to the state. To bring everyone out of their "self-incurred" lives of "immaturity," Kant contended, an upper-class, educated, and rational group of leaders was needed. It was the work of the state, in other words, to lead its people into enlightenment and modernity, and, notably, away from the hopeless shackles of tradition.

Coming more than half a century later, Hegel's *Introduction to the Philosophy of History* also elevated the state as the inevitable institution of rationality and human perfection in the world. According to Hegel, it was indeed rationality for which humanity was destined and in which God in the form of *Geist* was manifest. A faith in progress became concomitant with a faith in the God of history, with the workings of God in the world. The state was the institution charged with allowing progress to continue, especially as Hegel claimed that Protestant states in moderate climates were most likely to achieve rationality and perfection.[18] The nascent predecessor to development, here the manifestation of an ideology of inevitable progress, was in some way godly and increasingly tied to national governments.

As Hegel's rhetoric demonstrates, however, development was never entirely subsumed into a secular state. Rather, development evolved with two faces, taking on a double life as it represented the goals of the modern state even as it remained encamped in Christian discourses of divine will.

Most histories of development recognize the invention of this double life but focus exclusively on development's secular aspects as they became allied with colonial, and later, republican powers. Arturo Escobar, Gustavo Esteva, Wolfgang Sachs, and other scholars point to the introduction of Spencer's and Darwin's concepts of evolution in the Victorian era as a catalyst that fused notions of development, rationality, and progress with the idea of colonial governments as institutions that bore the "white man's burden" of bringing the world's peoples from their condition of savagery, tribalism, and idolatry into the "modern" world shaped by the Industrial Revolution. From their childlike condition of clinging to traditions rather than embracing the (obvious) improvements of industry, the peoples of the colonial world, Europeans believed, could and inevitably would become like the enlightened Europeans, on the road to progress and a better life for all.

It is at this point that development and postdevelopment scholars presume that development departed the religious realm, crossing over to the secular state in the Enlightenment period. Escobar discusses a Christian idea of salvation as an early model of development rhetoric, arguing, for example, that development retained the language of Christian eschatology without the substance of that eschatology.[19] He presumes that the overtly religious roots of development no longer mattered as development became independent, engendering its own eschatology of progress as an entirely secular institution.

Gilbert Rist agrees, though he harkens back to the theological roots of development by calling this new eschatology "religious." Development not only crossed over to the state, Rist argues, but transcended the state as it become an object of faith in and of itself. Development is religious, he concludes, because we believe in it. Moreover, it is eschatological. We believe in it not because of its effectiveness in bringing the world out of poverty, but because we have a curious faith that someday, in a mythic future, its kingdom of goodness and prosperity will finally be realized. We have become blind, he says, to our relationship with development as our own teleological invention.[20]

Rist and Escobar are correct in this description of development eschatology, an invention that continues to shape global realities from health to economics. However, they ignore the genuinely religious aspects of this invention. Truman's "Point Four" development was not simply a technological solution to the "problem" of a world gripped in material want, it was a moral and distinctly religious duty. The reason the United States and its allies in Western Europe were to "make the benefits of [their] scientific advances and industrial progress available for the improvement and growth" of Third World countries is clear in his address. "It may be our lot to experience," said the newly inaugurated president,

> and in a large measure bring about, a major turning point in the long history of the human race . . . The peoples of the earth face the future with grave uncertainty, composed almost equally of great hopes and great fears. In this time of doubt, they look to the United States as never before for good will, strength, and wise leadership.
>
> It is fitting, therefore, that we take this occasion to proclaim to the world the essential principles of the faith by which we live, and to declare our aims to all peoples.
>
> The American people stand firm in the faith which has inspired this Nation from the beginning. We believe that all men have a right to equal justice under law and equal opportunity to share in the common good. We believe that all men have a right to freedom of thought and expression. We believe that all men are created equal because they are created in the image of God.
>
> From this faith we will not be moved.[21]

While a secular notion of progress may appear to have replaced an overtly religious eschatology when development emerged as global policy, Truman's speech shows that the religious elements of development were not entirely subsumed into a secular state. Rather, religion was quietly elided with the state in a neo-Hegelian eschatology that envisioned the democratic, capitalist, and Christian West against the Communist East. Many of the development programs instituted by the United States in the "development decades" of the 1950s through the 1980s targeted countries in Latin America in order to win the "hearts and minds" of the civilian population and halt the spread of Communism. That this was a religious as well as a civil task is perhaps most clearly reflected in the words of U.S. Secretary of State John Foster Dulles, who proclaimed that the world was divided into two parts, "the Christian anti-communists, and the others."[22]

More recent trends in international economic development, explored more fully in chapters 3 and 6, have only continued this amalgamation. In the 1980s Women in Development (WID) and Gender and Development (GAD) programs attempted to recognize both the contributions of women to economic development and gender as a factor in development success. Amartya Sen's and Martha Nussbaum's "capabilities" approaches to development, which focused on "social capital," "freedom," and "participation" as key factors in implementing and evaluating development programs, have allowed women's practices and societal "traditions," including religion, to gain currency as valuable foundations for successful development.[23] The liberation theology movement, especially in Latin America, also combined religious and economic values through a "preferential option for the poor," which encouraged faith communities to work for the economic and social advancement of their members. Religion, once elided with "tradition" and "backwardness" in development thought and academic critique, became a broader part of "social capital," or even an asset in its own right. A conference held by the Templeton Foundation in 2003, for example, examined the possibility of "spiritual capital" as a development resource.[24]

Religion, then, was (and is) clearly a discourse that operated in the same space as development, sometimes working under the cloak of government and political systems, and sometimes disrupting and exposing the linkage between development, political, and religious ideologies, bringing the hidden into view. While development has emerged as a hegemonic faith complete with its own eschatology of salvific advancement, it has never been a completely secular endeavor, removed from the auspices of organized religious institutions, perceived religious values, or religious experiences and sensibilities.

Religion and Development in San Marcos

Certainly, this is true in San Marcos, where histories of contiguous religious and technological change have shaped social and physical landscapes from times before European contact. Long before oil revenues allowed the Ecuadorian government to smooth the way from Guaranda to Guayaquil in the 1970s, and then to pave the route to San Marcos in the 1980s, roads running into and out of San Marcos served as thoroughfares for trade and travel, making a physical link between people and goods from the area to their counterparts on Ecuador's coast. Located at the place where the Andes begin their steep descent to the ocean, cold *páramo* plains above town give way to warm and dense jungles below, and people from isolated communities come into contact with larger populations and political centers in its streets and markets.

Indeed, the roads and paths that bring people and goods into and out of San Marcos have always been an important part of life in the region. Before the arrival of the Inca state in the late fifteenth century, people traded the maize that grows abundantly in San Marcos for items they could not grow or manufacture, including salt, cotton, hand axes, and capsicum red pepper. Some of this trade appears to have taken place between independent chiefdoms, conducted between groups with the aid of traveling *mindaláes,* or trades people. Some of it seems to have taken place within related communities deliberately placed to have access across a wide array of ecological zones. This "vertical archipelago" structure, as Andean scholar John Murra first called it, ensured that members of family or community groups living in the extreme highlands had lowlands products such as corn, cotton, peppers, and *cabuya* fibers for making ropes.[25] At the same time, people in the coastal and temporal zones had access to the grazing lands and tubers that the highlands offered.

This trade and necessary cooperation joined San Marcos to the many small economic/political units that composed pre-Inca Ecuador, weaving them together as loosely connected, independent entities. While we do not have a complete or particularly detailed account of Ecuador before the arrival of Spanish *conquistadores* in 1531, early Spanish records, including chronicles, tax and land registers, and other documents, do lend a clue as to who was in the territory before European contact. These records, along with archaeological evidence, support a generalized picture of the San Marcos region as one in a loose affiliation of independent chiefdoms. Each chiefdom consisted of families and a single native lord (*señor natural*) to whom families paid tribute and labor in exchange for protection and access to prized goods such as high-protein foodstuffs, peppers, coca, cotton, and hand axes.[26] Walking in the hills around town, one can still find evidence of these old ways. An ancient, rock-lined path twists to the top of the hill where a cell phone antenna rises to meet the sky, linking new networks to old. Nearby, a hypothetical grave of a Puruhá chief is a favorite mountainside destination for San Marcos schoolchildren with a few hours to kill.

Marqueños are proud of this perceived Puruhá heritage, and explain with obvious delight that the road near the antenna once connected San Marcos to Cuzco, the grand capital of the Inca Empire. The remnants of the road are the physical remains of a historic, hybrid connection that shaped landscapes and ideologies and brought significant changes to the area. The Inca brought new technologies, including the roads, centralized administration of agricultural production, and a new emphasis on weaving. They also brought a new religion. Whereas pre-Inca societies did not seem to maintain distinct places for devotions, most likely centering religious activities in the houses of native lords, Inca religious practices were performed in separate places of worship and tribute.[27] Several fields in every Inca community were dedicated to the maintenance of Inca temples, and also to the *aclla*, young women who attended to temple rituals and the spinning and weaving of the fine *cumbi* cloth nobles wore. Tambos (state warehouses) and temples stood by the side of every Inca road, built and maintained by the labor of Inca subjects.

Indeed, Inca domination linked religion and technology inextricably in daily life. Inca administrators forcibly removed local deities, in the form of idols and other ritual objects, to the Inca religious center in Cuzco, thereby necessitating long journeys for newly conquered subjects who wished to worship and properly care for their gods. Communities were also required to send young women to become *acllas,* and to contribute the service of their young men to temple fields and cultivation, often far away from their homes. This *mit'a* system tied communities to Inca control as bodies, given in labor, were exchanged for state services and protection, and also for state ideologies. To be a part of the empire, to reap the rewards of the efficient state systems of storage, irrigation, agriculture, and distributed labor, was to participate at least nominally in the state religion.

When the Spanish first came to San Marcos in the mid-sixteenth century, then, and established the *corregimiento* (political subdivision) of Chimbo with San Marcos at its border, Marqueños were used to living at the end of a road that linked them to the state, and to its concomitant technical and religious influences. In many ways, the Spanish continued Inca modes of organization, introducing the *encomienda* system of *mita* labor that granted Indian lives, along with their land, to Spanish settlers. Some 820 Indians from the Chimbo and neighboring Riobamba *corregimientos* were assigned to work away from home in southern Cuenca mines. The first *obraje* (textile factory) in the newly formed Audiencia de Quito opened in the Chimbo *corregimiento* before 1564, once again obligating families to donate their labor in places far away for the good of the state.[28]

Roman Catholicism also came with Spanish rule, linking San Marcos to Europe as the state required *encomienda* Indians to attend Mass and receive religious instruction. Today, Marqueños remain literally and metaphorically connected to Rome. The Catholic church in the center of town is the ecclesiastical "head" (*cabeza cantonal*) of the region, and the main road out of town is a physical representation of that connection as it links San Marcos with Guaranda, the regional and ecclesiastical seat of government. As it has been since Inca times, the road linking San Marcos to the state is also that which links it to religious centers, allowing the simultaneous and overlapping flow of techno-logical and religious goods and ideologies.

Indeed, the main road into town, paved since 1985, remains the principal connection between San Marcos and the rest of Ecuador. Several bus companies run the route daily, carrying people and goods into and out of town every couple of hours from five in the morning until late evening. Although several graded dirt tracks depart in other directions, the road is the only asphalted route into San Marcos, evidence that the town is the last major population center at the end of a network of highland highways. Though one can see the lights of Guayaquil from San Marcos on a clear night, the roads that lead directly to the coast are seasonal and unreliable, secondary vectors that fall away quickly and become hidden in dense tropical foliage growing on the steep terrain.[29]

That the main road into San Marcos is so recently paved is indicative of more recent histories, of stories and experiences worn into the landscape by colonial, republican, and modern feet. Although the town is at a slightly lower, and agriculturally favorable, elevation compared with other cantonal capitals in the area, its location on the coastal side of the western cordillera makes it rainy and often cold in the winter months when the sun may be hidden behind a thick layer of clouds for weeks at a time. This climate, along with its remote location, must have made San Marcos unappealing for early European settlers and their later colonial counterparts. The owner of a large nineteenth-century *hacienda* that occupied much of modern-day San Marcos is rumored never to have visited his holdings. When the Ecuadorian government enacted land reform in 1964 as a response to the U.S. Alliance for Progress, which tied economic aid to internal political reform, there were only two large haciendas to divide among local inhabitants.

The comparative paucity of people living in the San Marcos region after land reform is the basis of its diverse population today, and of many connections that link San Marcos to neighboring areas. A small migratory wave from the other side of the Chimbo River valley brought people into San Marcos to take advantage of parcels newly available after land reform. Lucía's parents, Juan and Antonieta, made the journey to their farm from an agricultural community about thirty-five kilometers to the north and east of San Marcos, and many of their neighbors claim ancestral roots in Chimborazo, an adjacent sierran province.

These variegated immigration patterns resulted in a diverse ethnic population in and around San Marcos. While Juan and Antonieta consider themselves mestizo campesinos, or peasant farmers of mixed indigenous and European heritage who speak Spanish, many of their neighbors are Runa, easily identified by distinct indigenous dress and their use of the Kichwa language in their homes and communities. Settling in small villages and scattered farms in the valleys and hills around the growing town, both mestizos and *indígenas* (indigenous peoples) began to build San Marcos as an autonomous political region in the years after land reform, gaining recognition as an independent canton in the mid-1960s. The space at the end of the road became, with official state recognition and autonomy, a place on the map, a new center for the functions of church and state at the beginning of Ecuador's development era.

So far, this discussion has suggested that this development era has included religion; that development both has roots in and remains tied to religious institutions, ideologies, practices, and discourses of salvation. This is certainly true in San Marcos, where religious, political, and technological changes have come together since pre-Columbian times, and where people continue to negotiate those linkages today, particularly in the context of modernity. It is to these negotiations—their contours, locations, logics, and agents—that we now turn.

TWO

LA LUCHA

Negotiating Desire, Community, Religion, and Progress in San Marcos

On a dark night in September 2002, we were headed to one of the places on the edge of the map, but we were having difficulty reaching it. Dust and the low clearance of our four-door sedan prevented easy passage to our destination. High-centered and spinning our wheels, we could not make the climb from San Marcos to Juan's house outside of town with all eight passengers aboard. In an effort to lighten the load, Angel and I crawled out of the car and pushed, sending the vehicle on its way before climbing the steep slope under our own power, aided by the dim beam of my flashlight.

We were en route to the fiftieth wedding anniversary celebration of Juan and Antonieta Garces. Family had come from all over Ecuador for the party, gathering in San Marcos for a private Mass and then traveling to Juan and Antonieta's farm to dance, eat, drink, and honor the couple. Lucía, the eldest of Antonieta and Juan's children, invited me to the Mass and party so I could get to know the family and they could get to know me. Brian would soon be joining me in a small cement house that Juan and Antonieta had built in San Marcos for their retirement. We would pay rent for the use of the building, but the common dirt courtyard between Lucía's home and ours meant that we would live as extended family, sharing water, garden, and laundry facilities, and also the care of the guinea pigs caged next to our toilet and shower.

Angel asked how I came to know Lucía as we ascended the hill, working to find footholds in the slippery layers of dust and in our new relationship. I explained that Sam Martin, a Peace Corps volunteer who had done agricultural work in San Marcos in the mid-1990s, was a friend and colleague of mine. He had recommended that I contact Lucía, Angel's sister, when I arrived in town to do fieldwork. "Sam Martin," puffed Angel, out of breath from the exercise at 2,400 meters. "He's good people. Very Catholic."[1]

Angel's description of Sam is indicative of the daily, intertwined positions religion and development maintain in San Marcos life. Sam, a professional farmer in the United States, spent most of his two years in the San Marcos area in local fields, helping to grow and market experimental vegetable crops and to develop small fish farms. By all accounts, Sam was one of the most technically skilled extensionists—Ecuadorian or foreign—that the town has ever seen. Yet he is remembered first and foremost not for his prowess with agricultural matters but for his regular attendance at Mass. For Marqueños, at least for Catholic Marqueños, Sam's religious identity and practices were as important as his professional activities. There was no talking about Sam as an extensionist without talking about Sam as a Catholic.

San Marcos is a place where such talk is common. The mingling of Sam's identity as a Catholic with his role as an extensionist is indicative of the negotiations that the confluence of religious and development discourses spark in the course of daily existence. San Marcos has long been a place where religion and development overlap: in pre-Columbian social structures, in state development programs, and more recently, in the reinvention of development as a moral duty of Christian churches. Understanding San Marcos as a place where people negotiate these overlaps requires a working familiarity with these histories and with the ideals people use as they make sense of them in daily life.

Throughout this chapter, we will examine these ideals, particularly as they manifest in three sites of negotiation where Marqueños encounter, contest, and reproduce religious and development discourses: community, desire, and the tension between infrastructure and social progress as development modes. While none of these are fixed physical sites, they are ideological locations that are contested, coveted, and represented in the documents, practices, and ideals religion and development generate. They are the places that breed the collisions of networks Bruno Latour argues characterize modernity, places where the negotiation of modernity is required.[2]

Such sites are multiple and are as mundane as city council meetings and casual conversations or as elevated as Catholic Church councils and IMF (International Monetary Fund) policy meetings. Because of the ways in which religious and development discourses are navigated in local time and space, we will look at particular places where they are apparent in San Marcos, including the market, social constructions of "*la lucha*," and in historic, cultural, development, and religious networks that have shaped San Marcos. Examining these particular sites of negotiation will lead to a better understanding of their wider scope and importance, before we later turn to the points of connection that cause people to fuse them together, and to break them apart, in households, buildings, bodies, and rhetoric. In these spaces religion, development, and histories of all kinds come together, creating a modernity revealed in talk about a Catholic Peace Corps volunteer, potentially Protestant earthworms, and colorful signs by the side of the road.

Community and Desire in Public Places: The San Marcos Market

Held on the same day every week, the San Marcos market is a central site of negotiations necessitated by the assemblage of many aspects of global and local forces, including neoliberal capitalism and trade, internal and international migration, and community structures that encompass class, ethnicity, and systems of barter for basic goods and services. As in many places in rural Ecuador, the market in San Marcos is an important hub of economic and social activity in the region, attracting people and goods from near and far. Rural farmers carry in animals, fruits, and grains from local communities. Commercial vendors, often from large cities, bring products made in Ecuador as well as those produced in places as far away as Colombia, Chile, and China.

These goods are on display in San Marcos's three market plazas, which are spread throughout town. The uppermost plaza offers commercially produced clothing, blankets, and household items manufactured both locally and abroad. These and similar goods can also be

Figure 1. Lower market of San Marcos, 2002. Photo courtesy of Dave Dumaresq.

purchased in the streets in the center of town near the Catholic church and municipal building. The lower market plaza, paved in the late 1990s and covered in the late 2000s, offers fresh fruits, vegetables, fish from the coast, and staple household items such as flour and soap, as well as fresh meat from several small slaughterhouses. Animal and wholesale grain transactions are conducted in a specialized warehouse on the southern edge of town, often in the form of barter, with farmers trading sheep for seed corn or homemade cheeses for large bunches of bananas from the coast.

Where money is exchanged, the transaction takes place in U.S. dollars, another reminder of the larger financial networks that encompass San Marcos, and indeed all of Ecuador; and of some of the negotiations that have taken place at national levels to ensure Ecuador's participation in modern systems of global exchange. As the target of global development initiatives, Ecuador is deeply enmeshed in IMF policies and international politics spanning the U.S. war on drugs to global antiterrorism, free-trade, and environmental campaigns. The Ecuadorian adoption of the U.S. dollar as its currency to stem runaway inflation in 2000; the presence of U.S. military forces in Ecuador as a part of Plan Colombia, which aims to eradicate coca and cocaine production in Ecuador and neighboring Colombia; U.S. Peace Corps volunteers, and tourists in the Galápagos Islands all create inroads that bring North American money and people into Ecuador. These same vectors increase Ecuadorians' participation in world markets as some of the money that soldiers, development workers, and tourists bring to Ecuador finds its way north again, placed into the coffers of multinational corporations when Ecuadorians buy televisions, cell phones, and Nestlé candy bars, now common items in Ecuadorian life and in the San Marcos market plazas. Even where these pathways are blocked, as in the proposed and rejected 2006 free-trade agreement with the United States, they remain highly visible, the stuff of protest and public debate.

Such engagement with the global marketplace is particularly apparent on market days, when many people come to the San Marcos market with cash from remittances, the money sent from family members who have emigrated and found work abroad. An estimated 7–10 percent of the Ecuadorian population worked overseas in 2001, mostly in Spain, the United States, Italy, and Canada.[3] Many of them send part of their earnings home, funding the construction of new houses, the purchase of automobiles, and increased participation in the global economy.

Emigration also spawns new connections that bring Madrid, Quito, and San Marcos into conversations on telephones, through photographs sent in the mail, immigration laws, and wire services. The lines at the phone company, cell phone dealerships, and private homes that hire out their telephones for public use are long on market days as rural campesinos, many of whom are still without basic land or cell phone service, await calls from relatives living in Barcelona, Rome, and Chicago. Market days are also a time for relatives and friends living in diverse places within the region to gather and share the latest news of loved ones who have left to pursue a living outside of the area; a time for building shared imaginations and experiences of the modern, global world in which Marqueños both near and far participate.

This snapshot of the San Marcos market demonstrates some of the ways in which community and desire—for goods, economic prosperity, progress, and social change of various kinds—arise as sites of negotiations where global networks come together, continually forming the modernity of which Marqueños are a part. It also reveals that these hallmarks of modernity—connectivity, migration, and Appadurai's shared imagination—do not guarantee equality or the easy ability to move along the pathways international networks create. Many young men and women reappear at the market after a short absence from San Marcos as they are defeated in their attempts to emigrate. Since an influx of Ecuadorian immigrants in the late 1990s, Spain has revoked automatic visas for Ecuadorians wishing to enter the country, and the line of visa seekers around the U.S. embassy remains long and discouraging for most who apply. While many Ecuadorians emigrate legally, having gone through the lengthy and expensive process to obtain working papers, many cross borders illegally, picking up what work they can find if they make it to their destinations. Some fall victim to Central American *coyotes,* creating more international connections, and local gossip, as they are sent home from cargo containers and illegal ships in Costa Rica, Honduras, and Mexico.[4] In the first decades of the twenty-first century, Ecuador faces its own immigration crisis as its political and physical connections to Colombia and Peru are becoming strained in the face of illegal immigration. Citizens of these border countries are coming into Ecuador in unprecedented numbers,[5] seeking work that pays in dollars, and forcing public debates about community, citizenship, and human rights for refugees and the poor or unemployed.

Such negotiations around community, belonging, and the desires that cause people to cross borders are common in market spaces as people congregate at food vendors' stands, laying out fifty cents for a meal of soup, pork, and rice, or for the corn tortillas stuffed with cheese that are a specialty of the region. The social aspects of the market invite give-and-take as people assess the value of staying in San Marcos or the perceived differences between Ecuadorian and Peruvian labor habits over cups of coffee or grain transactions. In discussing the impacts of global, especially economic, forces on their lives, and by participating in and creating those forces with purchases and phone calls, Marqueños navigate their positions as global citizens, as people who often desire the perceived technological progress on display in market stalls and economic progress that drives the movement of their friends and family. The market is a place of possibilities, and the evaluation of those possibilities as desirable, realistic, or potentially harmful to social relationships, families, and community.[6]

Part of this navigation has to do with the negotiation of identities. Class and ethnicity are apparent as the bright wraps favored by Runa women blend in market spaces with the wool and acrylic sweaters that cover most mestizo shoulders. Campesinos—indigenous and mestizo—are easily distinguished from their urban counterparts by their footwear. Throughout central Ecuador, knee-high rubber boots are the unmistakable uniform of the peasant farmer. While many Marqueños are comfortable shopping in their boots, many others deliberately dress up on market days, claiming the identity of a "*blanco*," or a "*blanco mestizo*," one who lives in town and has the luxury of clothing not intended for physical labor.

Such disparity in footwear points to pervasive tensions in racial and ethnic relations in rural Ecuador, tensions highlighted in scenes of arrival and departure on market days. Most people come to the market in trucks, usually small passenger vehicles modified to hold a crowd via the addition of tall, wooden-planked sides. Each truck serves a particular community in the greater San Marcos region, though drivers will pick up extra passengers from the side of the road as they go to and from their destination. With few exceptions, the trucks are divided: Runa people go to and from Runa communities and mestizo folks ride to or from their own clusters of homes and farms. Despite the fact that most families arrived in the area at the same time and share common agricultural, political, economic, and religious heritages, pervasive perceptions of ethnic difference, linguistic differentiation, and a blatant racism that insists on indigenous inferiority work to recreate lines of separation, and discrete social networks, between Runas and mestizos. The community where Juan and Antonieta have their farm and raised their children is considered mestizo although several Runa families live and work the land there. A nearby community is Runa, and few mestizo families live or own property in the immediate area.

This type of segregation and many of the racist attitudes behind it are well documented. Ronald Stutzman's seminal 1981 essay on *mestizaje,* or racial mixing, begins with a description of Ecuadorian president Guillermo Rodriguez Lara's 1972 speech in which he defended Western-style development of indigenous lands by eliding progress with whiteness. "There is no more Indian Problem," the president declared. "We all become white when we accept the goals of national culture."[7] Ethnographies that study the Ecuadorian indigenous communities of Otavalo, Salasaca, and Saraguro trace this ideology to the present as they detail indigenous struggles for autonomy and cultural preservation in the face of *blanqueamiento,* or a national culture of "whitening" that equates "whiteness" with progress, education, and prosperity.[8]

Certainly, such racial issues and the networks that sustain them are at play in San Marcos. "*Indio*" is a common insult among mestizos, and indigenous people are often the first suspects in thefts committed in the mestizo community. At the same time, however, ideas of race, especially among nonindigenous Ecuadorians, are blurred by an equally compelling demographic indicator: class. Whiteness, as President Rodriguez Lara's statement and the choice of footwear by San Marcos market-goers make clear, is tied to wealth and to lifestyle. Wealthy landowners, businesspeople, professionals, and urban residents are far more likely to be considered "white" than peasant farmers, even if they share the same complexion. As in most of Latin America, race has less to do with physical characteristics than with the crosscutting determinants of ethnicity and class. Even when they have the whitest of skin and bluest or greenest of eyes, campesinos in central Ecuador are not "white" but are distinguished by their comparative poverty.[9]

To be a campesino in rural Ecuador, then, is to be a part of an active and cross-cutting ethnic and economic class, one that people are constantly defining in the course of everyday life, and one that may or may not encompass both mestizos and their Runa counterparts. Some of this identification comes in opposition. The word "poor" (*pobre*) is a common addendum to "campesino" in everyday speech as campesinos refer to themselves as "*pobres campesinos,*" "poor peasants" who work hard and honestly in the face of great hardship.[10] In contrast, campesinos, both mestizo and indigenous, often hold up "*los ricos*" (the rich) as a lazy group out of touch with genuine values and the redeeming moral fruits of real labor. When I teased a family that I am close to when they moved to a nicer home, asking if they would forget me since they had become comparatively wealthy, the mother immediately replied, "We've got more money than we used to, but we're not *plásticos!*" Despite their better fortune, she wanted to let me know that the family had not taken on what she assumed to be the values of the rich, whom she characterized as "plastic," concerned only with material things and superficial appearances.

Most of the people in this book identify themselves as mestizo and campesino, and most of them wear rubber boots on market days, though they come from both the town of San Marcos and several of the outlying communities in the canton. The mestizo campesinos in San Marcos share in assumptions about class and ethnicity which are at times privileged—as when some make jokes about "*indios*" over coffee and tortillas in the market stalls—and at times from the point of view of the oppressed—as when they engage in conversations about the impossibility of turning a profit with the corn harvest due to government import policies, lack of basic services to small communities, or a generalized lack of attention from national politicians from urban areas. Unlike indigenous communities in recent years, which have used ethnic identity and pride to mobilize politically across the country through the creation of panindigenous institutions, mestizos, and particularly campesino mestizos, must forge identities and alliances along different axes. Shared experiences of work, particularly agricultural work, is one of these axes, one that is particularly open to the imagination of development and its role in modern ways of being.

Campesino identification with work and an appreciation for things of "real value," then, highlight the roles of desire and community as sites where many Ecuadorians negotiate identities and actions as constituent parts of modernity. In identifying as campesinos who understand the value of hard work, most of which is performed locally on farms and in agricultural endeavors, Marqueños and other rural Ecuadorians forge identities around shared experiences of capitalism and consumption; around displays and discussions of desire for technological, economic, and social progress. At the same time, local struggles and local work create local ties and a sense of common, shifting, and not entirely unified communities. In the market, desire, community, and their boundaries are on display, open to negotiations, reinterpretations, and rejections as people make sense of their positions and possibilities as actors living, connecting, and laboring in a globalized world.

To Live Is to Fight: The Struggle of Daily Life

This element of struggle — work in a hard world — is a leitmotif in narratives of San Marcos life and is tied to a common working-class identity.[11] During the toasts at Antonieta and Juan's party, when all of the guests took a break from dancing to national music and gathered on the roof to salute the couple formally with sweet muscatel wine in one hand and a store-bought cookie in the other, every speaker mentioned the struggle (*lucha*) Juan and Antonieta had been through in raising their family and keeping their marriage intact over the years. Dancing together, friends and relatives asked after one another and acquaintances, often answering the queries with a breezy "*luchando, luchando*" (struggling, struggling). "One has to struggle" (*Hay que luchar*), the conversation continued as the dancers shuffled in time to band music coming from the CD player, "*vivir es luchar*" (to live is to fight).[12]

Women are especially fond of the phrase. When I would comment that Lucía seemed particularly tired after a long day on her feet, making and selling tortillas in the market, working in one of her many small fields or at the store she and her children keep in the lower level of her house, she would shrug, holding up her hands in a gesture of helplessness. To struggle, she reminded me on several occasions, is better than to die. Women in the Santa Anita cooperative, including Lucía's twenty-four-year-old daughter, also used the image of the *lucha* as they described the toils and tribulations of keeping the group together and solvent. The only way to improve or to meet their goals, they would often say, is to *luchar*, to struggle and overcome the problems at hand.

Men also invoke the lucha as they recount the details of their lives. Don Geraldo Ortiz, a shoemaker who lives in a cantonal capital not far from San Marcos, used the word frequently as he narrated his ninety years of life to me one afternoon. Sitting in the dark living room of his pressed-earth (*tapia*) house, Geraldo, whose increasingly blind eyes became teary as he remembered the loss of his wife to cancer in 1995, talked about his glory days as a trombone player in a local band. Describing how the band would play through the night at fiestas all over the province so people could dance and "forget their struggles," Juan lamented that things only seemed harder these days. "One has to struggle," he said, taking my hand and leaning forward to let me into his confidence, "until *Tayta Diosito* [God] decides to set you free."

As Geraldo's reference to God indicates, the lucha is replicated and in many ways reinvented in religious life. Good Friday processions in Quito and San Marcos, for example, recreate Jesus' struggle and suffering in relation to his crucifixion. Penitents, dressed in robes and masks for anonymity, walk barefoot on long routes bearing the weight of heavy wooden crosses on their shoulders. Many marchers add to the burden by wrapping their ankles in chains or by flagellating themselves as they go along. Crowns of thorns made of barbed wire are not an uncommon sight during the processions.

In Protestant circles, the lucha is also present, though private exertions often replace such public displays. Ignacio Cayambe, a Runa evangelical pastor in a small community outside of San Marcos, described his conversion to Protestantism as a series of struggles. God called him to become a preacher with a sudden illness, he said, but his greatest challenge was to accept Christ as "his personal savior in spirit." "I didn't accept him quickly," he recalled when I asked how he became an evangelical after having been orphaned and raised by Catholic priests. "I didn't accept him. I only walked and walked and after a time, after what must have been a year with the church here, I didn't accept him . . . And in the Bible it says that you have to accept Jesus Christ as your personal savior in spirit. You have to be born again. But I didn't have this . . . It looks easy to follow Jesus Christ. It looks easy, doesn't it? But I fell off the wagon plenty. I fell off the wagon plenty."[13]

Luchar also has a political dimension, one that often leads to discourses visible in political parades and speeches timed to coincide with the market. One may struggle against corruption, the privatization of social services, or compulsory military induction. Since the major indigenous uprising in 1990 and the subsequent formation of political action groups and formal political bodies, indigenous political parties have often invoked the image of the lucha as they have protested economic liberalization and privatization with marches, nationwide strikes, a lengthy occupation of Quito's El Ejido park in 2000, and in several strikes and occupations since that time.[14] Their platform has appealed to many campesinos, who have voted the multicultural Pachakutik party into office in Guaranda, Riobamba, and other locations with a high proportion of rural suffrage. In San Marcos the Pachakutik party paraded every market day during the 2002 campaign season, using the market as a venue to expand its influence in the region.

In speaking of the lucha as an identifying factor of life, then, Marqueños and others are invoking a broad spectrum of ideals and actions, from activities necessary for agriculture and basic survival to religious experiences to political struggles. Often, they are speaking of these experiences as ties that bind, as the common struggles that unite them as couples, families, and communities working together to overcome a wide variety of institutional and environmental challenges. Visible in political parades, in rubber boots, and in greetings between friends, the lucha is just one expression of Marqueños' reaction to the many discourses, large and small, that influence their lives. In the trucks, goods, and gossip that make up market day in San Marcos, Marqueños visibly forge and maintain local and global identities, and communities, as they negotiate the changes and challenges that life in a global world can bring. Whereas San Marcos has always been connected via roads and trading networks to outside places and forces, the influx of foreign goods and pressures of emigration demonstrate that the nature of those networks has changed, calling for new struggles, a different kind of lucha ideal and praxis, in the increasingly connected world of the early twenty-first century.

Enduring Processes: Development, Struggle, and Community

Development, which includes aspects of demanding work and many connections to the political realm, is a discourse that expresses many of these lucha ideals. Aid workers and clients frequently conceive and describe development projects using familiar terms of struggle, justice, and moral righteousness. They describe development as a continual fight for improvement in basic living conditions, thereby incorporating ideas of struggle into local experiences of global forces. Carmen García, a woman working with Plan International's health education division in Bolívar, called development "an enduring process. It isn't just today and tomorrow. It's something that continues day after day after day." Sofía Flores, a thirty-seven-year-old woman who helps to coordinate women's savings and loans cooperatives for Promoción Humana and serves as a technical adviser to the Santa Anita knitting program, answered my question about the state of local development by pointing to the difficulties she has had to struggle against as a development worker. "Look," she said, "when you look at how development is in San Marcos there are a lot of things, right? There are people in authority that don't, that don't give us support to make ourselves, to develop ourselves. We want to do something; they put an obstacle in our way." Carmen and Sofía characterize development using lucha language, highlighting aspects of long work against continual forces of resistance.

Development organizations often go beyond this characterization and institutionalize the lucha as part of their programs. Habitat for Humanity, for example, requires people participating in their projects to contribute "sweat equity" to their low-cost houses, ensuring that the physical element of struggle is not lost on participants. Working on the experimental nursery project in Sinche, the *alcalde* and municipal extensionists in the canton often invoked images of the lucha as they described their own position, "struggling for the people."

At the same time, development programs and institutions, especially as they are allied with neoliberal reforms such as the privatization of basic services and health care, are often the target of organizations that invoke the lucha as a unifying social condition of shared hardship and oppression. When the Ecuadorian government proposed to privatize health care as a part of an IMF-mandated economic reform package in 2001, members of the IESSC (Instituto Ecuatoriano de Seguridad Social Campesino, Ecuadorian Peasants' Social Security Institute), a government-supported organization of rural health cooperatives and clinics, protested with strikes and petitions. Rather than being the end result of lucha as a slow process of improvement, development in the form of economic liberalization and privatization was depicted in this case as an oppressive institutional force that must be overcome through struggle and fighting.

In San Marcos development programs are and have been similarly wrapped up in images and experiences of struggle, especially as they relate to the very real conditions of poverty. Most of the roughly fifteen government and nongovernmental (NGO) aid organizations that serve the nineteen thousand people in the canton work in the areas of infrastructure, health care, and education, and cite these as the "basic needs" of the people they serve.[15] The struggle campesinos speak of is often directly related to the monumental task of fulfilling those needs. While San Marcos has had a government-run health clinic since 1947, and a small hospital with a surgical suite since 1984, health care, especially preventative health care, remains rudimentary. Children die every year of preventable intestinal illnesses, and acute respiratory infections remain the leading cause of death in the region.[16] In a similar manner, the public high school and newly opened branch of the University of Bolívar have lifted literacy rates and education levels, but serve only those who can pay matriculation fees. In these areas, and in more recent programs that emphasize sustainable agricultural practices and small businesses, development shares with the lucha some of the stark qualities of survival. Not a simple solution to poverty as it is experienced as a lack of resources and access to power, development is, rather, poverty's offspring, another (institutionalized) part of the struggle to survive and thrive. It is one place where a global ideal meets and is transfigured by local understandings.

Indeed, development serves to illustrate the ways in which infrastructure is a site of negotiation where tensions arise over the aims of those ideals and their reality in the hard and visible stuff of bricks and hoses, or the softer ideals of social progress, equality, and environmental sustainability. Infrastructure is a place where power relationships and their changing contours are particularly visible, and where the meaning of development is often on public display. As small communities in the canton must petition the government in San Marcos for projects, San Marcos in turn petitions regional, national, and international bodies for roads, bridges, optic lines for Internet access, and the towers that make cell phone service possible.

These power relationships are wrapped up in particular histories. Because the canton was not independent until the mid-1960s, early development projects, including basic roadwork and the beginning of electrification, were managed at a distance in the old cantonal capital, necessitating a give-and-take of paperwork, equipment, and plans for the future. Today, infrastructure breeds similar relationships between San Marcos and its citizens and agencies of the Ecuadorian government, as well as state and private organizations in the United States, Spain, Italy, Japan, and the European Union.

In many cases, these global linkages are visible, easily traced through the signs on latrines, water systems, and bridges which detail the date of the project, the political administration that sponsored it, and any NGOs involved in implementation and design. Aside from the credits, however, what is also visible is the ongoing debate about the logic and contours of development, and especially the tension between the "cement things" of bridges, roads, and metal objects, and forms of development aimed at sustainability, community, and social growth.

Indeed, signs are one place where the tension acquires an unusual, physical form on the landscape. Coming into San Marcos, one is greeted by a slab of concrete five meters high and four meters across which features a painted reproduction of the local scenery. Plowed-up cornfields at the bottom give way to sparsely vegetated hills rising to a neat blue sky at the top. In the middle of the picture, a campesino waters a few small trees as a thought balloon encompassing an ear of corn and three small potatoes rises above his head. "Protect life," lettering toward the bottom of the sign advises, "plant a tree." A boy and a girl rendered in simple geometric shapes and a set of initials under the message indicate to viewers familiar with local development logos that the sign was sponsored by Bolívar's provincial government and Plan International, a Canadian NGO that runs child-sponsorship programs, and which has built many of the community houses and school cafeterias in the province. The new signs, which are, of course, cement things in their own right, are meant to signal a shift in Plan's emphasis away from infrastructure and to "social development," away from buildings and toward education, health care, and sustainable agriculture programs.[17]

As one leaves town on the way to Juan and Antonieta's house, a rusted metal marker gives notice of an experimental farm operated under the auspices of Proyecto Bolívar II, a long-term project funded by the European Union and the Ecuadorian Ministry of Agriculture (MAG). This project, like the newer endeavors of Plan International, had a large sustainable agriculture component, and promoted natural fertilizers, integrated pest management, and animal husbandry, though many Marqueños remember it best for the roads to some rural communities that the project provided as a way to aid farmers in moving produce and animals to market, and for a latrine-building campaign in several rural communities. For many Marqueños, the rusting sign on the remains of the experimental farm is marking the least successful and least desirable aspect of the international effort. The painted banners on the sides of the latrines and the faded paint on the marker for the new road are the bona fide symbols of progress, the proof of what "real" development can do.

The signs of course are also representative of the intangible connections that development creates, be it in infrastructure, agriculture, hygiene, or social areas. Canada, Japan, and the European Union all find representation on the signs by the side of the road, drawing San Marcos into global debates over development strategies, aims, and outcomes. The signs and the projects they represent are visible evidence that development projects act as paths, as well-defined routes that people, goods, and ideals travel as they go between San Marcos and places near and far, tied together into communities both permanent and temporary by the institutions, ideologies, and discourses made visible, and negotiable, in paint, metal, and cement.

In San Marcos these communities are many and varied. Small and temporary groups organize to petition for and then work on projects such as water systems or the acquisition of improved corn seed, coming together for the duration of a project and then disbanding at its completion. In other cases, development is institutionalized in continuous, morphing communities that grow up to sustain long-term projects, goals, and social organizations. These two types of communities—temporary and continuous—persistently overlap, their borders bleeding together as they share members, sponsors, physical spaces, and ideologies in the course of daily life.

Take, for example, guinea pigs. Members of the Santa Anita women's group, literacy workers from an indigenous community along the road to the coast, two Peace Corp volunteers, and the entire staff of the San Marcos Municipal Unit for Technical Assistance in Small-Scale Agriculture (UMATA) formed a small, temporary community around the diminutive animals. Traditionally raised on Andean kitchen floors as a ready source of protein, guinea pigs were the subject of a short workshop (*taller*) the municipio sponsored with the intent of demonstrating the finer points of moving them out of the house and into the market as profitable, low-risk commodities.

For the two days of the workshop, the participants ate breakfast and lunch together, talked together, and shared in a rhetoric that linked development in the form of household rodents to markets, modernity, and change. "The big problem," said an UMATA extensionist as he began the first of the two days with an overview of conference goals, "is the market." Everyone had come to the workshop about guinea pigs because they wanted to change something, he continued, and then added that change for the sake of change itself was useless. If the men and women in the room wanted to improve the way they raised guinea pigs, they had to do so in a way that would be effective. They had to do so in a way that takes market forces into account, forging new and profitable connections between households and the forces of capitalism.

The guinea pig workshop is an especially good example of the way UMATA, as the newest incarnation of local, government-sponsored development, uses development networks to form new, often hybrid communities in San Marcos. Founded in 2001 in the second year of a new administration, UMATA bills itself as a "new kind" of development that supports sustainable agriculture rather than "cement things," the infrastructure projects traditionally taken on by the municipio's development wing. Employing a staff veterinarian as well as two extensionists trained at an agricultural technical high school in the province, UMATA functions in much the same way as older, more traditional extension programs. The program forms local connections to disperse goods and information from centralized, authoritative sources to local people. Indeed, this is how UMATA's work in Sinche functions. The community there invited the extensionists to help their nursery project, seeking knowledge and funding in the form of connections to the municipio. In this and in similar instances, the community involved is stable, though groups formed specifically in the name of a project will often disappear at its conclusion.

The act of dispersing knowledge and resources through development networks creates other, less permanent kinds of communities as well. Sometimes, as in the case of the guinea pig workshop, the extensionists plan a program and invite people from the canton to attend, forming an ad hoc group of clients that disperses at the end of the program. In this kind of temporary community, the most constant relationships exist among the extensionists themselves as they act as a unified source of government funding and information, the brokers between shifting groups of clients and the state.

Certainly UMATA acted as a broker for my work in my earliest days in San Marcos. The guinea pig workshop took place on September 11 and 12, 2002, at the end of my second week in town. By attending the meetings, I got to know the UMATA extensionists as well as the resident Peace Corps volunteer who was working with them. I also made the acquaintance of community members and people from other development projects participating in the workshop. At the same time, the participants got to be more familiar with my project and modes of operation as I took notes, asked questions, and took part in the proceedings. The guinea pig workshop allowed me to form connections through the communities, both immediate and extended, that it created.

One of these connections was to the Santa Anita cooperative. Santa Anita is an example of a continual, morphing community formed around long-term development activities. Founded in 1989, the group is a local branch of a much larger parent organization, Promoción Humana, a liberationist Catholic charity that specializes in small credit unions and microenterprises. The San Marcos cooperative started as a knitting collective, buying yarn and selling its finished products through Promoción Humana. When the members met with success in their knitting endeavors, they moved into cheese making and built a two-story production facility in 2002. Money for the building came from an Italian charity, Mani Tese, an arrangement brokered by Father Antonio Polo, the Italian Salesian priest in charge of Promoción Humana in Bolívar.

Cooperative activities include cheese production, which employs three women full time, microlending, cultivation of crops, small animal production on the land around the cheese factory, and needlework. Women meet once or twice a week, knitting needles and crochet hooks in hand, to work on projects, learn new skills, and to discuss future orders and current sales.

Most of my interaction with the group came at these meetings. Anamaría Carvajal, the president of the cooperative, invited me to attend after we met at the guinea pig workshop, and I was more than happy to join the women. I had learned to knit during my time in the Peace Corps and had since taken up spinning with a guild in North Carolina. Sitting in a room full of women, knitting needles working steadily amid conversations ranging from intricate patterns to politics, was familiar to me and came as a welcome activity to fill the hours of San Marcos's frequently rainy afternoons.

The needles in my hands also gave me a ready entrance into conversation. The women could ask me what I was working on, and for whom, using the socks, hat, or sweater I was knitting to query my relationships and connections to others in the community. I in turn could strike up similar conversations based on the piecework we were doing, learning about Magdalena's sister-in-law in Quito and her daughter in Guayaquil. In many cases, the critical give-and-take we would engage in over the technical aspects of a piece was the basis of later collaborative efforts. As I began to analyze materials for this project, and wanted the women's opinion on my analysis, we were already well practiced in holding up work for evaluation.

Much of this analysis had to do with the cooperative's emphasis on community. To join the group, a woman must pledge that she will be actively involved in all cooperative concerns, and agrees to pay a fine if she does not attend work sessions or the many planning and strategy meetings that the group holds. Long-term success, and many conflicts that I witnessed, centered on the creation of an enduring, committed, and continually active community capable of outliving any specific project.

This emphasis on a core, if changeable, group, rather than on particular activities, makes the group another significant node in the network of development activities that take place in San Marcos. The cooperative and its members are often involved in a wide variety of projects. In the year that I observed and worked with them, many of the thirty Santa Anita members made an appearance at other development activities I attended, from the guinea pig workshop with the municipio to health care and water meetings in neighboring towns. In doing so, they created new communities and networks within networks, allowing the transfer of ideas, goods, and expertise within and beyond the borders of the community they worked so hard to create and maintain, opening up possibilities for new communities, as well as the destruction of old ones.

This kind of construction, with the negotiations it brings, is not created or experienced ex nihilo. Like the many proliferating and overlapping paths that the women and development move along, such communities are not always original, do not always require forging new ways through social and physical wilderness. Rather, the women and the ideas they carry with them often move along preexisting ways that connect and cut through varying social groups and circumstances. The women in the cooperative come together along the path fashioned by Promoción Humana as a Catholic organization. In a similar manner, the HCJB medical caravan did not blaze its own trail as it set up for business in the evangelical town of Puyupamba, but instead followed a well-worn route of Protestant missionaries. Money for Sinche's nursery likewise traveled the beaten paths of election year campaigns. As in all networks—in all places where things and ideas move—established ways are those that offer the least resistance, those where memories and experience aid in quicker modes of exchange.[18]

In this sense, then, the guinea pig workshop and the Catholic women's cooperative demonstrate that development projects and discourses are particular networks capable of proliferating and creating communities in San Marcos. As such, they often forge new, though recognizable, connections between well-worn paths. The hybrids that form when Catholic women participate in municipal events are thus unsurprising, are even predictable, as new, intermeshed communities of people active in development projects come together and then go their separate ways, exchanging common experiences and ideas.

San Marcos has long been a place where this exchange happens, where hybrids are created as the goods, people, and ideologies from one well-worn path join with another to create new ways, new connections. Angel's assessment of Sam Martin as "very Catholic" on our way up the hill, HCJB's work in rural medicine, and the existence of a Catholic development cooperative signal some of these hybrid connections. Development in both its global and local settings seems frequently to travel the same paths, becoming entangled in the same networks, competing for some of the same spaces, and demanding some of the same negotiation as institutional Christianity.

The Road from Rome: Catholicism, San Marcos, and Religious Discourse

Catholic and Protestant discourses in San Marcos have molded histories, beliefs, bodies, and communities in San Marcos as they have traveled along and created pathways in the area.[19] Catholic symbols and gestures unify landscapes and shape perception and bodies, and both Catholic and Protestant organizations create communities in San Marcos, many of them hybrid concoctions that mix religious aims with development or other ideals. And of course both Protestantism and Catholicism have extensive histories, histories that go a long way toward explaining the kinds and qualities of ideals that both strains of Christianity bring to town. Inextricably tied to political, social, and technological forces, San Marcos's Christian communities are an excellent example of the ways that religion never stands alone but engages with and becomes entangled in the forces that surround it.[20]

Like most places in Ecuador, San Marcos possesses a long and vital Catholic heritage that ties the town to outside forces and places, as well as to a continuous sense of time and community. The parish of

San Marcos was established in the late eighteenth century to serve a regional population of about eight hundred people, when a parish priest began constructing the area's first church building. From the beginning, the church was an important social and cultural center in the region, and the Villa de San Marcos (Village of San Marcos) grew out from the edifice. Parishioners came to worship, receive the sacraments of the church, and then conduct business in the stores, streets, and market plazas that sprang up around the religious center. A spiritual hub, the church also acted as the political and economic center of the region until the crown assigned a civil administrator in 1800.

In the early twenty-first century, the Catholic Church retains a vital place in San Marcos life. Flipping through a photo album one afternoon with Lucía's daughter, Mercedes, I was given a tour of the family's memories. Christening pictures were among the first photographs taken of each of Lucía's three children. The children's godparents, a different couple for each child, smile in the snapshots. Because Lucía is a single parent, their support has been essential in helping the family pay school matriculation fees, medical costs, and other expenses as the children have grown and progressed through high school.

Other photographs featured family members as they participated in parades and processions that take Catholic liturgy to the streets. In one image, Lucía's sons, dressed as Middle Eastern shepherds, accompany their classmates, similarly attired as Mary, Joseph, and assorted angels, through town. Another picture captures the boys dressed as Otavalo Indians, decked out to take part in the annual Carnaval parade. A more recent photograph shows Lucía, her brothers, and the extended family walking with intricately woven garlands of palms, reenacting, along with a few hundred other Marqueños, Christ's entrance into Jerusalem on Palm Sunday.

These festivals, along with Day of the Dead celebrations, a Good Friday procession that recreates the stations of the cross, and other events, make Catholicism and the Catholic calendar a highly visible, public, and shared aspect of life in San Marcos, and indeed in most of Ecuador. Roughly 93 percent of Ecuadorians identify themselves as Catholic, and even for those who are not, there is little choice when it comes to at least an oblique participation in major holidays and events.

Annual processions honoring the apparitions of the Virgin at Cisne and El Quinche shut down major roads for days at a time, making travel difficult for Catholics and non-Catholics alike, and government offices are closed on Catholic feast days.

The festivals are also a time when evidence of pre-Columbian religions and religion's ability to reproduce discourses and their concomitant identities through time are apparent. Molds people use to create "bread babies" that Ecuadorians share with deceased relatives on the Day of the Dead bear a strong resemblance to mummies paraded on Inca feast days honoring dead ancestors. The blending of Inti Raymi, the Inca festival celebrating the summer solstice, and the Catholic holiday of Corpus Cristi, celebrating John the Baptist, is also well documented.[21]

Quotidian Catholicism, what people do in the course of being Catholic on a day-to-day basis, is less visible, though it too was recognizable in the photo album Mercedes and I perused. Each child had a First Communion photo, again featuring a smiling set of godparents chosen especially for the moment, and Mercedes proudly showed me a certificate of recognition given to her in honor of her work as a catechist. Several pictures recorded a family visit to a shrine in Guayaquil. In many instances, it was not the subject of the image but the background that showed some of the warp Catholicism provides to life, some of the threads around which people weave their existence. Mercedes, on a school trip, sits on a bus in front of an image of Jesus' sacred heart; a large cross rises over a soccer field where the family picnics in Quito.

Similar snapshots could be taken in San Marcos, revealing images, edifices, and gestures that connect Catholic Marqueños to one another and the town to points and peoples beyond its borders. Catholicism, as a large and visible religious network, works in a manner similar to development to create and reify communities and identities as the church and its activities often bring Marqueños and people from outlying communities into the same space, creating new ties and connections that give shape and color to daily life. Catholicism in San Marcos is a reminder that religion has substance. It is often incorporated, shaping bodies and the ways bodies move in space and time. Market trucks generally wait until the early Mass lets out before returning people to their homes, and Juan rides into town from the farm every market day, buying, selling, and then bending to pray with other parishioners at Mass before starting back, his horse loaded down with supplies.

In addition to bringing people together in the space of the church, Catholic symbols unify a diverse and changing landscape, and many identities within that landscape. Every exit from San Marcos is marked by a cross, protected from the elements by small enclosures along the sides of the roads. These points of arrival and departure memorialize the uncertainties of moving in new directions even as they provide a continuity housed in familiar religious iconography and physical gestures as people passing the shrines make the sign of the cross. Networks the church creates—of shared beliefs, experiences, space, and histories—become visible in the movement of hands. Catholic identities, and the Catholic identities of one's neighbors, are worn into experience and memory as they are traced onto bodies.

Catholicism and the connections it creates also serve to reinforce community organizations. Even though most households in San Marcos proper now have telephone service, television, and radio, and a handful have Internet access, the church remains the most reliable source of local information. Community announcements ranging from school supply lists to events such as the guinea pig workshop are made after Mass. Tolling bells ring the first, mournful notice of parishioners' deaths.

The vestiges of these experiences, the residues and products of Catholicism's long history in San Marcos, are apparent in the wide variety of connections the church opens between the town and the rest of the world. Ecclesiastical structures and church doctrines, as well as the far reaches of the Inquisition, joined Catholics and indigenous peoples living in Catholic areas of Ecuador to Europe from the early days of colonization. Today, posters on the inside of the church feature African children as they advertise the work of Catholic charities and encourage donations. In the money parishioners give and in the prayers they offer for the church in the world, Catholic Marqueños use connections that the church has created, linking themselves to a global body of Catholics and those whom the church touches through its many aid programs.

Many of these connections break through ecclesiastical boundaries. When church and crown were united in the time of the Conquista, it was the church that first placed San Marcos, in the form of a parish, on a Spanish state map. And it was through the church—in birth, baptism, and marriage records—that Marqueños became formally linked to and recognized by the state.[22] Indeed, the 1869 Ecuadorian constitution chartered under Gabriel Garcia Moreno solidified the ties between church and state by stipulating that only Catholics might become citizens. A new constitution under liberal president Eloy Alfaro established respect for religious minorities in 1897, and in 1906 yet another constitution abolished Catholicism as the official religion of Ecuador, placing church and state in separate domains. The ties binding the two remain strong, however, and in 2002 the San Marcos municipal government erected a statue of the Virgin Mary in a city park at taxpayer expense.

While Catholicism is and has been an important force shaping landscapes, communities, bodies, and lives, other forms of Christianity have also affected Marqueño experiences. Protestant missionaries first came to Ecuador in 1895 when the North American Gospel Missionary Union (GMU) established a church and school in neighboring Chimborazo province, using funds donated by North American churches to maintain their operations. The GMU was joined in this early period by Seventh-Day Adventists, the Christian Missionary Alliance, and Methodist missions.

These organizations, with the exception of the Methodists, were part of a late nineteenth-century protofundamentalist movement in the United States that emphasized a belief in biblical inerrancy and the doctrines of Christ's redemptive sacrifice, resurrection, and imminent return. Indeed, there was a special emphasis on overseas missions in this period as many protofundamentalists believed that Christ's return to earth would be precipitated only by the conversion of the majority of the world's inhabitants. Converting the world "in this generation" was a real goal for evangelicals of the time, one that created ties between Ecuador and the United States in the form of the missions, their personnel, and the protofundamentalist doctrines they espoused.

In this early period (1895–1960), Protestant activities in San Marcos were limited. None of the evangelical missions had resident personnel in town, and Protestant presence in the area seems to have been slight. While HCJB sent out its first evangelical radio broadcast from its Quito station on Christmas day in 1931, there is little evidence that people in San Marcos had access to a radio with which to receive the signal. It is likely, however, that they had some contact with one of the organization's itinerant missionaries, engaged in preaching an evangelical message of salvation from the organization's "gospel sound bus," which traveled over most of the country.[23] With such sparse contact and little or no evangelical infrastructure, it is unlikely that anyone living in San Marcos in the first half of the twentieth century would have identified as a Protestant Christian.

With land reform and in-migration of evangelicals from Chimborazo in the early 1960s, however, small, mostly indigenous evangelical communities began to appear within the boundaries of the canton. In the 1960s and early 1970s, these small communities were connected to larger organizations through national and international evangelical networks via visiting missionaries and local pastors trained at the Colta evangelical seminary in Chimborazo. In 1986 these ties were strengthened when Ruth Bauer and Joyce Davis, North American missionaries employed by HCJB and Unevangelized Field Missions International (UFMI) respectively, moved into a small house close to the public high school in San Marcos.

Ruth and Joyce were the first resident evangelical missionaries in San Marcos, and they came to the area at the beginning of a period of unprecedented growth for Latin American Protestants. Between 1960 and 1985, Brazil's Protestant population more than tripled, increasing from 4 percent to more than 15 percent. Scholars noted a similar shift in religious identity and practices in Guatemala, Peru, and El Salvador.[24] While much of this activity came from a marked increase in the number of Pentecostals, churches sponsored by theologically conservative, nondenominational organizations such as HCJB and UFMI were gaining members as well. A small congregation sponsored by HCJB formed in the San Marcos area in the early 1980s, leading to new intra-Christian diversity and fears of Protestant "conquest" on the part of Catholics.

Aside from active congregation building, Protestant organizations were also engaging in development projects as never before. Ruth has been able to take advantage of HCJB's Community Development division, added in 1979, to sponsor basic infrastructure projects as well as training for rural health coordinators. Indeed, some of her first projects in the area were in infrastructure. She has helped several communities, mostly Runa and evangelical, fund and build potable water systems. While still active in these projects, Ruth now spends the majority of her time in health care. She trains rural volunteers to handle first aid, routine checkups, and fast response in the case of medical emergencies, and serves on the San Marcos hospital board.

Ruth's activities, like those of Sam Martin and the Catholic women's cooperative, tie San Marcos into overlapping and tangled networks that connect the town to a wide variety of people, institutions, and ideologies, necessitating a continual negotiation of those ties and ideologies. Several churches and individuals support Ruth by pledging enough money to pay her basic salary and expenses every year. In exchange, she writes letters and sends pictures of San Marcos and the people with whom she's worked. In a similar manner Joyce, who runs religious classes for children and adults and helps to manage an evangelical summer camp, keeps in close contact with her supporters in UFMI and in the United States. An April 2002 bulletin from a Bible church that supports her, for example, asks that church members pray for Joyce and the people she works with. "Pray for a permanent job for Violetta [sic]. Right now, she buys clothes in Quito and sells them in San Marcos to make money," the bulletin suggests. Joyce also asks that the congregation pray "that the high school kids will put the Word into practice," and "for Teresa's husband, Marko [sic], who appreciates Joyce's work with Teresa and their children, but he has no interest in the Bible himself."[25]

While these sorts of exchanges tie San Marcos evangelicals to their religious counterparts in the United States, the infrastructure work that the missionaries conduct also joins area communities to development organizations and ideologies. Ruth brokered the funding for her first water systems through USAID (U.S. Agency for International Development) and has trained her most recent health coordinators under the auspices and financial umbrella of Ecuador's Ministry of Public Health (MSP). Mobile clinics, such as the HCJB caravan at Puyupamba and an evangelical dental and surgical team that set up in San Marcos at the behest of the missionaries in the late 1990s, create temporary but equally conflated channels that bring religion and development to town in a single package. Even the Jehovah's Witnesses, who have maintained a permanent North American missionary presence in town since 1997, and two more recently established Pentecostal churches, describe some of the work that they do as "development," joining in development discourse even though they do not engage any of its larger, more formal institutions such as infrastructure or health care projects. Their freedom in using "development" as a descriptor for religious teachings points both to similar goals with development organizations (salvation, charity), and to similar histories that have resulted in shared genealogies and networks, and thus the family resemblances Wittgenstein noted.

Religion and development, then, share many of the same paths and employ many of the same actors as they come into, shape, and are shaped by San Marcos and its surrounding areas. Guinea pigs, cheeses, and water systems are at once secular and religious, the hybrid products of Cold War development programs and Christian charity filtered through the processes of daily struggle. Small animals, food, and water pipes are points of connection, the subjects of conversations, policies, and economic exchanges that link San Marcos to its national and provincial government, U.S. foreign aid programs, Japan, Canada, Italy, the EU, and a Bible church in the midwestern United States.

These connections are modern, spawned by modernity's emphasis on "progress" as well as by the systems that modernity, in the form of technologies ranging from plastics to the Internet, has put into place. As we have seen, however, these connections are not entirely new. The old road leading up to the communications tower above town tells the story of comings, goings, and hybrid productions far older than Truman's doctrine or Protestantism. The inroads religion and development share today are just a few in a series of highways and byways that have connected San Marcos and its people to the world and to each other since pre-Columbian times. They are just some of the latest in a series of influences Marqueños have negotiated, defined, and changed in the course of the struggle for daily life.

Outside of Juan and Antonieta's house, the sun had come up over the imposing wall of mountains on the other side of the valley as we finished making a tape of the popular "Carnaval Song," for Maria, Juan and Antonieta's daughter in Spain. Instead of using standard lyrics, we had reinvented the words, singing verses to describe the anniversary party in detail. In couplets, we commented on the beauty of the Mass where Juan and Antonieta renewed their vows, and then on the party afterward, which consisted of dancing to Ecuadorian national music; toasts to the couple; speeches by Juan, Antonieta, and several family members; and an elaborate meal of soup, chicken, and potatoes served at almost three o'clock in the morning. We worked on the masterpiece, enduring the harsh criticism of a cousin in charge of the recording, until Antonieta emerged from a side door, insisting that we come into her kitchen to eat lunch before dispersing back along the roads that had brought us to the party. Crowded at the wooden table, we ate in semidarkness, in the middle of a hybrid structure boasting a modern cement roof on one side and traditional wooden thatch on the other. Like many campesina women, Antonieta cooks using both a metal gas range and a raised fire pit (*leña*). The chicken soup she served had been simmering on the gas stove, but the hominy came fresh from the fire, one of thousands that had left the inside of the kitchen walls covered in an ashy black creosote that defied the most valiant efforts of the single, 60-watt bulb.

As a point of contact, a place of production, and negotiation, Antonieta's kitchen points to the ways in which the discourses and histories outlined in this chapter come together in people's daily lives. The bulb hanging over our heads connected us to modernity in the form of the local, if still unreliable, power grid, even as the creosote we brushed off our clothing as we walked down the hill to catch a bus back into town was a reminder of older ways. We came together, dancing, singing, and eating as family, and as part of larger communities, include those spawned by Catholic identity and practice. In the speeches, dancing, and eating, people expressed desire as a common element of local life, even as they linked that desire to processes of struggle and progress.

This discussion has outlined many of those processes and their routes, defining and tracing the ways that religion and development have traveled as they have come together in San Marcos history, and in the specific sites of the San Marcos market, the lucha, community, infrastructure, and religion. Next, we will turn to development discourses and histories in the context of Peace Corps training, and then examine the way in which the discourses of religion and development come together and are negotiated in spaces like Antonieta's kitchen as Marqueños reform the modernity of which they are a part.

THREE

PEDAGOGIES OF POWER

Alternative Developments

Several years after Juan and Antonieta's party, and at the end of a relatively distant road, I found myself once again thinking about kitchens as a part of ethnographic work. Seated at the back of a crowded apartment living room in Cayambe, a cantonal capital in the north of the country, I joined twenty-five Peace Corps trainees, along with a handful of Ecuadorian language and culture facilitators, playing a game. "Bingo!" one pair of trainees shouted, coming perilously close to tipping lentil markers off a playing card. They collected their prize, pieces of chocolate wrapped in foil, only after correctly sorting the foods depicted under their lentils into the nutritional categories a current Peace Corps volunteer had outlined in an earlier *charla,* or educational talk. "Do you see," the volunteer asked as she ended the session, "how active games like this one get people excited about the topic? This is my third set of cards!"

Understanding nutrition bingo, and its importance in places like San Marcos, requires understanding its genesis and deployment as a part of power constellations I term here "alternative" development, approaches that include "participatory," "empowerment," "capabilities," and "community" development ideologies and practices that emphasize information and integration as much as direct economic aid or infrastructure. In using pedagogy as a strategy, I suggest, "alternative" development does not make a clean exit from the imperialist models it seeks to escape. Instead, by becoming a discourse focused on knowledge and knowledge transfer, the renovated ideology of "alternative" development perpetuates uneven power relationships even as it creates the conditions for a widespread reimagining and renegotiation of those power relationships as information replaces infrastructure as the economic basis of the postindustrial age.[1]

The Pedagogical Turn: "Alternative" Development in the Information Age

Knowledge transfer, linked to material progress, has been a formative concept of development from its beginning. Truman wished to make Western "scientific advances" available to people in the developing world so that they might learn to "realize their aspirations for a better life."[2] John F. Kennedy envisioned the U.S. Peace Corps as part of a "New Frontier" of American policy that would bolster an expanding American capitalist economy against Communism while "help[ing] those [underdeveloped] nations to help themselves" through improved technical skills in order to establish greater global security.[3] In keeping with the classic Enlightenment schema that envisioned the West as teacher (those with intellectual and material resources), and the rest of the world as eager pupils (those lacking knowledge and thus the ability to exploit material resources), early models of economic development emphasized knowledge transfer through training as the heart of the enterprise.

But training, specifically training with an emphasis on information as the key to economic and social salvation, has taken on a new role with the advent of "alternative" development. Classical development models conceptualized hierarchical knowledge transfer as a necessary step toward optimal social and material outcomes, and to worldwide "modernization" more generally. Many contemporary, localized development programs have reconceptualized both the importance and mechanics of knowledge transfer, however, making it synonymous with development itself. Much as Kevin Kelly pronounced that "communication *is* the economy" in his 1998 monograph describing the effects of network on global economic processes, pedagogy, as a mode of development designed to optimize a decentralized, integrated, and multilateral transfer of information, has become the heart of "new" development practices.[4]

The roots of this shift to pedagogy lie in the genesis of "alternative" development, loosely defined as development strategies that privilege bottom-up local initiative, implementation, and independence over top-down modernist models based on a Western teleology of progress. "Alternative" development is rooted in the 1970s critique of global economic development, when critics of the modernist, top-down approach cited statistics showing a net increase in world poverty, leading them to argue for local solutions to local problems. This "basic needs" approach to economic development focused on minimum standards for food, clothing, and shelter at the individual and household level, casting aside a previous emphasis on the broad and indiscriminate dispersal of new technologies.[5] By seeking local strategies, alternative development proponents sought to save the primary goal of international economic development—the end of global poverty—by altering the mode of development. What had not been effective at the macrolevel, they argued, could succeed if shifted to the microlevel. Not coincidentally, the invention of alternative development corresponded with the implementation of programs designed to include women in development processes. Women in Development (WID) and women's empowerment initiatives attempted to bring women, and "women's issues" such as child and family health, into the sphere of development discourse and influence.[6]

Alternative development strategies were also implemented as a response to the postcolonial critique of development in the 1980s and 1990s, when those who still supported development as a general good imagined local initiatives to be an effective counterpoint to development as a tool of empire. This emphasis on local efforts also reflected economic theories that suggested import substitution as the best remedy for hemispheric or global dependency structures in which developing countries were perceived to be exploited by "developed" northern and Western countries through systems of production and export, limiting their potential for economic advancement and independence.

Though dependency theory has given way to concerns over globalization, cultural extinction, and neoliberal economic and political policies at the beginning of the twenty-first century, the ideals of alternative development have flourished, along with a proliferation of NGOs, both secular and faith based, which implement them in daily practice. Indeed, it is through the practices of these NGOs and the practices of larger state organizations such as the U.S. Peace Corps that information, conveyed through pedagogical practices, has often come to replace infrastructure as the central currency of localized development work. Be it in roads or Nutrition Bingo, development is often a tie that binds peoples and states perceived as lacking material or intellectual goods to those perceived as having such resources, and all of the power that controlling such resources entails. Development is and has been a tool of empire, a certain mode and mechanism of control, as well as a way people with genuine need attempt to access and use ill-distributed global resources.[7] Documented here is the changing scope and method of this control and the spaces it opens for the negotiation of the modernity which spawned it and which it represents, both from those being "developed" and those actively engaged in the project of "developing."

As a U.S. government organization, the Peace Corps is not an NGO, unlike the majority of the development programs that work in San Marcos. As one of the earliest and largest development entities in Ecuador, however, the Peace Corps is often held up as a model, both good and bad, of localized foreign assistance. The Peace Corps' policy of partnering with Ecuadorian agencies means that it has considerable influence on what might best be termed the culture of development practice in the country. Ruth Bauer, one of the evangelical missionaries in San Marcos, lamented that strategies of both secular and faith-based NGOs remained top-down but cited the Peace Corps as an example of local, alternative development that she works to emulate. "I think development should be from what people feel, their needs, and then that's what you work on," she said after I asked what an ideal development model would be. "Whether it be a road or whether it be a water system or whether it be a place for their pigs [guinea pigs], whatever . . . There's got to be a sense of theirs. I think that with the Peace Corps, there's still that mindset of trying to help people where they're at. And not to come in with all these ideas, grandiose ideas, 'I'm going to help you do this,' you know. That's what I like about this kind of development." While the Peace Corps cannot represent all development organizations working on an alternative model, then, it is emblematic of a certain kind of development in contemporary Ecuador, one that consciously emphasizes a "grassroots" approach that seeks to respond to some of the critiques of development detailed above.

The Peace Corps has been active in Ecuador since 1962, when 156 volunteers worked in community development, an enterprise that comprised everything from community organizing to large-scale infrastructure projects. In 2012 there were roughly 200 volunteers in Ecuador working in habitat conservation, sustainable agriculture, and small business, as well as in the youth and health programs. The Peace Corps in Ecuador trains two groups of recruits annually, one specializing in conservation and agriculture, and one made up of trainees who will work with youth and families or rural public health/HIV/AIDS. The small business development program works and trains concomitantly with the other four areas. Once they have completed training, volunteers begin two years of service in designated work sites throughout the country.

The bulk of this chapter is based on fieldwork I conducted with the Peace Corps in Ecuador in the years around 2005. Specifically, it is based on my observation of training for new volunteers in the youth and families and the rural health/HIV/AIDS programs. In observing training, I was interested in investigating how the Peace Corps, as one of the oldest secular transnational development agencies in Ecuador, articulates and replicates development ideologies and methodologies, and how these ideologies and methodologies have changed over time. Participating in training also allowed me to explore how the Peace Corps, at once a pioneer of localized development and an official branch of the U.S. government, handles the relationship between state and transnational power structures and the push for local alternatives in the early twenty-first century.

Working with the Peace Corps also allowed me to cross-reference field experiences with an extensive documentary history. As a publicly funded entity, the Peace Corps submits annual reports to the U.S. Congress in order to gain budgetary approval. These reports, in addition to training manuals, histories, and didactic materials given to volunteers, document Peace Corps ideals and strategies through tallies of programs, countries, volunteers, and basic needs, as well as mission statements and interpretations of the success and failure of programs. An examination of this documentary history, in conjunction with field observations, highlights the changes in development ideologies—including a new emphasis on pedagogy—which open up spaces of negotiation around desire, community, infrastructure, and social progress.

Doers to Advisers: Pedagogy and the Peace Corps, 1961–2007

Coming more than a decade after the genesis of the U.S. "Point Four" development policy, the Peace Corps was launched in the form of a late-night campaign promise. John F. Kennedy, speaking to several thousand University of Michigan students who had waited past midnight in the October cold in order to see him, asked the crowd, "How many of you who are going to be doctors, are willing to spend your days in Ghana? Technicians or engineers, how many of you are willing to work in the Foreign Service and spend your lives traveling around the world? On your willingness to do that, not merely to serve one year or two years in the service, but on your willingness to contribute part of your life to this country, I think will depend the answer whether a free society can compete."[8] Though it would not be dubbed the "Peace Corps" until a November 2 speech in California's Cow Palace, Kennedy's vision for an international volunteer service organization that would send young, educated Americans abroad to work in the development sector was instantly appealing to the American public, garnering favorable reviews from the *New York Times* and other media outlets.[9] While U.S. Senator Henry Reuss (D-Wisconsin) and others had envisioned an international volunteer "Point Four Youth Corps" prior to the 1960 election, Kennedy's Peace Corps was enacted with the power of the presidency, coming into fruition under the guidance of Sargent Shriver in a remarkably short period. Kennedy signed the order establishing the Peace Corps on March 1, 1961, and the first group of volunteers began training later that year.

From the beginning, part of the appeal of the Peace Corps was its image as an organization involved in local, direct, "hands-on" development work. Peace Corps architects framed Peace Corps superstructure and operations using decidedly active tones. The 1962 *Annual Report to Congress* detailed operating procedures that placed volunteers only in countries that requested them, and only with host country agencies or other organizations working within host countries, preferably with host-country nationals.[10] After these stipulations, volunteers were to work directly in the field. Volunteers "would not be 'advisers,' but 'doers,'" a phrase that stands alone in the report, and signals an ideal of development as a hands-on enterprise, with volunteers working where they may be directly, locally effective.[11] This was in notable contrast to Point Four institutions, such as the World Bank, which made policy recommendations but left the nitty-gritty of implementation up to grantee governments.

This ideal of the Peace Corps volunteer as a "doer" ran deep in early Peace Corps programs, and early volunteers were involved in dam design, road construction, building community health centers, psychiatric nursing, and civil engineering.[12] "Doing" also included less technical activities. Community development volunteers, usually liberal arts graduates with no technical expertise, were charged with community organizing, a vaguely defined enterprise through which poor communities were to position themselves better to request and use state and nongovernmental resources via the formation of formal social entities.[13] Community development volunteers were to assist target populations in organizing these entities, and then in aiding them to undertake projects for the good of the community. That such organizing was considered a form of direct action, of "doing," is clear from the early Peace Corps reports, which describe community development as a series of events, beginning with mental energy in the form of thoughts and words that were then translated, through the work of the volunteer, into tangible results. "The work is beginning to roll along to successful advances," the *Annual Report to Congress* states in describing the community development program in Colombia for 1961. "The first few months have been perhaps the most difficult in getting things organized. Almost all the work has been in thought and word, but now these are being reproduced in bridges, schools, roads and public health centers. Colombia has a great future. So does the Peace Corps in Colombia."[14]

Though volunteers were only talking at first, they were eventually perceived as doing, making projects and infrastructure happen.

Certainly, then, pedagogy played a role in early Peace Corps visions of "doing" development. In the example above, the volunteer is imagined by the report's authors to be in the role of teacher, helping Colombians to "help themselves" by organizing communities to the point that they might build roads, bridges, and health centers. He or she is an alchemist of sorts, lending the knowledge required to turn thoughts and words into bricks and asphalt.

Often, however, the role of pedagogy in Peace Corps programs was more direct, and more limited. More than 50 percent of all Peace Corps volunteers served as classroom instructors in the 1960s. "Doing" for them was teaching, development encapsulated in direct knowledge transfer in subjects as varied as English and biology. Many volunteers in teaching positions during the first decade of the Peace Corps, however, complained that administrators in Washington did not regard classroom instruction as "genuine" Peace Corps work, citing persistent images of Peace Corps volunteers digging latrines and working in construction projects, as well as the expectation that teachers would engage in extracurricular projects in addition to their normal classroom duties.[15] Peace Corps administrators, and the public to whom they owed their funding, were so wedded to an ideal of development as material production that teaching, in and of itself, was seen as preliminary to the real work of the program.

This emphasis on doing as opposed to simply teaching began during training. Volunteers being sent into community development and teaching positions received extensive instruction in physical conditioning and infrastructure construction, but very little in pedagogical or political technique. As Paul Cowan, a community development volunteer working in the municipal offices in the Ecuadorian city of Guayaquil from 1966 to 1967 put it, "There was no reason at all why a man who would spend two years working in the Department of Taxation in Guayaquil's municipio should know how to build a storehouse with a Cinveram machine."[16] So much emphasis on doing, imagined as construction and other forms of physical labor, left volunteers untrained for the jobs they would actually perform.

Cowan's critique of training was widely shared by early Peace Corps volunteers, and the training process, coupled with volunteer selection, remains one of the most malleable, and controversial, portions of Peace Corps service. In part, this is because training is the place where the changing ideals of the organization and the political climate in which it works are most directly implemented. The earliest training programs in the 1960s reflected the image of volunteers as pioneers in the "new frontier" of the Third World, and included significant physical fitness and Outward Bound components, as well as constant testing and evaluation by staff psychologists. Under the conservative Nixon administration, which placed the Peace Corps under the administrative control of ACTION, a government agency created to oversee volunteer service, the Peace Corps recruited older and more technically skilled trainees, and training programs were moved from their original sites at (presumably activist and liberal) U.S. university campuses to locations overseas. By 1973 all trainees in North Africa, the Near East, Asia, and the Pacific completed all of their training overseas, and 75 percent of trainees in the Africa and Latin America regions received all or most of their training in their country of service, up from less than 50 percent in previous years.[17] Community organizing, often categorized as "community development," was also downplayed, and the 1973 *Annual Report to Congress* does not list "community development" as the primary occupation of any volunteer.[18] The report does comment on the continuing debate over generalists and specialists as ideal volunteers, however, noting that the organization "need[s] to find a middle ground somewhere between the early 1960s when 70% of volunteers were generalists and the early 1970s when almost 70% were specialists."[19]

The history of the Peace Corps in Ecuador mirrors these trends, and also broader debates over the place of development as a part of U.S. foreign policy. When Paul Cowan entered training in 1966, he spent three months at the University of New Mexico taking classes in physical fitness, Spanish, community development, and industrial arts, which included construction in latrines and the aforementioned storehouse. After their time in Albuquerque, his group did "field training" for a month with a community development organization in Ciudad Juárez, Mexico, and then completed the process in Guayaquil, where the entire training group of twenty-nine was slated to work with the municipio, trying to serve better the poor populations at the city's periphery.

Cowan's description of training, one echoed by Moritz Thomsen, another early volunteer who has written about his service in Ecuador, is dystopian. Both men were disdainful of the constant psychological testing the Peace Corps employed, and Cowan, especially, had difficulty connecting the tasks required of him in training with his vision of what a productive volunteer could or should be doing in a work site. As an activist and worker in the civil rights movement, Cowan shared the predominant and institutional ideal of the Peace Corps volunteer as "doer," and was highly skeptical of what he saw as an imperialist assertion that volunteers would be effective simply by being present. In his memoirs, he describes Benitez, a Mexican-American consultant who had worked with the municipio in Guayaquil and who was managing Cowan's training, as having "distilled his belief in America into a somewhat mystical faith in our project."[20] That this faith was imperialist is demonstrated by Benitez's comment to trainees that

> when you get to Guayaquil you'll realize that your background is the most important thing that you're bringing to the municipio: the training you have absorbed just from living in the United States—from your high schools and your colleges, from your Boy Scout troops and summer camps.
>
> Those people will follow the example you set. Here's an illustration. I always observed when I worked in the municipio that if a man had ten pieces of paper on his desk he'd make ten trips to the wastebasket to throw them all out. Now, I know that all of you would only make one trip. That's the kind of efficiency you'll teach, sometimes without knowing it.[21]

For Cowan this was not the best of American know-how but the worst of American conceit, racism, and imperialism under the guise of "development."

Where Cowan was concerned with the Peace Corps as an instrument of ideological or cultural imperialism, then, he was also concerned with more overt connections between the agency and U.S. foreign policy.[22] Though the Peace Corps has remained independent of the

State Department and direct policy implementation, this position has been continually revisited as the agency's mandate is in the hands of liberal and conservative administrations. Nixon and Reagan, for example, wanted the Peace Corps to be more direct in promoting "administration priorities," while Sam Brown, the head of the agency under President Carter, worried that the Peace Corps was "at the vanguard of American cultural imperialism" and needed to take human rights records and relative levels of economic development as much as geopolitical aims into account when choosing host countries and programs.[23] Presidents Bill Clinton and George W. Bush both expanded the Peace Corps, which supported more than eight thousand trainees and volunteers in seventy-four countries in 2007.[24] Much of this expansion in the Bush presidency was to support the President's Emergency Plan for AIDS Relief and Prevention (PEPFAR), an initiative designed to combat AIDS in sub-Saharan Africa through the coordinated effort of the U.S. government and a wide variety of secular and religious NGOs.

The participation of the Peace Corps in PEPFAR programs is indicative of the agency's new role in the post–Cold War era, and also of its emphasis on the "alternative" modes of development discussed above. In 1991 the Peace Corps added freestanding programs in WID and youth. Of the 7,733 volunteers deployed in 2004, 20 percent worked in health and HIV/AIDS, 34 percent worked in education, and only 6 percent were employed in agricultural projects.[25]

While the Peace Corps still promotes an image of direct action, and of providing "practical assistance" to needy people around the world, the wisdom of doing that has changed. New idealized modes of localized development work—pedagogy, integration, and limited action—have created a tension between direct action and information brokering that compels Peace Corps volunteers and their peers in development agencies across the globe to become precisely that which the architects of the original Peace Corps denigrated: advisers, people with a store of information and organizational skill who teach but who do not necessarily "do" the projects with which they are involved. It is education and small-scale economic development more than feats of engineering or miraculous agricultural change which are presumed to "help people to help themselves" in the developing world in the early twenty-first century.

Crafting Competency: Pedagogy in Peace Corps Training

This heightened emphasis on pedagogy, and the tensions this creates in Peace Corps ideals and methodologies, is evident throughout the training process in Ecuador. In the weeks before new Peace Corps trainees (PCTs) arrive in Quito, Peace Corps staff members, both people in permanent positions and short-term contractors brought in to handle language and culture education, come together to craft a course of study that will sufficiently orient trainees, many of whom do not know Spanish or anything about Latin American culture or history, to be effective development workers.[26] The process is, in many ways, a race against time. Aspiring volunteers must prove proficiency in fourteen technical, cultural, and linguistic skills by the end of the nine-week training period. If they fail in any of these areas, they will be "administratively separated" from the Peace Corps and sent back to the United States, a process referred to by volunteers and local staff as "early termination."

Peace Corps trainers, usually North Americans who have served as Peace Corps volunteers (PCVs) or in related positions in the host country, are responsible for coordinating technical training with other areas, and for making assessments of the trainees' abilities and well-being. In Ecuador the trainers are assisted by teams of co-trainers, currently volunteers who take time off from their regular duties to help direct training and to give trainees a more "realistic" view of life in the Peace Corps. Language, culture, and safety training is done by Ecuadorians, some of whom have permanent staff positions, and many of whom are hired as contractors only for the length of training, though many work both training cycles for a total of six months' employment every year. In addition, Peace Corps medical staff, program directors, and permanent staff members in charge of equipment, financial resources, information resources, and administration take part in preparing trainees for service.

Much of the emphasis during this pretraining period is on pedagogy: what are the best ways to teach newcomers to development work, and to Ecuador, the best ways to do their jobs in the limited time available? In pretraining meetings for the health program, staffers worked to create a schedule that balanced competency requirements in language, culture, and personal safety with technical training in subjects as varied as breast-feeding and family gardens. For the two volunteer co-trainers, Terry and Ashley, this meant modeling behaviors and sharing knowledge they had found to be effective in the development field. For head trainer Alejandro Vásquez, a young man with an extensive background with the Ecuadorian health care system but no volunteer experience, this meant a direct style reliant on charts and statistical information. As they hammered out a course of study, debates emerged between Alejandro and the co-trainers about what information trainees would need to have in order to be effective, and when they should receive it. The co-trainers argued for an experiential approach, whereby they would model what they believed to be effective development techniques that the trainees were expected to emulate and adapt in the field; the head trainer favored a model of information transfer designed to equip trainees with a broad base of facts and figures they could use to build their own programs.

While they disagreed somewhat about some of the content and technique of training, Terry, Ashley, and Alejandro were united in their assumption that the primary duty of health volunteers is to amass and distribute information that will help people to prevent illness and to promote health. When the health team met to begin forming a training syllabus, for example, Alejandro proudly produced contraception demonstration kits he had procured from Plan International. The kits were cloth bound and contained samples of condoms, IUDs, spermicidal foam, contraceptive sponges, and birth control pills. The training team was quite excited about the possibilities of using the kits to teach about contraception and decided that they would instruct the new health PCTs in their use. The newly trained PCTs would then teach their counterparts in the youth program in the proper use of the kits in the field. Alejandro also brought out a film made by Ecuadorian NGO Pajaro Pinto, *Debes y Puedes* (you should and you can), which outlines fourteen legal rights for youth in Ecuador. Once again, his idea was to train PCTs in its use as a teaching tool. Alejandro produced both sets of didactic materials for view several time in the pretraining process, each time to great excitement. Good pedagogical tools were considered invaluable to a process that emphasized teaching as the core of the endeavor.

The greatest evidence that training staff and volunteers see themselves as educators, however, comes in the centrality of the *charla*, or educational talk, in Peace Corps methodology. The manual given to all volunteers in the health program consists largely of outlines for charlas about disease prevention, nutrition, sexuality, health, and hygiene, and the Ecuadorian health care system. Pretraining exercises also highlighted the charla as the central mode of development work. In one exercise, a youth co-trainer pretended to be a PCT giving a charla in community settings, something all trainees must do in order to become full-fledged volunteers. The language and cultural facilitators were to watch her performance and then offer critiques so that they might become proficient in the art of public, constructive criticism before meeting actual trainees.

The performance of the co-trainer, and the response of the facilitators and other training staff, highlighted not only the valuation of pedagogy as the central mode of development within the Peace Corps, but also assumptions various constituencies in the room held about the relationship between pedagogical and cultural processes. Rebecca, by all accounts a successful and culturally competent volunteer in a poor coastal suburb, gave a convincing performance as a volunteer so out of touch with local customs that her intended lesson was obscured by cultural missteps. Scantily clad in a halter top, short skirt, and flip-flops, she failed to introduce herself or the Peace Corps to the group, and simply launched into a charla on sex, asking the assembled facilitators embarrassing questions, responding to questions with rude and halting Spanish, and being generally disorganized. When the woman in charge of the facilitators asked them to critique Rebecca, they did so hesitantly, quietly explaining that "things are a little different here" but offering no strong condemnations of the performance.

The facilitators' reluctance to offer a strong critique, a response common in Ecuadorian culture where tactful indirection is the rule, prompted the facilitator coordinator and the North American trainers to ask why the facilitators had not been stronger in their corrections. Both emphasized "teamwork" as an essential element of a successful training. Helpful and accurate critique, they maintained, was an essential part of that teamwork. With this prompting, the facilitators became more direct in their critique, and Rebecca gave the charla again, this time in a markedly improved form that displayed greater cultural awareness and conformity to Ecuadorian social norms, better command of "grammatical" Spanish, and superior organization.

The negotiation around facilitator responses to Rebecca's presentation is indicative of the ways power and pedagogy came together as staff members planned training, and of the way they continually come together in broader development settings. The facilitators, the lowest-paid and most transient members of the "training team," were essentially being chastised for not being North American enough in their responses to Rebecca's presentation. They were not part of the "team" because they refused to model that which they were meant to criticize: Rebecca's sometimes blunt responses. What was intended to be, and what on many levels was, a free give-and-take of ideas about the best way to teach trainees to be teachers was also a lesson in the flip side of any pedagogical process: discipline. In emphasizing charlas and other pedagogical mechanisms, pretraining and training programs imagine development as a discipline: a controlled, hierarchical, and reproducible body of knowledge and actions designed and deployed to form behaviors, bodies, and ways of thinking.

"That's Not How We Do Things Here": The Discipline of Development

Indeed, many scholars criticize development because of this disciplinary element. Critics such as Escobar and James Ferguson examine development as a mode of economic and social conformity imposed by powerful Western countries which has little flexibility or respect for local cultures or conditions. In these analyses, development furthers the hegemony of powerful states by introducing dominant discourses about social and material "goods" that favor capitalist production, individuality, and consumerism. In the most biting of these critiques, development refashions communitarian or locally centered lifestyles into "poverty," a condition from which people must be rescued. Development, in these accounts, functions as a disciplinary device that refashions the ways in which people, both "developers" and those who begin to think of themselves as being "in need of development," construct reality.

Of course, development has functioned and does function as a conduit for international relationships and power brokering. Development funds are often used by donor governments or institutions to reward or punish recipient states. In recent years the International Monetary Fund has mandated neoliberal policy changes favoring privatization, open market policies, and a decline in state subsidies. These policies are often framed in a language that invokes discipline as a form of restraint, as in a requirement of "fiscal discipline" and transparency on the part of recipient governments. Restrictions on condom distribution, a mandated preference for "abstinence only" sex education programs, and an explicit prohibition of needle exchanges also point to discipline—read in this case as "self-control"—as an organizing principle in PEPFAR programs for HIV/AIDS reduction in Africa.[27]

Pedagogy in contemporary development, then, is a primary practice that is particularly well suited to reinvent, reproduce, and recreate modes of discipline. Michel Foucault described discipline as a naturalized, "organic" hierarchy that works through institutions such as military regiments and classrooms to create "docile bodies" suited to serve powerful individuals and institutions. Formal education, in Foucault's model, promotes an ostensive veneer of equality and egalitarianism that is "supported by these tiny, everyday physical mechanisms, by all those systems of micro-power that are essentially non-egalitarian and asymmetrical that we call the disciplines."[28]

Development, and particularly pedagogically based development, as a discipline holds egalitarian and liberating ideals, along with a place in systems of political and ideological power. To have knowledge about alternative crops, contraception, and markets is to have some control, or access to mechanisms of control, denied to those without such knowledge. But to presume that the "clients" development programs are designed to serve lack knowledge also assumes at some level that they lack discipline, be it defined as self-control or the mastery of specific, necessary bodies of knowledge. Recognizing development as a discipline highlights its role as a form of modern hegemony that both inspires and limits genuine human freedom.

As the pretraining exercise above indicates, pedagogy is the central metaphor Peace Corps staffers employ to describe the process of preparing (disciplining) volunteers to do development work in Ecuador. During the exercise, staff members were concerned that the facilitators who did not criticize Rebecca strongly enough were not, at the base of things, *teaching* correctly. Trainers for the health program also invoked pedagogical metaphors as they referred to their outline for the training program as a "syllabus." The "Training Plan" for the health and youth programs also invokes common pedagogical tropes as it lists "problem analysis," "problem solving," and "critical thinking" as key components of the training program.[29]

Certainly, the nine-week training period reflected these ideals. Pedagogy was a central and critical practice. While the Peace Corps in Ecuador has not trained volunteers in an independent center, complete with classrooms, desks, chairs, and chalkboards, since 2000, PCTs continue to come together on a daily, highly regimented basis to listen and learn. Each weekday, PCTs, assigned in groups to several rural towns surrounding Cayambe on the basis of program and language ability, gathered together to learn a combination of Spanish and/or Kichwa, cultural, technical, and safety skills. While these sessions took place in community centers, churches, and other nontraditional learning spaces, they were nonetheless reminiscent of a high school or college classroom, with instructors in roles easily recognized as that of "teacher."

PCTs in one community, for example, gathered most mornings in the local community center for three hours of language instruction with the facilitator assigned to that group, and occasionally with one of the co-trainers in a combined language and technical session. On a morning that I joined them for one such combined session, about two weeks into the training period, the PCTs, like students in any typical classroom, shuffled in from their meeting place in the park outside, found chairs facing a stagelike area in the front of an open room, and settled in for the morning by opening notebooks and uncapping pens.

The session, planned by the training staff, focused on the Ecuadorian health care system and the UN Millennium goals for health. Speaking in Spanish, the co-trainer asked the PCTs what they thought the purpose was of the Millennium goals, a document that outlines targets for universal education, the eradication of violence against women, the end of extreme poverty, and improved maternal health, among other things. As the PCTs spoke, a PCT wrote their answers, also in Spanish, on a whiteboard at the front of the room. Once they had some ideas up on the board, the group continued to discuss, as best they could in limited Spanish, the ways the Ecuadorian health system and local beliefs about health both helped and hindered the attainment of those goals. As they went along, the facilitator corrected both written and spoken Spanish errors, and also contributed stories about her own experiences with health care in Ecuador. She explained beliefs about folk cures, including personal accounts of being taken to alternative healers, and also basic preferences in and constraints on Ecuadorian diets. The group then worked together to think of meals that would include more fruits and vegetables than they were eating in typical meals with their home-stay families in town, and concluded the session with some drills and questions about Spanish grammar, as well as with recitations, once again in Spanish, of the goals, address, and phone number of the Peace Corps in Ecuador. When the morning session had ended, the PCTs went to lunch in Cayambe, and then to the co-trainers' apartment, where they spent the afternoon learning about and implementing charlas on nutrition, breast-feeding, and cooking, including the spirited round of Nutrition Bingo described earlier.

A typical day of Peace Corps training, then, is one centered on the act of teaching and learning. Though much of Peace Corps training is conscientiously "hands on," fashioned on an "adult learning" model of education, it is clearly reminiscent of the formal education the PCTs have completed in prior circumstances. Days are regimented, there is homework to complete, and PCTs are subject to the judgment and authority of the training staff, particularly at mid-cycle and final reviews. As in high-stakes testing in U.S. classrooms, PCTs must "pass" fourteen "competencies" in order to commence service as a volunteer, and they must not violate specific prohibitions against unauthorized travel, drug use, tardiness, sexual relationships with training staff or persons under eighteen, driving, political activities, religious proselytizing, or failing to take required (usually antimalarial) medications. Again, pedagogy is a form of discipline, a way of molding and modeling subjects. As trainees graduate from being students to being teachers, to becoming volunteers in the field, they take with them the idea that knowledge transfer is the core of their endeavor. Their power lies in their ability to sufficiently hold, create, and impart information—to master the discipline to which they have been subjected.

A focus on pedagogy as a central practice, then, does not seem to shift Peace Corps development practice—or indeed the "participatory" or "alternative" models on which it is based—entirely away from the top-down or classical models the organization rejects. Indeed, the ability to have and impart information remains a central commodity in the training that aspiring volunteers receive regarding development goals and ideologies. In the training cycle in which I participated, for example, the five sessions dedicated to community development focused on becoming a "student" of the place where one works, approaches to development (top-down, grassroots, etc.), identifying community resources, recognizing that "the only thing that can change is the volunteer," and "self-care." While such an approach has undoubtedly stemmed some of the imperialist conceit of the early Peace Corps about which Cowan complained, it elevates information as the commodity of the new development era. One gathers information in order to gain a certain position of power, and then to use it in the exercise of that power, though this exercise of power is at the behest of and in cooperation with the community. Knowledge in this model is power distributed in the disciplinary practices of pedagogy. The business of development is the business of this distribution, with the person "doing the development" largely in charge of the process, though in a conscientiously community-centered and cooperative model.

This is not to say that processes of development function as hierarchically, or as smoothly, in practice as they do in the idealized realm of Peace Corps training. Volunteers often complain about acts of resistance, small and large, that Ecuadorians enact by withholding or disclosing their own information resources, or by questioning the desirability of some development programs. While the development ideology promoted by the Peace Corps presumes the universal value of information, in other words, not every Ecuadorian shares this view. Nutrition Bingo is popular, the volunteer giving the charla told the group, because it allows participants to suspend some of the more overt hierarchical elements of the pedagogical endeavor. By integrating play and teaching, the volunteer and her clientele could each engage in the activity without sharing a mutually agreed-upon goal. Participants in the exercise may just want to have fun and play the game. The beauty of Nutrition Bingo, the volunteer asserted, was that participants would probably learn some nutritional information in spite of such alternate objectives.

By making pedagogy a central practice of development, then, organizations such as the Peace Corps open up a field of action that remains hierarchical and tied to colonialist power structures. The field, however, is ripe for negotiation and multiple, overlapping interpretations and actions, and such negotiations and interpretations are especially encouraged by integration and limited action.

Rural Development to Global Markets: Integration as Development Ideal

While pedagogy holds sway as the primary practice of Peace Corps training and subsequent work in the field, *integration* emerges as a predominant organizing concept employed by Peace Corps trainers to describe ideal training processes and development itself, a flexible and multifaceted term that reflects general development practice and histories, some of which are documented later in this chapter. Because of this flexible, idealized nature, integration is often a point of contestation and negotiation among development workers, a term that encapsulates the changes and contours of development as a continually evolving discourse.

As the Peace Corps trainers use it, "integration" primarily refers to combinations of skills and knowledge sets that reflect the entangled, interrelated, and culturally contextualized nature of the realities that spawn the perceived need for development work. Unlike hybridization, where new understandings or entities are created through processes of combination, integration in the Peace Corps model focuses not on fusion but on contextualization. By teaching technical skills in Spanish and stressing the need to gather local understandings of illness, as well as placing training in the context of rural communities, Peace Corps staff hope to prepare trainees to identify the contexts in which health and economic development problems arise, and thus to give trainees better, more locally rooted skills for handling those problems.

In the small group class I described earlier, for example, the facilitator combined a lesson on explanations for illness with instruction in Spanish and nutrition, working at the same time to probe trainees' assumptions about illness, nutrition, and their own roles in creating better health environments. "When people put potato peels over their eyes to treat a headache, do you think it really works?" the facilitator asked the assembled group of trainees in the community center. When one trainee assented, comparing the potato peels to a wet washcloth, the facilitator went on to describe her own experiences of being cured of *susto,* a spiritual malady caused by walking too close to restless spirits in places like a graveyard. "Be aware," she cautioned the trainees, speaking the entire time in Spanish with occasional translation assistance from the co-trainer, "that illness is cultural [*tiene algo de cultura*]. Health is cultural." The co-trainer supported these assertions, telling the trainees that they would need to ask people about the causes of health problems before they could start to find solutions.

As described by the co-trainers as they formed the training syllabus, sessions such as these were designed to introduce essential vocabulary and cultural knowledge together with technical skills, in this case nutritional information and the UN Millennium Development Goals, so that volunteers could begin to piece things together and have an accurate vision of the ways things "actually work" in local contexts. Indeed, there was great emphasis in the pretraining planning period on such integrated learning, both because of time constraints, and because of its perceived benefits to development outcomes. One pretraining exercise, designed to acquaint staff with charlas as preferred development practice and with "Positive Community Development" as a concept, focused on "causes and problems." During the exercise, a small group of facilitators led staff members through a series of situations and asked if they were a "cause" of community health problems, or the problem itself. The fact that most participants were evenly divided about things like polluted drinking water and the lack of affordable education was meant to draw attention to pluralities of perceptions in development contexts, and to the complexity of defining even "basic" needs within living communities. By focusing on the complexities inherent in defining development needs, the staff was also pointing to integration as a preferred strategy for adequately recognizing and then working to meet those needs.

Specifically, staff members in training and pretraining sessions highlighted integration by linking it to "alternative," "positive," or "community-based" development. When someone asked about the assigned roles of two floating staff members free to work with both training groups, the health trainer responded that they were tasked with "integrating" development theory and intercultural and linguistic issues into the general training routine, thereby "completing" the trainees' education. In other instances, the language facilitators were asked to "better integrate" their language and technical sessions. In all of these cases, staff members voiced their presumption that an integrated training would lead to the kinds of collaborative efforts, better communication, cross-cultural understanding, and project execution that would, in turn, lead to successful development efforts in Ecuador.

Indeed, integration was often cited by staff as an index by which to measure the desirability of the training activities. During a pretraining meeting to evaluate the current technical manual used by the health program, a co-trainer requested the addition of pertinent Spanish vocabulary words at the beginnings of chapters in order to "better integrate" Spanish language learning and the acquisition of technical skills. During a meeting with the facilitators, the head trainer for the health program asked that they be more involved with all training activities so that trainees would be learning Spanish not only in the mornings, the time when formal Spanish lessons are taught, but throughout the day. In the discussion that followed this request, one facilitator complained that while there was a lot of talk about integration, in reality people still broke down training into separate components. "We keep talking about tech time and language time," he complained, "it doesn't seem that we're really integrating the two."

The facilitator's comment touched off a lengthy and concerned conversation about the meaning of "integrated training" as the ideal for the upcoming weeks. For the head trainer, "integrated training" was primarily tied to learning language and technical skills. Technical skills were to be taught in Spanish so that trainees could learn, without translation, how to teach about nutrition, birth control, self-esteem, and other topics related to health. For the facilitators, however, integration went well beyond a unification of Spanish and health information. One facilitator, for example, was concerned that trainees were not spending enough time in their host communities during training, and thus were "not integrating" with those communities to the desired level. Another facilitator asked why more was not being done to "integrate" the health and youth programs, which often share similar training needs and development goals. In all of these cases, integration, as the unification and co-mingling of two or more sets of knowledge, was viewed as a pedagogical asset and ultimate good, though a good with variegated and contested meanings and modes of idealized implementations.

Some of integration's cachet, as well its flexibility as an operative term, comes to local training staff and volunteers via administrative structures that also support and promote integration as a pillar of effective development work. Rosa, the woman in charge of the language and cultural facilitators, told me that her job is "to integrate language and culture during the nine weeks of community-based training." Community-based training itself is an attempt by the Peace Corps administration to encourage more flexible and integrated experiences into the training period. By placing trainees into small communities, administrators hope that they will learn Spanish, cultural norms, and survival skills more readily than they would in a centralized training center such as the one previously located in a Quito suburb.

While integration figures as a key pedagogical trope for training, then, it is also an organizing concept for development work writ large. This is especially clear in Positive Community Development sessions that teach volunteers that they will fail in their development endeavors unless they are integrated, to the maximum extent possible, into the communities they seek to serve.[30] The *Training Handbook* for rural public health distributed to every health trainee, for example, informs readers that, "In addition to being familiar with the basics of child health, PCVs must be able to integrate themselves into and become accepted by their local community or neighborhood and be able to work with counterparts and other members of the community in carrying out activities and projects."[31] In this instance, integration shifts from being a descriptor of a mix of pedagogical disciplines to being a code for someone able to use those disciplines in the course of daily life. Being "integrated" signals the ability to use linguistic, cultural, and technical skills in order to judge a situation, form a plan of action, and then persuade people to participate in that plan.

While this is integration on a personal level, or at least on a relatively small scale, the concept also has significant currency on theoretical and policy levels, something Peace Corps practices and ideals have replicated. In the late 1970s and early 1980s, for example, integration referred less to local practice than to national and international structures. Integrated Rural Development (IRD) programs worked to combine agricultural improvements with economic programs and infrastructure initiatives in order to create "sustainable" rural economies. Of eight references to "integration" in the Peace Corps' 1982 *Annual Report to Congress,* for example, six were in the context of IRD. This reflected more extensive development and economic policies that supported significant debt accumulation in order to overturn the perceived problem of import-substitution through a push toward industrialization. By "integrating" rural production with urban industrialization, entities such as the World Bank theorized that economic development would more evenly benefit people across the developing world.

With the rise in popularity of laissez-faire and neoliberal theories after the 1982 debt crisis, however, integration became decoupled from Integrated Rural Development and took on broader implications. The term became a watchword used to describe a country's level of involvement in an "integrated" global economy marked by free trade. A decline in state subsidies, floating currency, and privatization became the hallmark of "integrated" economies, a positive sign of development for lending institutions such as the World Bank.

An examination of the 1984 *World Development Report* released by the World Bank, for instance, reveals only four references to integration. The 1990 *Report* cites "integration" or "integrated" eleven times, mostly in the context of Integrated Rural Development, which the report criticized as often being "too ambitious and complex" and not focused enough on a "policy framework."[32] By 1995 "integration" transformed from being a descriptor of combinatory local programs to being a defining global economic reality. The report, subtitled "Workers in an Integrating World," uses the term "integrated" twelve times, ten of them in the context of markets. In 2003 "integrated" gets nineteen mentions in the *Report,* many of them in the global market context, but many of them as descriptors for programs deemed successful because they are "integrated." By 2005 in a report subtitled "A Better Investment Climate for Everyone," "integration" was no longer linked directly to global markets (though the implication remained in the emphasis on investing) but retained its place as a positive descriptor for successful development work. Projects in South Africa, China, and Senegal were highlighted in stand-alone textboxes, all of them described as having "integrated" components.[33]

Integration, then, has become a key organizational concept for macrolevel economic development that reflects "Washington consensus" economic policies emphasizing free trade and a neoliberal ethic in the information age. Clearly it has also come to play an important role in localized development ideologies. The 2003 Peace Corps *Annual Report to Congress* mentions "integration" fifty-seven times, not once in the context of Integrated Rural Development. In many instances, integration itself has become a primary goal of Peace Corps work. Rosa, the coordinator for language and culture who oversees the facilitators during training, used "integration" to describe the primary function of her job, saying that her job is to "oversee" and to "integrate" language and culture into training. Perhaps more tellingly, she used similar language in describing the end goal for training as a whole. Training, she mused, "is a process that turns PCTs into integrated volunteers."

This is not to suggest that the Peace Corps and other entities that employ concepts of integration or its variant in "wholeness" (see chapter 6) are directly propagating Washington consensus policies that favor free-market approaches to poverty eradication. What is clear, however, is that a switch in emphasis from infrastructure to information within a broader conceptual framework of integration has created a formative imagination of development less likely to take on structural inequalities through programs focused on road construction or universal health care, and more likely to place an emphasis on individual responsibility, knowledge, and participation in "integrated global markets." Those who remain unintegrated are not those cut off from basic social services, but those who refuse to participate in the seemingly open and egalitarian world of knowledge.

Development, in this regard, continues to privatize not just at the policy level, where the World Bank and other entities insist on privatization as a prerequisite to aid as a part of Washington consensus policies, but at the deeper level of core, assumed ideologies of what development is and who its primary actors are. When "integration" becomes the goal of development, individuals and private entities are the presumed instigators of that development and its presumed beneficiaries. The Peace Corps manual for health describes the goal of development as "a multidimensional, ongoing process of enlarging peoples' choices which achieves social, economic, cultural, and political changes within the society itself and its interactions internationally."[34] In the shift from infrastructure (generally the realm of the state) to integration (a personal or corporate responsibility), development comes to favor the private over the public, the individual over the state, and personal choice over public policy. While an integrated development may not always serve as a direct application of power or policy, then, it certainly does reflect many of the values of those powers and policies.

Finally, an integrated development that favors pedagogy as a central practice also opens new connections between religion and development, especially in the case of evangelical Christianity with its emphasis on individual salvation through knowledge of the Scriptures and subsequent election of a personal relationship with Christ. Both integrated development ideologies and evangelical Christianity rest on the premise that knowing (the truth) is the first step toward freedom, be it from sin, poverty, ignorance, or a combination of all three. Agape,[35] a Christian NGO that focuses on children, measures development in equally spiritual and material terms, having participants fill out sticker charts that mark learning goals, physical progress, and, most importantly for the organization, the day one accepts Jesus Christ as a personal savior. HCJB, like many evangelical development organizations, is interested in developing "whole persons," that wholeness being defined as physical, spiritual, and psychological. For these organizations, in a way strikingly similar to the Peace Corps, ideal development is integrated development, one that seeks to create whole, educated, and connected individuals living in improved physical conditions that they themselves have created, and for which they themselves are responsible.

The Paradox of Integration: Positive Community Development as Limited Action

While integration is the positive organizing element that supports development-as-pedagogy, then, *limited action* is its negative counterpart. Like integration, limited action draws on the ideals of a development that is not top-down but rather comes from the needs, wishes, and circumstances of those being "developed." Where integrated development situates developer and developed in close quarters, placing the knowledge of the developer and local ways of knowing into a utilitarian combination, limited action eventually removes the developer from the project altogether. Once she has given her knowledge to those she has come to teach, the ideal development worker in this system fades away, having played the role of adviser but intentionally relinquishing that of the "doer."

Limited action as a development ideal is apparent throughout Peace Corps training and literature, especially in sections that focus on development theory. Currently, volunteers are encouraged to use a system known as PACA (Participatory Analysis for Community Action), developed by the Peace Corps and codified in the PACA manual in 1996.[36] In the PACA model, when volunteers arrive at their work sites, they are to refrain from beginning any major projects for the first three months of service. Development workers are facilitators, the manual states, and cannot be effective until they have a good understanding of the community with which they have come to work. According to the manual, "Participatory Analysis for Community Action (PACA) was developed to provide a set of gender-sensitive tools which could facilitate the implementation of an approach where projects and programs are shaped in a participatory process, with voices of the stakeholders themselves shaping the development process itself."[37] Staff members advise volunteers that rather than approaching development as experts who come to a community with a preformed "agenda," they should instead approach development in the mode of a student or researcher. PACA methodology encourages gender-specific community mapping, as well as surveys covering time allocation, household structures and capital, and community health resources. The introductory session on Positive Community Development, entitled "How to Be a Student," is designed to instruct trainees in the use of these methods.

While PACA is designed to forestall uninformed and inappropriate projects at the beginning of a volunteer's time in a work site, and to encourage a collaborative approach to project design and implementation, such restraint is also encouraged as a part of "good" development throughout training. The tech manual for the health program reminds trainees that they are not the "experts," and the trainer for Positive Community Development told trainees in one session that "you are the only ones who can change here." Volunteers, in this ideology, are not to be foreign experts but locally informed collaborators, facilitators for the "long and intentionally enduring process" that is sustainable development.[38]

Indeed, throughout the training cycle PCTs were reminded by current volunteers, facilitators, and training staff that any project they undertake should be primarily in the hands of the community with which they work. A knitting project in Mira, a small town in Ecuador's northern Imbabura province, has become the trademark of such collaborative, sustainable work. Emily and Peter Gladhart, volunteers in the town from 1964 to 1966, taught local women how to knit, and then helped to form a cooperative to market the sweaters to foreigners within Ecuador, and eventually beyond its borders. The project has been so successful that it has been replicated throughout the highlands, including in San Marcos, and is often held up as the shining example of U.S. aid in Ecuador. A July 2006 advertisement in the Guayaquil paper *El Hoy*, timed to coincide with ongoing negotiations over a proposed free-trade agreement between Ecuador and the United States, featured a woman knitting in front of a stack of the easily recognizable sweaters. The caption under the photograph read, "Ecuador and the United States. Friends. Partners." The text above described the original Mira project, saying that "this initiative is only one of many that, over the years, have marked the collaboration between Ecuador and the United States. In 2005, the United States contributed $21.7 million in economic development programs in the northern and southern border areas, and in poverty reduction programs throughout the country."[39]

And indeed it is "sustainability" that drives both PACA methodologies and the overall preference for not "doing" development projects which is prevalent in the Peace Corps and in contemporary development culture. As a movement closely linked to "alternative" development agendas in the late 1980s and early 1990s, "sustainable" development takes perpetuity, ecological responsibility, and indigenization as its core organizing principles. In an ideal world, sustainable development projects continue, evolve, and expand long after the development organization has left a work site. Development is maintained and internalized, as in the case of the Mira knitters, by the community the project is intended to benefit.

Certainly, the Peace Corps has become a proponent of such "sustainability," a term held up as a high ideal in training and in Peace Corps literature. During a training session for family gardens, for example, trainees were taught organic methods of planting and producing vegetable crops for home consumption. The trainer in charge of the session emphasized organics not only because they were "healthier" and "less dangerous" than chemically assisted gardening practices, but also because organic practices are "sustainable," requiring less economic investment from families and resulting in a reduced environmental impact. The trainer also emphasized the need to think about sustainability when choosing a garden site: water needs to be nearby and readily attainable, fencing materials need to be close at hand and cheap. Finally, he said, no garden will survive if the family it is meant to help does not want it, care for it, and own it. Volunteers could start the process and provide the necessary supplies and information, but the family the garden is intended to help would have to own it, to "do" the project in the end. During other training sessions, PCTs were reminded that while they had resources unavailable to most Ecuadorians, this did not make them experts. "Know your limits," one co-trainer advised. Again and again, trainees were advised not to do what an Ecuadorian could or "should" be doing, and not to overestimate their own roles as experts or resources. "You'll know a project is going really well," one volunteer told an assembled group during a session, "if it goes on without you, in directions you never intended."

The Power of Not Doing: Limited Development and Negative Theologies

As with integration, then, not "doing" a project is an organizing concept that both reflects and conceals power relationships at work in development processes. Though Peace Corps volunteers work via the power and the resources of the U.S. government, idealizing an indirect or limited involvement blurs the impact and the implications of that power. This is especially apparent in images of the local in rhetoric surrounding "alternative" or "sustainable" development work. Where development personnel, theorists, and the recipients of development efforts imagine development as localized, they may also imagine development to be naturalized; the inherent desire of people wishing for the greater "choices" such an idealized development may bring them. Gardening and knitting become idealized as locally desirable practices supported by outside intervention, rather than programs that may be fostered by a foreign government for its own political and economic interests, or in most instances, some complicated combination of the two.

Not "doing" projects as a part of "sustainable" or "alternative" development initiatives, then, does not completely unseat development as a vehicle that enables and maintains uneven power relationships and the structures that support them. For some, however, not "doing" development has become a conceptual vehicle for recognizing and challenging those power structures, opening up a space in which development, and the modernity of which it is a part, may be negotiated.

While some Peace Corps volunteers and staff use a formative concept of limited action to query the power structures of which they are a part, the ways in which faith-based development workers imagine inaction vis-à-vis colonial histories and contemporary state structures is indicative not only of the way they bring their religious histories and understandings to bear on their work, but also of the way that religious and development messages combine as faith-based NGOs bring them to San Marcos. By exploring what might be called the religious dimensions of an ideology of "not doing the project," in other words, we can see connections between religiously based and secular development projects, and their relationship to greater colonial histories and development strategies that they both resist and replicate.

Certainly, many personnel working in faith-based organizations engage "alternative" development language and concepts when speaking about their work. Ruth Bauer, for example, often made a point when describing her work of emphasizing her preference for "not doing" projects when establishing relationships with local communities, the Ecuadorian government, and the international organizations from which she draws financial and logistical support. She underscored that she does not undertake development projects unless they are specifically requested by a community, following a model of sustainability. And despite her frequent involvement with USAID as a granting agency, Ruth expressed strong reservations about such foreign support as a substitute for local systems. "You try to work with the [Ecuadorian] government, the government agencies," she said when I asked about her preferred partners for projects, ". . . because you want the people to go to their governments and find—you want them to develop somehow and not to be the patrón. That's our whole concept of development, not to be the patrón."

While Ruth would go on to describe development in positive terms when it comes to spiritual growth—something she frames in evangelical Protestant terms of having a "personal relationship with Jesus"— when it comes to what might be considered secular or traditional development focused on physical need, *not* becoming an authority figure with the sole ability to control resources was a major concern. Her "whole concept" of development was expressed not in positive terms of change or progress, but in preventing the reestablishment of a negative and disabling colonial relationship. In doing this, she decouples knowledge and resources from debilitating power relationships.

In a similar manner, Bob Newell, chair of the board of directors and one of the founders of Mercy Corps, International, a Protestant

NGO that does not engage in proselytizing, described the organization's approach to development by saying, "The whole idea is not to do the project," once again describing ideal development as coming not from a power center outside of a community but from the community itself. Like Ruth Bauer he was concerned with not reestablishing colonial systems of exploitation and dependence, though in his case the system he was concerned about was centered not in Washington but in Soviet Russia.

> The whole idea is not to do the project, the idea is to teach the process . . . That they can organize, that they can do stuff, that they can find the resources . . . And it's hard, I think it's hard for Americans to understand how paralyzing the Communist system was because everything flowed from the top . . . [But] we use a community-based model because we say, we've worked ourselves out of a job. We say that's our goal. It doesn't always work out that way, but sometimes it does.

Again, ideal development is imagined in terms of limited action, in countering colonial processes of intervention and centralization, even as Mercy Corps is heavily dependent on aid from Washington—the organization received $169 million from USAID between 2001 and 2005—to carry out its programs.[40]

Such a limited idealization of development among faith-based personnel is often accompanied by, if not partially rooted in, Christian theologies that favor a unique emphasis on divine power, tied to service to God and evangelical witness.[41] Henry Palacios, a doctor working with HCJB in Ecuador, described his view of development in theological terms, once again framed in a negative grammar. "I'm not here to impact a community," he said when I asked about his goals as someone working in the development field.

> And you know, the argument is still there. Why are you going to Ecuador? You're never going to change health care there. You're not going to change [the hospital]. I was at [the hospital] for an entire year, and you walk in there today, and it looks just like it did when

I left. But then the question comes, and I think this is the question that is critical for missionaries and people who do this work: Are you here because you can impact a community? Are you here because you can change a hospital? Are you here because you can get a result that you can see and measure? Or are you here simply to serve at the pleasure of your Lord?

While Henry does not address the colonial or neocolonial legacies of development, his theology, which emphasizes service to God over more traditionally quantifiable progress, counters the same kind of centralized and hierarchical development that Ruth Bauer and Bob Newell criticize in their responses. Once again, ideal development is expressed in terms that any Peace Corps trainee who has read the PACA manual would recognize: not in results that one can see and measure, not in impact, not in tangible change on the part of development clientele, but rather transformation of the person who has come in the name of service.

Henry's emphasis on service to God over quantifiable progress also points to one way in which concepts of development that favor limited action employed by faith-based development workers can engage and expose development's ties to colonial and neocolonial power structures, opening up negotiations about the implementation and legitimacy of those structures. Catherine Masters, a pastor at a mainline Protestant church in central North Carolina, uses negative theologies and imaginations of development to force college students participating in "alternative" spring break trips to recognize unequal global systems. Taking twenty-five to thirty-five students from several area universities to work in Haiti, as well as in poor sections of Washington, D.C., and Georgia, she describes her primary objective in organizing the trips is "to do no harm." "I think doing *for* can do harm," she commented when asked to clarify her goal. "I think that presuming what people need does harm. And I think we can be pretty disempowering. You know, creeping in with our assumptions and all of our haves. So I try to set it up with a lot of opportunity to listen. I want [the students] to have a sense of the political reality and of the impact our country has on wherever we are; the choices that the First World makes, and how that creates and sustains the difficulties that other people have." For Catherine Masters, good development is once again framed in the negative—doing no harm. And, once again, it is theologically rooted. "I think that the dominant misconstrual of Christianity today is an emphasis on the risen Christ that comes from the post-Pauline letters," she explained,

> where Jesus, where this sort of white-robed, shiny-faced cherub is sitting at the right hand of God the Father and judging us with mercy and kindness and gratitude as opposed to the . . . Social Gospel . . . where you have this historical Jesus . . . that really, quite frankly, held us a hell of a lot more accountable. It was the Jesus that actually walked in the dirt, you know . . . He actually lived with the people. So I think mission trips provide us with the opportunity to be converted from the sense that Jesus is just a nice guy who wants us to love other people . . . And also a conversion from a pretty un-aware understanding of what it is to be American and what the United States is doing in the world; to be converted to a much more deep understanding of our responsibility in history. It is no acci-dent, it didn't just happen that Haiti is the poorest country in the Western Hemisphere and that it was once the wealthiest colony of France. That took effort. You have to make that happen.

By framing development in specifically theological terms, both Henry Palacios and Catherine Masters strip development of its hegemony in the context of superior Western progress, resisting, either covertly in the case of the doctor or overtly in the case of the pastor, the Washing-ton consensus assumptions about the place and power of Western de-velopment policies. What Gilbert Rist calls a hegemonic "belief" in development as a salvific paradigm is uprooted by a theology of a differ-ent kind.

The invention of a development that favors pedagogy as a pri-mary practice and integration and inaction as organizing concepts has thus opened a large and active space in which the negotiation of development—its meanings, its deployment, and its consequences—may take place. In advising its volunteers that they are not experts, and in requiring them to wait three months before beginning a project, the Peace Corps signals that its volunteers, while equipped to be information brokers, must be information brokers in conversation with the communities they have come to serve, a practice that often leads, to the consternation of some volunteers, to conversations about what is useful, or desirable, about development itself. For Bob Newell and others in the faith-based context, an organizing concept of limited action not only allows them to negotiate a sustainable development that does not replicate repressive social structures, but helps to expose those structures, opening them to critique.[42]

Though they often reflect the uneven colonial power structures of their inception and current implementation, then, the development discourses that converge in San Marcos are clearly multiple, critical, and open to negotiation as to their meaning and implementation. This chapter has focused on the negotiation of meanings at the institutional level, from the experiences of those who work for and in development organizations. We now turn to the negotiations and understanding of development and of its confluence with religion from the experiences of Marqueños who receive, barter for, and reject development assistance as a part of their negotiations, and reformations, of modern life.

GOOD HOUSEKEEPING

Negotiating Religion and Development at Home

Negotiations, as human activity, happen in places. Where one can slow down enough to glimpse and perhaps go through the thin barriers between public and private life, one can begin to discern the points of contact and exchange where larger discourses meet and are transformed by local lives.

Doors often represent this barrier between the public and the private, marking the liminal zone between the inside world of the household and the outside world of commerce, government, and public exchange. The space immediately around doors is of neither one world nor the other. In San Marcos, most people keep wooden benches or stools near the entrances to their houses as ready places to sit when guests appear or when occupants of the household want to make themselves available for conversation with passersby. During my time in town, I could always count on a dialogue with Don Segundo, my seventy-year-old neighbor who spent hours every day on a bench in front of his house near the main market square. "Where to today?" he would ask as I made my way up the hill toward the center of town. "Stop by on your way back for a *copita* [of cane alcohol]!"

I often took Segundo up on his offer, pulling up one of his tree trunk stools and leaning against the outside wall of his house as we discussed local politics, weather, and his career as a horse breeder. As we talked, his wife, Sara, would frequently appear from the kitchen on the other side of the wall, bringing us a steaming bowl of hominy (*mote*) or some tortillas that she had made. We became good friends, but neither I nor Brian, who also made it a habit to stop by for an occasional drink or round of cards, was ever invited inside to the spaces reserved for family. We remained outside, in public territory. The door was a barrier most people would never cross.

Segundo's and Sara's door is not unusual. Double sided, doors in San Marcos often bear the marks of their occupants on their interiors as they support calendars, religious images, carved family names, or newspaper cuttings. On the outside, doors display the signs of more public interaction. Campaign posters decorated many domestic entrances in San Marcos in 2002, making it clear which political party the family behind them supported. Doors were also the markers of official government recognition and hegemony as mandatory census stickers from 2001 were joined by Ministry of Public Health vaccination stickers the following year.[1] In each of these instances, doorways worked to identify the household as a basic social unit at the center of attention from public powers and institutions. Campaign workers, census takers, and health officials all announced their contact with household members inside the doors with signs placed prominently on the other side, purposefully within public view.

This chapter is concerned with such interactions, and specifically with the household as a place where the larger networks that religion and development use and create come into contact. In the household, development organizations work in kitchens and bedrooms as they aim to modernize the ways people cook, eat, dispose of waste, sleep, and reproduce (or not). At the same time, many of these spaces are the object of religious discourses as evangelical Christian, Catholic, and older Andean sensibilities inform correct diet, family relationships, and ways of living in the house and on the land. Households in rural Ecuador are thus places where Ecuadorians encounter and negotiate many of the diverse and overlapping discourses that religion and development create. Sometimes Ecuadorians blend religious and development ideals into cohesive interpretive platforms that meld religious and scientific understandings of sexuality, households, and families. Sometimes, however, they explode those hybrids back into their previous, delineated forms.

These processes of fusion and explosion point to a larger interaction between religion and development which calls into question development's exclusive claim to modernity, and also religion's supremacy as the fount of tradition in domestic spaces. They also raise questions of agency and the contradictory place of desire as that which drives and is simultaneously stifled by religious and development discourses in the space of the home.

Households, in other words, are places where discourses collide, fusing into new realities that combine elements of "tradition" and "modernity," the sacred and the secular, or exploding back into separate domains. By looking at the ways that these fusions and explosions come about in household spaces, we can learn something about the relationship between religion, development, and agency in daily, private life.

Zones of Production: Hybridity in Private Spaces

The term "household" is used here in both its geographic and social sense, identifying households as physical places where people live and work, as well as social structures that may include members of extended conjugal families, fictive and affinal kin, and other entities such as livestock. A long line of academic and other discourses take households as their subject. Indeed, households share a similar status in religious, development, and anthropological rhetoric and ideologies, especially as they relate to community.[2]

Religious institutions, for example, often assume that households are the basic units of their communities. In Christian circles, church membership rosters list "families" or "households" as the basic social element of which their populations are composed, and many churches emphasize the role of family in maintaining a strong society within and beyond church walls.

Annual reports for development organizations also join in this view of communities, and list "households" or "families" as the basic components of society.[3] Indeed, households and communities are inextricably linked in development discourses. In a speech in a rural community in

2000, an agricultural representative from the Bolívar Provincial Council said that "every household has the right to food and development,"
notably emphasizing households over the individuals who compose
them. Manuel Míguez, one of the technical advisers to UMATA in San
Marcos, echoed these sentiments when he defined communities as
"groups of families."

Aid recipients also identify households as the starting points of community and of development as a community concern. In 2000 a woman
in a small Bolívar town defined development as "something that affects
the home," when I asked her for a brief explanation of what development (*desarrollo*) is. She then went on to explain that what affected the
home would eventually work to affect the community at large. This is
a formula often repeated in religious circles, where people point to religious conversion or rededication as the catalyst for changing family
relations, and then for the community as a whole. Indeed, the same
woman who identified development as "something that affects the
home" used the same words when I asked for her definition of religion,
placing development and religion in the same familiar space and at the
base of the communities of which those spaces are a part.

Academic descriptions and analyses join churches and development organizations in viewing society and its institutions as entities
based on component households. Many ethnographies on religious
change in the Americas, for example, have focused on household relations, and especially on the way that evangelical Christianity may allow
for changing gender roles first in domestic spaces, and then in society
at large.[4] A 1984 ethnographic study designed to measure the effects of
evangelical Christian development organization World Vision on Ecuadorian indigenous communities used similar language. The report described communities by counting households in a geographic area and
then subdividing the total number by categories that included religious
affiliation, agricultural activities, race, and ethnicity.[5] By so dividing the
community, researchers in the study replicated World Vision's methods
for measuring success, once again reckoned by the number of households with which the agency worked. The study, taken in combination
with the rhetoric of religious and development communities it documented, shows that across the spectrum the household is the stuff of
which people presume that communities are built, a sort of societal

Figure 2. Image of the Virgen de las Nubes in a San Marcos home. The image travels from house to house on specified days each month. Photo by author.

DNA made up of family units that combine economic, social, and religious concerns.

Households are volatile entities, however, and are never quite as perfect in practice as they are on paper, or in the multiple discourses that employ them as a basic unit. While churches and development organizations and some social scientific surveys describe households as single, united elements, in reality many households are composed of multiple, even disjointed parts. Rural Ecuadorian households often include several generations of family members, itinerant workers, guests, friends, and fictive kin, and may be missing members of a Western-style nuclear family as mothers and fathers emigrate to Ecuadorian or foreign cities in order to find work or educational opportunities.[6]

Indeed, many people describe households as including several generations, plots of land, goods, and properties. One woman living with her grown daughter and two sons in San Marcos, for example, sometimes included her elderly parents living on family holdings outside of town in her description of her household (*la casa*). Notably, pigs and other livestock she keeps for profit were also included in her descriptions, though none of this was replicated in the 2002 Ecuadorian census.

Ideological diversity is also rarely accounted for. Evangelical missionary Joyce Davis, for example, asked her home congregation in the United States to pray for the husband of a San Marcos family with which she studies the Bible. She sees the wife and children regularly, but the husband remains outside of formal religious activities. This particular household is counted as Catholic on local parish rosters as both the husband and wife were baptized and confirmed in the local Catholic church, but would be counted as evangelical in ethnographic surveys, especially those interested in religious affiliation and practices.[7]

Like the discourses and networks with which they interact, then, households are hybrid, moving combinations of people, objects, and beliefs that can fuse or collide in countless amalgamations. Rather than thinking about households as natural, contained entities, then, I have tried to conceptualize households as points of contact where people engage with a variety of material and intellectual flows.

This characterization stems partly from the work of Enrique Mayer, an Andean anthropologist who describes households in economic terms, calling them the "the basic units of production, distribution and consumption" in small Andean communities.[8] While I wish to trouble the idea of a "basic unit" that he employs, his work is particularly useful as he describes households, or affiliations of households that share land and other resources, as controlling a large "zone of production" where the basics of life, and society, are continually made and remade. Mayer describes production zones as communally managed sets of resources meant to fulfill needs beyond the reach of single households, though households remain the basis for their management.[9] This description builds on the work of John Murra, who argued that Andean societies were organized around four key concepts: control, maximum, vertical, and ecological levels.[10] It was through careful management of

multiple levels, Murra argued, that Andean societies, and the households that composed them, could obtain the variety of resources they
needed for continued existence, even when located at high altitudes
with limited agricultural potential.

While Mayer agrees with Murra that tiered production zones are an
integral part of Andean life, he feels that too much attention has been
paid to verticality and ecological levels as natural phenomena. Andean
peoples did and do maximize production by taking advantage of several vertical ecological zones, but they have done and continue to do
so via political systems of control meant to maximize use of those various levels. Production zones, Mayer contends, are not simply ecological
niches ideal for growing certain crops or animal husbandry. Rather, they
are societal and thus political creations, the result of human cooperation and contestation.[11] They involve agency in the form of daily negotiations that combine politics with the more concrete stuff of water,
soil quality, altitude, or fertility.

Something similar is happening with households. Like the larger
production zones Mayer claims they support, households are not purely
economic or biological entities, defined solely by plots of land, family
occupations, or the human needs of reproduction and bodily maintenance. Instead, their output expands well beyond physical, biological,
and agricultural spheres. Households are production zones where
political, ecological, and social resources combine, allowing—even
compelling—people to form worldviews and opinions that influence
experience and interpretation both inside and outside their doors.
Households are thus hybrids—biological and social—places where we
have never, despite the modernizing efforts of development and the
discipline imposed by religion, maintained what Latour recognizes as
the "modern divide" between nature and culture.

Households are also excellent examples of the problems inherent
in using the term "hybrid" as a metaphor for the things people create in
the spaces where discourses join and overlap. While we have seen that
hybrids are productive and able to reproduce and to affect the social
order, in their original, biological context hybrids were by definition
infertile, the sterile offspring of different species. In a similar manner,
the concept of hybridity brings with it a history in the linguistic sphere,

one linked to theories of creolization and the spontaneous creation of new dialects when two languages exist in the same, usually colonial, space. In both instances, it is difficult to give credence to human agency in the formation of hybrids and in their continuing utility as linguistic and epistemological frameworks. In Latour's model, for example, where networks come together hybrids simply result, partially because people need them in their drive to maintain the illusion of modernity, and partially because people are blind to their own motivations. Hybrids, productive though they may be, just happen among moderns, who, in his model, take the opposite stance of premoderns by denying hybridity even as they produce it. "While the moderns insure themselves that they are not thinking at all about the consequences of their innovations for the social order," writes Latour, "the premoderns—if we are to believe the anthropologists—dwell endlessly and obsessively on those connections between nature and culture. To put it crudely: those who think the most about hybrids circumscribe them as much as possible, whereas those who choose to ignore them by insulating them from any dangerous concepts develop them to the utmost."[12] By refusing to look at the places where nature and culture, science and tradition overlap, Latour asserts, moderns, and he would include contemporary Ecuadorians among them, create hybrids without intention. While there is agency in separation, we lose it entirely when our efforts at separation fail and hybrids proliferate, coming into the world under their own power, and mostly of their own accord.

Such descriptions of the origin of hybrids in points of contact are useful as we examine households as places where diverse, competing, and contradictory discourses come together. Here, hybrids are a *condition* of modern life, a useful descriptor of the way things are. But they are a limited descriptor in that they cannot take into account the places where hybrids fail, where people refuse to let the interconnected discourses in which they are involved come together. To understand better the place of hybrids, then, and also their limits as people sometimes prevent their formation or continuation, I employ a sense of hybridity that takes its cue from Bakhtin, who describes hybridity in dialectic terms.

"What is hybridization?" Bakhtin asks in *Dialogic Imagination*. "It is a mixture of two social languages within the limits of a single utterance, an encounter, within the arena of an utterance, between two different linguistic consciousnesses, separated from one another by an epoch, by social differentiation or by some other factor."[13] In Bakhtin's model, hybrids are the result of shared linguistic and conscious discourses, but they are not the inevitable result. Where people are able to see division, they are able to bridge it, subsuming one discourse into another, or separating them out again so they no longer share the same linguistic, psychological, or social spaces. While hybrids in this instance may be unconscious, the simple result of networks coming together, they may also be conscious, the result of fusion, or separation, at the behest of the actors who create them. Hybridity in these cases is not only a condition but a *tool*, something with which people negotiate and inform the conditions in which they live and act.

Hybrids in the context of households, then, are productive entities that are concomitantly and variably produced by Marqueños and others involved in religious and development organizations. Examining the ways that these discourses come together in household spaces such as kitchens and bedrooms, along with the hybrids that such convergences create and resistance to those hybrids, reveals the modes and zones of production that people use to give religion and development some of their specific texture, economy, and meaning in everyday life.

Cooking up Modernity: In the Kitchen

Within Marqueño households, kitchens are among the most obvious production zones. Be they interior structures with cement roofs and gas stoves, exterior buildings where the smoke from wood fires escapes through thatch, or one end of a single room in the smallest rural homes, women sustain their families in kitchens, turning raw agricultural products into finished sources of sustenance. Accordingly, kitchens are places where culture is created and sustained. Food, and the social roles surrounding its cultivation and preparation, help mark San Marcos as a unique location with its own cuisine—foods that taste of home. Most families own several hectares on which they farm both sweet and feed corn, and the provincial tourist pamphlet promotes San Marcos's corn tortillas, hominy, and steamed corn fritters (*humitas*).

While the men take charge of most large-scale agricultural matters, it is women who give the raw products shape, producing local specialties. Indeed, kitchens are one of the most gendered domains in Ecuadorian life. Women both produce and are produced there. As a single Peace Corps volunteer, I was often teased by my friends that I was ineligible for marriage because I was incapable of making a good soup or shaping a perfectly round tortilla.

For many women in rural Ecuador, then, kitchen activities are a primary occupation. Women rise before dawn to make tortillas and coffee, spend noontime hours cooking large pots of soup to feed the family and any extra workers at lunch, and then finish the day by providing a substantial meal of rice, salad, soup, and, when available, meat. For both women and men, kitchens are a center of family life. Men start and end their days in kitchens, eating the food women produce before and after spending sunlit hours in the fields as they work to provide more of the raw ingredients. Often kitchens are the only space in rural homes where the entire family will gather, talking over events of the day. As Mary Weismantel has documented, what a family eats reflects its economic and ethnic status.[14] Indigenous rural families, for example, will consume meals based on barley and quinoa, while most mestizo families, whether they live in the countryside or in small towns, fortify their soups with store-bought wheat noodles. What a family *is* has something to do with what, how, and where they eat—that is, with the networks that are involved in the foods that they use. Culture and families are produced in the kitchen.

I spent a fair amount of time in Ecuadorian kitchens, both as a Peace Corps worker and as an ethnographer. Since I was an extensionist, my role in kitchens was mostly social. Several women with whom I became friends got into the habit of inviting me in off their outside benches, making me family for the time it took for us to share a meal together. Their invitations, spurred by some combination of compassion and curiosity that my strangely single status engendered, allowed me access to the private spaces of kitchens. Able to see behind the scenes, I would watch women prepare food and wash dishes as we chatted about upcoming projects or the day's events. I rarely did formal work in the space of other people's kitchens during my time as an extensionist, my realm being clearly defined by my occupation and my unmarried condition. When I worked, it was in the outside world of fields and family gardens.

I was able to become more involved in kitchen work in my capacity as an ethnographer, however, since I had married and taken on work I could practice indoors. I helped the Santa Anita women make *humitas* for their trip to Guayco, for example, and Lucía occasionally allowed me to knead bread, grind corn, wash dishes, or dice some tomatoes for her salsas. I often used my time in kitchens to ask women questions related to gender, querying their thoughts on married life and children in a space where such talk is common. Cooking areas became perfect workspaces for me, comfortable places in which to discuss the roles kitchens help to produce.

While I had to switch positions in order to enter kitchens professionally, then, development workers dedicated to nutrition, health, and alternative technologies often begin there. Development workers in health programs, for example, frequently give talks about sanitation, cleanliness, and nutrition focused on the kitchen, seeking to educate people about washing their hands, food choice, and preparation. In a similar manner, the structure of the kitchen itself is a primary concern for many development organizations, both secular and religious. Plan International has built dozens of cinder block kitchens with gas stoves in schools and community buildings in Bolívar province. Staffers from HCJB joined in this concern the night of the home birth in Puyupamba as they considered a lecture on ventilating cooking rooms as an accompaniment to a showing of the *Jesus* film, a standard evening activity after a day in the mobile medical clinic.

Much of this development attention toward kitchens has to do with "modernizing" or "improving" the ways in which families produce and store food. Traditional Andean kitchen spaces are dark, with dirt floors, thatched roofs, adobe walls, and a raised brick fire pit taking up one side of the structure. Food hangs from forked sticks suspended from the ceiling, and most of the cooking is done in large pots placed on stout wood or, more recently, on rebar rods directly over the fire. Water for cooking and washing is stored in buckets residents place strategically around the room. For many residents of rural Ecuador,

Figure 3. A "hybrid" area of a San Marcos home, with traditional cooking fire and modern washing machine. Photo by author.

especially those living in places smaller than the town of San Marcos, these kinds of cooking spaces remain in use, even as they may contain functioning lightbulbs when communities connect to electric grids, and are often the home to a family's radio or television set.

When the Ecuadorian Ministry of Public Health and Plan International joined forces to implement a program in nutrition education in 2000, however, traditional kitchen spaces were strikingly absent from the didactic pamphlets they produced. In one pamphlet aimed at improving storage and preparation of basic foods, the cover and inside pages feature pictures of fresh produce being washed under a tap located inside the kitchen space, and all of the cooking scenes take place over the distinct flames of propane stoves. In another scene, a woman inspects an egg by holding it up to an electric light bulb suspended from the ceiling.

In the series of six pamphlets, the only scene featuring "traditional" cooking over a wood fire is in the context of a warning. "DON'T eat street food," warns the caption beneath a rendering of a market scene in which a woman cooks in a markedly traditional Andean pot. Next to her, a boy deposits the food he has just purchased into a trash can as flies buzz over his head amid the floating labels of "hepatitis," "cholera," and "typhoid." In all of the pamphlets clean, healthy kitchens where people produce nutritious foods are depicted as "improved," with propane stoves in place of wood fireplaces and potable water piped directly to a tap in the room. Not coincidentally, these "improved" kitchens are also depicted as havens of gender equality. Every pamphlet in the series features men doing traditionally feminine tasks, including cooking, marketing, and washing dishes.[15]

As the object of development discourses and actions, then, kitchens become one place where modernity is imagined and enacted. Food becomes the object of science, analyzed for its nutritional value and possibilities for disease or cleanliness. Culture, in this case embodied in gender roles and behaviors, is also the explicit object of development critique as progressive, developed kitchens produce progressive, developed men able and willing to take on egalitarian roles. Clean, safe, and nutritionally improved, modern kitchens (and these more recently include refrigerators, microwaves and commercial ovens) produce modern families, the children of which, in the words of one of the pamphlets, "develop normally, as much physically as intellectually."[16]

Kitchen spaces in San Marcos often replicate, at least to a small degree, those depicted in the pamphlets. The town of San Marcos is electrified, and the gas truck makes its way up and down San Marcos streets offering replacement propane cylinders for household stoves once a week. But kitchens are also spaces where traditions are produced and preserved in a hybridity unrecognized or even discouraged in most development projects aimed at cooking spaces. Both Antonieta and Lucía, for example, do their cooking over both propane stoves and fires, using gas flames for small batches of soup and rice, and the fire pits for making large pots of hominy and morning tortillas. Indeed, both women have split kitchens designed especially for such expansive cooking options. They use their propane stoves in cinderblock rooms while maintaining fire pits that are paired with thatched roofs in separate but attached structures.

There is a method behind the duplication. No propane stove, Lucía explained to me one day as I joined her for coffee and tortillas, could adequately render the lard of a pig or boil corn into the hominy people need to properly serve guests. "It doesn't know how!" she clarified, the joke glinting in her eyes. Even for life in the modern world, one needs traditional implements and the spaces in which to use them; some improvements would be no improvement at all.

If kitchens are one place where people negotiate, and sometimes reject, development discourses about improvement and modernization, they are also places where they negotiate religious identities and understandings. In Catholic kitchens, the sweet blueberry *colada morada* people make for Day of the Dead, corn *humitas* they eat for Carnaval, and *fanesca*, the fish and grain stew they consume around Easter, are all made in conjunction with feast days, cooked when possible over wood fires. In addition to consumption, people often pray before they eat, and it is not uncommon to see children preparing for catechism classes around the kitchen table. Even the decor marks kitchens as religiously connected spaces. Many Catholic households feature a reproduction of da Vinci's *The Last Supper* on a kitchen wall, and crosses fashioned from fronds carried in Palm Sunday processions are common adornments. Kitchens are points of contact where indigenous, Catholic, and Protestant religious networks and practices meet with those of development, spawning hybrid and conflicting ideologies that people interpret and negotiate, reintroducing religious elements in some places where secular ideologies have left them unrecognized, and separating them in other spaces where either religious or development ideologies would place them together.

Take, again, guinea pigs. As native Andean food animals, guinea pigs carry indigenous religious significance, though they are also the object of development rhetoric focused on production and marketing. When someone is ill, it remains common to find a local healer willing to deduce the cause of the sickness by reading the entrails of a guinea pig that has been passed over the victim. When the *curandero/a* has determined the cause of the illness, he or she will recommend an appropriate remedy, one that is often targeted at spiritual maladies.

One of the reasons guinea pigs are believed to be efficacious in their diagnostic abilities is their place on the kitchen floor, underneath the warmth of the raised wood stove where they eat scraps from the family's food. Guinea pig entrails can tell the story of human ailments partially because they share similar spaces and similar foods. They are culturally related. Indeed, when someone is ill, guinea pigs kept on kitchen floors are preferred to those which have been moved to cages outside the house, even if the person seeking a cure or explanation for an illness is simply going to wave or rub the guinea pig over the ill person without killing it. "How could a *cuy desarrollado* ['developed' guinea pig, raised outside and meant for the market] know what's wrong with us?" one rural woman asked when I inquired about her mixed system that incorporated guinea pigs both on her kitchen floor and in cages outside.[17] "Only the *criollos* [natives] understand who we are." It is kitchen spaces that give guinea pigs part of their cosmological significance and efficacy, even as they are also associated with development programs and market strategies designed to increase both home protein consumption and family incomes.

Kitchens retain this hybridity in Protestant circles and are common spaces for religious teachings and activities conducted by San Marcos Jehovah's Witnesses, Pentecostals, and evangelical Christians. Patricia Chandler, a Jehovah's Witness missionary who lived with her husband in San Marcos for five years, often read the Bible with women in kitchens as a part of her door-to-door ministry. Frequently, the readings she conducted included lessons on cleanliness and the role of women in keeping a sanitary household, beginning with food handling and preparation. "When we study the Bible with people there is a lesson about being clean," she explained when I asked about activities that people might see as related to development work. "Simple things like washing your hands after using the restroom or before manipulating food . . . We feel that health is very important. We feel that God requires his servants to be clean, clean people." Witness missionaries also mimicked the Ministry of Public Health, distributing an *Awake!* pamphlet in February 2003 entitled "Malnutrition: The Silent Emergency." Articles inside advised women on correctly feeding children, quoting UNICEF and the World Health Organization as well as the Lord's Prayer ("Give us this day our daily bread") as it outlined a theological basis for practical action to end world hunger.[18]

In a similar manner, evangelical missionary Ruth Bauer often finds herself in kitchens, teaching about nutrition and domestic infrastructure as a part of her work in San Marcos and its surrounding communities. Ruth often quotes biblical passages, linking a relationship to Jesus with health and longer life. "Teaching about water and having clean water and boiling your water and so forth, I use the passage in John 4 [the parable of the Samaritan woman at the well]," she explained. "Jesus is the water. He said that 'I am the living water.' With nutrition, Jesus is the bread of life out of John. That's basically how I try to teach." Pentecostal pastor Edgar Lorenzo is also concerned with linking what people consume and do in the spaces of their kitchens with what he terms a "sanctified life." Seeing my husband, Brian, and me exchange an empty case of beer bottles for a new, full set one day, he came knocking on our door the following afternoon. He wanted to be sure I knew that what I did in my house would affect my spiritual and physical health, he said, indicating our kitchen where the new beer bottles reposed. "How is your soul today?" he asked every time he saw me thereafter. "Are you feeding it properly?"

Kitchens are thus places where people encounter and negotiate understandings about proper living that sometimes combine and sometimes break apart discourses that originate from widely varying sources. When Edgar Lorenzo warned me about alcohol as an abuse of the body God had given me, for example, he combined theology with discourses about the effects of alcohol on biological structures. "Some people say that because God made alcohol, it can't be bad," he told me during an interview in which he repeated his concern over the beer in my kitchen. "Don't fall into that line of thinking. Your body is a gift from God, and if you poison it, you are sinning. You have seen the effects of alcoholism on people here. It ruins their livers and their minds. It ruins families. This is the one of the drunkest provinces in Ecuador. People here are *torcido* [twisted] in their understanding of religious truths!" For Pastor Lorenzo, his religious argument was strengthened by a biologically based rhetoric that would look familiar to the most secular development personnel.

In a similar manner, Catholic women also combine discourses when talking about faith and household matters. Magdalena Lopez, a forty-eight-year-old mother of five children, spoke admiringly of Santa Rita de Casia, patron saint of a local parish. Unable to join a convent due to her parents' insistence that she marry, Santa Rita was forced to endure an abusive marriage to a drunken husband who did not provide for the family. Rather than let her children or her spouse starve, she is said to have cut pieces from her thigh to feed them.[19] Magdalena was especially impressed with this act of generosity and sacrifice, noting that Santa Rita provided her children with "protein" and "good food" in the face of severe adversity. "She is a wonderful example for the home," Magdalena concluded. "As the Word of God says, as mothers we have to provide . . . in the home more than anything."

For both Edgar and Magdalena, biological explanations of consumption and nutrition lend credence to religious beliefs, lend support to broader cosmologies. The biological models of nutrition and sanitation that dominate secular development rhetoric become religious in the social spaces that kitchens provide. That this is a negotiated hybridity, one that demonstrates a certain agency on the part of rural Ecuadorians, is made clear by the woman who could not easily combine scientific practices with religious beliefs in kitchen spaces. For her, guinea pigs could not be both religious objects and market products. Through mechanisms of negotiation, Ecuadorians construct worldviews that reflect not only physical reality, but also a cosmological interpretation of that reality that takes religious beliefs and experiences into significant account.

(Re)Production Zones: Bedrooms in Religion, Development, and Household Life

Kitchens of course are not the only place in households where religious and development discourses and personnel come to touch. As the particular focus of both development work and religious attention, sleeping areas are also specialized zones of production where people create hybridized understandings of their lives and worlds, understandings that illuminate the complex relationships people create between religion and development.

Most of the focus of both development and religious discourses in bedrooms is aimed at bodies and health, both spiritual and physical. Development lectures on family health, for example, reflect the fact that entire family units often share a single bed, and frequently include a diagram for placing people with heads next to feet so that they are less likely to share colds or parasites. Sanitation and cleanliness also play major roles in charlas about proper behaviors in bedrooms. Health care workers from Plan International, the Ministry of Public Health, HCJB, the Peace Corps, and other organizations often emphasize the importance of washing bed linens and airing mattresses in their presentations.

By far the greatest emphasis on bedrooms in both development and religious discourses, however, comes in talk about families, familiar relationships, sexuality, and reproduction. While the specifics of proper behavior vary and are openly contested between Catholics and Protestants—and between religiously affiliated and secular development agencies—there is a widespread agreement that what goes on in bedrooms affects the rest of the household. Like kitchens, bedrooms are zones of production where Ecuadorians create, contest, and maintain households and gender roles.

The emphasis on bedrooms, and specifically on sexuality and reproduction, is deep-seated in both development and Christian doctrines. In development, "population" and "overpopulation" as terms used to describe global crises based on human reproduction came into use after Truman's 1949 inaugural speech.[20] In 1952 John D. Rockefeller III established the Population Council to study the "problem" of growing global populations and human reproduction, especially in countries deemed "underdeveloped" in Truman's inaugural address. Despite this, initial U.S. development policy was ardently removed from the area of human reproduction. In an article on population as a part of development policy, Barbara Duden quotes Dwight D. Eisenhower from a 1959 address, when he stated, "Birth control is not our business. I cannot imagine anything more emphatically a subject that is not a proper political or government activity, or function or responsibility."[21]

With the popularization of "family planning" as a preferred term in the 1960s (at roughly the same time "family values" began to gain currency as a descriptor of conservative moral stances), the prevailing attitude among development agencies shifted. Duden quotes George H. W. Bush in 1973, when, acting in his capacity of U.S. representative to the United Nations, he declared that the "population problem" was "no longer a private matter . . . [It] commands the attention of national and international leaders."[22] As Duden documents, "birth control" became "family planning" in the course of becoming an international development concern, something that has not changed as state and private development agencies have begun to address the worldwide epidemic of HIV/AIDS, often through religious agencies. PEPFAR, George W. Bush's President's Emergency Plan for AIDS Relief, for example, reported that between 2004 and 2005 its faith-based partners increased from 20 percent to nearly 25 percent, a trend that reflects a U.S. policy that makes faith-based groups "priority local partners" in the implementation of AIDS and HIV treatment and prevention.[23] What people do in their bedrooms, and what government and religious agencies should do about it, became as important within religious and development discourses as what people do in their fields, their factories, and their houses of government. Households and their size came to be front and center in larger debates over effective development and its goals. Bedrooms were institutionalized.

Human reproduction and sexuality continue to play important roles in the goals of many development agencies, and most people in San Marcos have had some interaction with development personnel who speak about reproduction and sexuality in the context of personal and household health. For example, Plan International distributes a pamphlet entitled "Improving My Family" in conjunction with UNICEF and the Ecuadorian National Institute for Families and Children (INNFA). While it never directly addresses birth control, one chapter is entitled "Being a Better Couple." Words underneath the title inform readers that to be a better couple is "to respect ourselves, help ourselves, and accept that both of us have equal rights and responsibilities together. So long as there is love, the rest is unimportant." The following two chapters address "The Rights of Pregnant Women" and "Becoming Better Parents."[24] Improving one's family starts with improving one's relationship with one's spouse, a relationship that includes love and then children (though, notably, not necessarily material wealth) in the scenario the pamphlet lays out.

Other development organizations are more direct in their approach to familial relationships and issues of reproduction. The U.S. Peace Corps in Ecuador often sends volunteers to work with NGOs in health care, many of which are involved directly with family planning and birth control.[25] HCJB also offers reproductive advice and medical assistance in its clinics, and Ruth and Joyce frequently counsel women and families who come looking for family planning advice. On market days, it is not uncommon to see a small line of people knocking at the missionaries' front gate. Business can be quite lively. Ruth recalls that she spent a particularly memorable Christmas Eve teaching a woman how to use contraceptive foam.

Work such as Ruth's and Joyce's points to the fact that reproduction has never been a simply secular issue. Christian doctrines and social teaching also have something to say about reproduction and its place in family structures and correct living. What happens in the bedroom is a reflection of people's understanding of their relationship to God and to church teachings on human sexuality and the family. For Marqueño Catholics, this includes church doctrines that proscribe premarital sex, artificial birth control, abortion, and homosexual relationships. It also includes family roles as defined and reinforced by church teachings. Magdalena's description of Santa Rita as an example for women in the home, for instance, reifies church teachings about women as nurturers and sacrificial mothers.

Evangelical Christians also discuss appropriate sexual relationships in the context of their doctrines and teachings about correct living. None of the Protestant groups in San Marcos prohibits birth control for married couples, and Ruth helps women obtain it in her work as an HCJB missionary, but all encourage abstinence until marriage. Anita Martinez, a Vicenteña Jehovah's Witness, gave voice to these teachings one day as we were talking casually about world affairs. "We wouldn't have problems with AIDS," she opined, "if people would just do what the Bible says and not have sex before marriage. It's all there, it's in the Bible, they just don't know." Her sentiments were echoed by Edgar Lorenzo, the Pentecostal pastor, who pointed to his family as his greatest pride and joy after a service. "People are so twisted in their thinking," he remarked, "they think sex is about pleasure. That's just Satan's way of confusing people. It's really about family. It's about doing God's will."

Joyce Davis also brought up sexuality and church teachings as she discussed her work with young girls. When I asked what her most successful effort had been in her more than twenty years in San Marcos, she replied, "Just feeling like maybe the spiritual influence I've had in their [her pupils'] life has helped them to become a better person. Or it's helped them from falling into some of the problems a lot of other kids do . . . even seeing some of the girls wait until they're married to become involved in active sex. And not ending up pregnant at fifteen." For all of these people, sexuality is linked to right behavior, to right relationships with God, and to families within traditionally defined household relationships. What happens in the bedroom is to happen according to doctrine, and then to be nurtured in the kitchen with the support of church and family structures.[26]

What happens in bedrooms in relation to sexuality and reproduction, then, can be related to the networks that both development and religion create. Sex can be modern in the context of the "better relationships" that human development organizations such as Plan International promote, and it can be traditional in its relation to the nuclear families supported by Christian doctrines. It is also contested, making the bedroom another place where people negotiate religious and development ideologies and their relation to the multitude of other factors that make up modern life.

Often this negotiation focuses on the ways in which religious doctrine and development goals and practices conflict. Miguel Artola, director of the Health Education Program for Peace Corps Ecuador, cited sex as a sticking point when it came to collaboration with religiously affiliated development organizations.

Miguel Artola: When we work with nutrition, we don't have a problem [working with religious organizations]. Not with mother-child programs either. But when we talk about family planning, or work with the prevention of sexually transmitted diseases, with behavior and the use of various methods that aren't accepted by the church, then yes, we've had some trouble.

JD: With the Catholic Church?

MA: And with the evangelicals, too.

JD: Really?

MA: Yes. For the majority of the evangelicals here, abstinence is one of the things that they promote. But, the use of condoms, they don't use them. The use of spermicides, of contraceptives, they don't use them. So we have certain limitations.[27]

A staff member in the Community Development division at HCJB also mentioned issues of sex and reproduction as stumbling points when it comes to collaboration between HCJB and other organizations, including the Ecuadorian government. "It [our evangelical identity and commitment] isn't a huge issue," she said,

> But we did run into a problem in that one of the things that we've been asked to do mainly in San Lorenzo is tubal ligation for the women. The hospital is a Catholic mission hospital in San Lorenzo, so we have a clinic with an operating room, and one of the things that people ask us for is family planning advice, and tubal ligation is one of the things that's indicated.
>
> We did apply to the government at one point to bring down a couple of North American surgeons that we could rely on and a general surgeon [to do the ligations], but that was denied . . . It doesn't make any difference to us now because our general surgeon will have an Ecuadorian license and we can do what we like. But we decided to comply with that ruling there.

For both the Peace Corps and HCJB, sex and reproduction are points of contact where ideologies collide, where the hybrids they would like to create between religion and development break down. The Peace Corps cannot quietly reconcile its desired biological and behavioral education with the religious doctrine of the Catholic and evangelical organizations with which it collaborates, and HCJB, which already offers medical services for religious purposes, finds that its own brand

of hybridity does not match that of the Catholic Church or the Ecuadorian government.

In a similar manner, Marqueños and other Ecuadorians also challenge hybridity in bedroom spaces, sometimes choosing options that
development provides in spite of contrary church teachings, and sometimes ignoring development advice for religious reasons. Angelina
Cruz, a woman in her midforties living in a Quito suburb, chose a tubal
ligation after her seventh child had been delivered via caesarian sec-
tion. "I know the church doesn't approve," she told me when I asked if
she had any reservations about the procedure, "but God gave us the
technology, right?" She then went on to explain that though she and her
family were Catholics, they felt that there were some areas in which the
church had no business interfering.

In another instance, Luz María Carvajal, a woman in her midthir-
ties living in rural Bolívar province, ignored the advice of visiting doctors. Though she has six children and frequently says that her family is
complete, she did not accept any of the forms of birth control visiting
physicians offered in an effort to spare her from another pregnancy
they feared would be difficult if not dangerous. "I know they are trying
to help," she said when I asked why she was unwilling to use artificial
methods to prevent another pregnancy, "but God is in control. There
are some things in which we shouldn't interfere. It would be a sin." Even
in the bedroom, there is a limit to the combinations that religion and
development create. Some lines are not easily crossed.

The bedroom, then, is a good example of the ways that intercon-
nection does not always result in an easy hybridity that goes unnoticed
or entirely uncontrolled by those who are affected by overlapping discourses. At some points, the same discourses that blend and recom-
bine as they come together also cause friction, separating out again in
the crucible that placed them together. Some of the combinations that
religion and development forge, in other words, are explosive, capable
of causing conflict and greater definition of difference rather than
seamlessly melded forms.

In this way, bedrooms are places where it becomes apparent that
neither religion nor development stays comfortably camped in the larger
metanarratives of progress and tradition with which they are usually

associated. As the "Improving My Family" pamphlet so obviously dem-onstrates, heterosexual love and marriage are the center of even the most progressive of households in development ideology. By the same token, the Enlightenment notion that religion is somehow restrained by the traditions of which it is partially composed is genuinely challenged when an evangelical woman uses a medical pathology to support church teachings on sexual morality, and a conservative missionary organiza-tion finds a way to confront the Ecuadorian government and offer sur-gical birth control. Not only does it appear that development has never been modern in the context of bedrooms, it would appear that religion has never been entirely traditional as it engages scientific understand-ings of the body to bolster doctrine and to challenge the most modern of institutions, the nation-state.

Negotiating Desire in Religion and Development

Kitchens and bedrooms, then, reveal the common deployment of reli-gious and development discourses in household spaces. They are also places where desire plays a unique role in the conceptualization, im-plementation, and negotiation of religious and developmental ideals.

Certainly, desire is a central component of Ecuadorians' experiences with religion and development as ideological movements, one place where their convergence may be observed and theorized. In his work on colonial constructions of culture and human difference, Christopher Herbert calls attention to desire as culture's uneasy dialogical partner, claiming, "The doctrine of culture can be said to take form as a scien-tific rebuttal to this myth [of the ungoverned state of human desire in 'primitive' societies], but it has never succeeded in dispelling it, for it is invoked in various extreme forms in theoretical and polemical writing, and in colloquial parlance as well, to this day."[28]

For Herbert, the invention of "culture" as a way of explaining human diversity never quite broke away from Victorian rhetoric about desire as a defining trait of "primitive" peoples. Rather, desire became subsumed into culture, lurking in everything from anthropological depictions of the other to colonial encounters in which modern men and women found themselves longing after their native hosts. The sexiness of the foreign became codified in modern rhetoric about exotic cultures and places.

Something similar is at work in development. Though an ostensibly modern invention focused on "progress" through economic and material betterment far from the realm of emotion, desire plays a large, if often unacknowledged, role in development imagery and practice. One needs to want a gas stove or ventilation holes in kitchen walls before one can take action; one must choose to move guinea pigs into cages out of doors. To become "developed," one must desire, and then take action to enter into, a personal relationship with modernity as defined by some kind of material or ideological "improvement."

Indeed, and as Chris Shepherd has documented, a fundamental assumption, and frustration, among development workers is that development clientele should have a natural inclination toward the "improvements" they offer.[29] Women, and to a certain extent men, are expected to work toward the goal of clean, bright, and gender-equal kitchens because they are expected to desire these things over traditional kitchens, conceived in development rhetoric as deleterious, unsafe, and repressive. In the past, Ecuadorians, especially rural and indigenous Ecuadorians, have been expected to desire these things for the good of the nation, something codified in Ecuadorian president Rodriguez Lara's 1970s speech in which he described development as a process by which all Ecuadorians would come to share a standard (mestizo or white) culture that would unify the nation.[30]

In this respect, a specific kind of development desire can and often does function in a similar way to religious and specifically missionizing desire. In households, development workers and institutions assume and propagate desire as a basis for a change in lifestyle, one that professes salvation from ill health, gender inequality, and the dangers of being "left behind" technologically. At the same time, religiously motivated missionaries use development rhetorics of nutrition and improved living standards to uphold their theological and missiological claims, integrating religious understandings of the presumed universal need for transcendental salvation with more mundane circumstances.

Cleanliness is not only next to godliness but the way to God and a sanc-tified life. Desire is thus one mode where the religious roots of devel-opment are on display, one place where connections between changes in daily practices are connected with cosmological motivations and consequences.

A focus on desire as it manifests in religious and development dis-courses, however, also reveals that the deployment of desire is uneven. By attempting to constrain desire, either through doctrine or by lim-iting sexual practices, religion and development discourses in the bed-room are in an antithetical role to that which they play in the kitchen. While desire is still at the base—one must want to control family size, for example, or comply with what one assumes is God's will in order to reach a larger, metaphysical goal—desire in the bedroom is not based on positive expenditure or consumption but on the paradoxical condition of restraint. One reaches what one desires by constraining one's desire. Development is taken out of its usual mold of concrete improvement and placed instead into the spiritual realm of ascetic discipline.

While much has been written about hegemonic assumptions of the desirability of development, then, Ecuadorian households reveal an equally important facet of contemporary development practice: that of an ascetic constraint of desire that often conflates religious and de-velopment goals. People produce understandings of religious and de-velopment goals using both positive and ascetic notions of desire, using both modes to reproduce, and occasionally to subvert, the dominant discourses.

It is thus this dual application of desire in religious and develop-ment discourses in Ecuadorian households which opens up the possi-bility of agency. If development is not so modern as it seems, nor reli-gion so traditional, if desire is multifaceted and contradictory, it has something to do with the way early twenty-first-century Ecuadorians understand and reproduce these discourses in the spaces of their homes. Unlike Latour's hybrids, which he claims proliferate despite moderns' best intentions of separation, Ecuadorian households reveal some-thing closer to Mayer's production or "alternative" development's ide-alization of integration: an often conscious, strategic blending of ma-

terial, cultural, and intellectual resources which works toward continued survival. Where religion and development discourses deploy modernity through interventions designed to change existing practices
under the rubric of improvement and desire for this improvement,
Ecuadorians fashion something that might best be termed a negotiated and subsequently reformed modernity, one that both accepts and
subverts certain claims about the desirability of a secularized notion
of development or its implementation. Santa Rita's act of sacrifice becomes one motivated and described in the context of nutrition; birth
control is chosen or rejected on the basis of (sometimes heterodox)
theology. Desire and its constraint are translated into local terms and
conditions that are not always in accordance with the ideologies whence
they spring.

Zones of Reproduction: Households and Community in Religion and Development

Finally, the production, reproduction, and constraint of desire in religion and development contexts are not limited to private spaces. As
we have seen, households are the breeding grounds for the hybrids of
religion and development which people create and contest in private
life, and for their negotiations in private spaces. But households also
present a public front. There is leakage in and around the door. Border-
lands between public and private spheres, households offer a glimpse
into the ways in which Ecuadorians work to inform and create concepts about community as an integral part of both religious and development practices and ideals, concepts that allow for agency and negotiation at the level of society.

   One sign of this leakage is the way in which religious organizations
and aid agencies replicate households and familial structures in the
work that they do. Religious organizations, for example, often call up
images of households and families as they use familial language to describe larger communities, both within and outside of the immediate
church setting. In a sermon he gave on the occasion of St. Mary's (Mercedes's) feast day, for example, the Catholic priest in San Marcos likened

the nation of Ecuador to a large family with Mary as its patroness and loving mother. "She came with the Conquest," he noted, "and led us to independence, to the status of adults with our own house." His image of Mary as the mother of Ecuador bound the congregation, and indeed the nation, together as Mary's children, and also reproduced the household as he depicted his audience as children with filial responsibilities. As Catholic Christians, as children of God, Ecuadorians were to take care of the house Mary had helped them to build.

Protestants invoke similar images as they use household and familial language to identify fellow *creyentes* (believers). Runa evangelical men, for example, refer to each other as "*wawki*," or "brother." In a similar manner, Jehovah's Witnesses use the terms "sister" and "brother" to refer to fellow members of the church, and further recreate household roles by adhering to gendered tasks in church activities.[31] Women study with women, and only men are allowed to read Scripture in public settings. Just as men and women have specific places within the household as defined by Witness doctrine and interpretation of the Scripture, so do they have specific, determined places within the church. Worship spaces are replicas of the household, one of the places where private spaces are reproduced in public settings.

Development organizations also reproduce household spaces and actions in public realms. Perhaps the clearest example of this replication of the household in development work comes from Plan International. Founded at the end of the Spanish Civil War to aid orphans, the agency reproduces both household spaces and relationships in the public sphere. While the agency has recently begun extensive education projects in health, nutrition, and human rights, all of which touch on household spaces including kitchens, bedrooms, and latrines, its earlier efforts were focused on infrastructure. Most communities in Bolívar have "*casas comunales*," community houses, that Plan built to host local meetings and recreational functions. Almost every elementary school in the province, despite being federally funded and constructed, has a new kitchen building complete with several propane stoves which bears the unmistakable Plan logo on the outside. The agency has reproduced household structures in public community spaces, replicating traditional spaces in the name of (modern) community development work.

This kind of replication is not limited to infrastructure. Plan also replicates family structures as it collects funds based on a familial model of patronage. Plan asks men and women in donor (Western) countries to act as "godparents," donating money to children in the developing world. Godparents are encouraged to write letters to their "adopted" children, and the children in turn are required to write to donor parents at least twice a year.

At its most basic level, this arrangement reproduces and extends the household as it replicates basic parent/child relationships within families. Plan's adoption of the term "godparents" to describe donors also calls up strong images of *compadrazgo* (godparenthood) structures put in place and maintained by the Catholic Church. Families enter into godparent relationships on the occasion of a child's baptism, first Communion, and marriage, and godparents are expected to contribute to the financial, emotional, and religious well-being of the child throughout his or her life. Indeed, parents often use godparent relationships to cement friendships or shaky family ties, as well as to improve family fortunes. *Compadrazgo* is one way that families are extended beyond the borders of households, coming together into larger reciprocal communities on the basis of shared faith, religious practices, and economic ties. By invoking this relationship in the work that it does, Plan replicates and reproduces this arrangement, further cementing the household as a basis of community life even as it inadvertently introduces religious images into its work.

Indeed, the requirement that children write to their sponsoring "godparents" can lead to the reproduction of the household and religious obligations in public, community spaces. When I arrived for a weekly Santa Anita knitting session one Thursday in December 2002, I found the upstairs table at the cheese factory—normally covered with pattern books and skeins of yarn—heaped instead with paper, glitter, glue, and paints. Rather than the usual crowd of women, ten children sat around the table, busily turning the craft materials into Christmas cards with the help of attending adults, most of them members of the cooperative.

The younger kids drew scenes on the outside of the cards they made, mainly representations of local life. The adults and older children then wrote messages on the inside of the cards. "Dearest Godparents," most of the cards were addressed, "I wish you a very Merry Christmas and a Happy New Year." The adults then referred to a list of the children Plan sponsored in the local area and signed their names to the cards, one child per card, until each of the sixty or so children was represented.

It would be easy to read this scene as a sort of grand deception; or as a condemnation of the women's group and the community that accepts Plan funds without, apparently, taking their obligation to communicate with Plan sponsors very seriously. Yet the production of the Christmas cards is an accurate reflection of the way that Plan uses sponsor funds within the communities in which it works. No child receives the money his or her godparents donate directly. Rather, Plan monies are divided up by community based on the number of sponsored children within that community. The kitchens, latrines, *casas comunales,* and education programs that Plan sponsors do not go to households but to the communities of which households are a part. Community Christmas card production, then, especially in a space that closely resembles a kitchen table with parents lovingly guiding their offspring along, makes a certain amount of sense. Households in this instance are a tool, a fiction everyone is willing to live with and to reproduce for the greater good of community life.

While Plan is the only development agency in San Marcos to use extended kinship terms in describing donor/recipient relations, it is not the only agency to reproduce and reinforce the household in the work that it does. Proyecto Bolívar II, an infrastructure development project funded by the European Union, counted recipients by "heads of household" within designated communities and distributed aid only to those listed accordingly. In the UMATA project in Sinche, "households" were also the presumed beneficiaries, and at the initial meeting the extensionists asked the president of the Sinche organization "how many households" the organization included.

Household images are further enhanced by the presence of food and even kitchens at many development events. At the guinea pig conference sponsored by the municipio, for example, we shared a common lunch, coming together, family style, around the space of a table. Every time the UMATA extensionists traveled to Sinche in order to work on the nursery, they ate a sumptuous lunch prepared by the wife of the association president. Santa Anita cooperative members also ate together frequently in the course of their work, crowding together into the smoky kitchen at the cheese factory in order to cook meals made with the rice, tuna, and oil that Ecuador's Ministry of Social Welfare donated to registered community groups such as the cooperative.

In all of these examples, kitchen spaces and activities were reproduced in the spaces development creates, blending them together so that the private, traditional spaces of the household were given public currency in development settings. Some of this is practical—people need to eat during activities that last several hours away from home—but some of the reproduction is done with a conscious eye toward community formation. The food donated by the Ministry of Social Welfare, for example, is explicitly intended to aid in "creating community" in small social and development organizations.[32]

In reproducing household spaces and activities, then, both religious and development organizations seek, paradoxically, to create public and communal settings by replicating private spaces and functions. Whereas household kitchens are spaces for intimates, for the production of families, the kitchens development creates and uses aim to break down some of those walls, creating something that goes beyond family into the realm of community. As with Christian discourses that broaden nuclear families, opening them up to larger communities in the space of the church, development also redefines and recreates family units, idealizing them as the building blocks of society even as it redistributes them in new, public groupings. In both religious and development reproduction of the household, community is emphasized as the natural expansion of household, a grand family that works together and makes decisions to better collective circumstances.

The similarity in the ways that religious and development agencies replicate households thus often leads to a mixing of religious and development discourses, and often to their easy convergence. Marqueño children have both religious and secular godparents. Adults move through recreated household spaces that both religious and development organizations encourage as part of the work that they do.

The replication of households by religious and development organization also leads to the paradoxical situation in which development, as a "modern" construction, helps to create and proliferate the traditions that both religion and the household represent. The Santa Anita women, for example, do their cooking over a fire, maintaining old ways even as they use development funds and food designed to "improve" just such practices. Indeed, the women in the cooperative retain such traditional cooking practices to the point of pain. The kitchen in which they cook is of new construction, and has no ventilation for the smoke preparing food over the large central fire produces. Often we would cook and eat with tears streaming from our eyes, the propane stove the cooperative owns unused in a back corner. Funds from the government, meant to encourage community in the women's process of "advancement," quite literally fueled the flames of tradition. In a similar manner, the UMATA extensionist's use of the "household" as a basic unit when asking about the makeup of the Sinche agricultural association, and the generalized use of "households" as a basic element in development practices and plans, all lead to the reification of the household, a traditional space, as the basic unit and requirement of progress. As in the case of private households, where those households are replicated in the public sphere, people engage in negotiations that result in a modernity with a striking array of traditional elements in some instances, and their absence in others. The same women cooking over smoking fires with eyes tearing from the effort reject the fictional, if traditional, structures imposed by a development organization intending to help their children.

The reproduction of the household into the public sphere, then, reveals a negotiation of religion and development that serves to push against a modernity defined and enacted solely from without. In public as in private, an examination of households and their reproduction in public spaces shows us that while development may be rightly characterized as a Western-dominated, global hegemonic system, this system is frequently challenged when it comes into the space of the home, be that home at the individual or communal level. Certainly many rural Ecuadorians believe in development, much as many of them believe in Protestant or Catholic doctrine. They desire it. How these beliefs and desires come together and break apart in the space of the households, however, defies any easy logic that describes Ecuadorians as simple "victims of the miracle," be that miracle agricultural, medical, or ecclesiastical.[33] Rather, Ecuadorians tailor the realities that appear in the private spaces of the home and public spaces of their communities as they go about the work of negotiating, and reforming, a modernity they can live with, a modernity that defies not only the predictions of the death of God but also any easy removal of God from development's ideologies and products.

FIVE

CEMENT THINGS

Imagining Infrastructure, Community, and Progress

Buildings. Easily visible from the side of the road, buildings are among the most obvious signs of development and institutional religion in the modern Ecuadorian landscape. On the highway from Guaranda to San Marcos, a nursery complex sponsored by a Catholic development organization dominates a hectare with raised seedbeds, cinder block storage sheds, and multiple greenhouses. Not far down the road, a small metal sign announces the turnoff for a new Pentecostal church, its walls just discernible in the distance. Off the highway, the Plan International office occupies a large, three-story white structure next to a school in Guaranda, the logo on its roof competing for visual space with the Catholic spire in the central town square. In San Marcos, the slaughterhouse and a community center, both covered with the emblems of their sponsoring state and nongovernmental organizations, are clear symbols of the presence of development enterprises and the role of government in local projects. The town's several churches attest to longer and changing histories of religious identities and affiliations.

This chapter explores the role of buildings in development and community life, fleshing out the ways in which what Ecuadorians call "cement things"—large infrastructure projects such as bridges, buildings, and roads—act as public points of connection, exchange, and negotiation between religion and development ideals. Like the kitchens and bedrooms of the previous chapter, buildings are focal points where religious and development ideals are produced and enacted. Be they community centers, water stations, commercial-grade animal pens, churches, or houses of government, buildings provide telltale evidence of community as a physical and ideological entity. They are monuments to the many interactions between Marqueños and larger discourses, and to the interpretations and productions of reality that these discourses foster. Buildings are public commodities, spaces where overtly communal conceptions of religion and development are produced and codified. These processes of production enacted through the imagination, construction, and maintenance of buildings serve to create spaces where Marqueños negotiate religion, development, and ideas of progress in the context of the communities in which they live.

Bricks, Blocks, and Buildings: Infrastructure in Ecuadorian Life

Much of development's history is tied up in what Ecuadorians have come to identify as *cosas de cemento,* the "cement things" that were the focus of early religious and development efforts in the country. As discussed in chapter 2, San Marcos sprang up in the late eighteenth century as a colonial town formed around the original Catholic church building. The physical structure of the church, as well as the religious, social, and economic communities institutional Catholicism created, served as a center for a new kind of community life, one that tied San Marcos to Rome and to the Spanish state. In a similar manner, bridges, roads, dams, and buildings—the stuff of basic infrastructure—were and are the building blocks upon which development progress has been constructed and defined. The Ecuadorian Ministry of Public Works, for example, calls this kind of infrastructure "the motor of increasing progress in all of the regions and provinces of the country."[1] Cement things create community horizons and give form, function, and meaning to progress and modern life.

Beyond this, cement things such as the cinder blocks commonly used in Ecuadorian construction projects serve as tangible evidence of institutional success. World Vision, Plan International, and other development organizations often use building supplies as a quantifiable marker of program execution, carefully counting the number of cinder blocks and bags of cement they have delivered to the communities they serve. Religious groups, developmentally oriented or not, also measure their effectiveness in structural terms. Every new church a community erects is a victory for the sponsoring denomination, physical evidence of metaphysical gain.

The real advantage of focusing on buildings and construction materials, however, comes from the opportunity to examine the way that these entities, as nonhuman actors introduced by religious and development organizations, come to interact with and affect the most human of constructions: communities. As physical enclosures, buildings and other structures give the communities that religion and development create identifiable form. Cooperative members working in the Santa Anita cheese factory are walled off from the rest of San Marcos, their membership clearly marked and enacted, when they gather in the space the group has created. Working in the nursery in Sinche, UMATA creates new markers of community as association members are allowed to pass onto the private land donated to the project, their hands working together to construct bamboo seedbeds and shade structures. And, of course, Catholics, Jehovah's Witnesses, and Pentecostals in San Marcos enter into a clearly defined and demarcated community when they enter into their churches, stepping into the spaces where people perform actions and articulations that create group identities around religious understandings and practices.

This relationship between infrastructure—in this case buildings and the materials that compose them—and community/national identity is adeptly captured by political theorist Benedict Anderson. In his analysis of nation-states as amorphous yet powerful entities in the modern world, Anderson argues that ideas of a "nation" are often generated in the context of communal imagination. Media and other global conduits allow an articulation and unification of language and ideas across space, time, and cultural differences such that disparate groups of people may come together in the common, imaginary spaces that they produce. Many Marqueños, for example, experienced the beginning of the 2003 U.S. invasion of Iraq through Ecuadorian media, connecting to the event through stories of the more than five thousand Ecuadorians serving with the U.S. military.

Anderson argues that states codify this collective imagination through the production of national maps and other materials such as museums and censuses that create a sense of nationality and common heritage.[2] What Latour designates as nonhuman actors, the stuff of God and nature, becomes common property, the stuff of collective imagination and identity, through the implementation of censuses, maps, museums, and widespread participation in capitalist markets. Nationals became those who share a common but readily reproducible sense of ownership, history, and participation in the state imaginary.[3]

While Anderson never touches on religion or development as collective enterprises (though he does credit the expansion of print media to the Protestant Reformation), his concept of imagined communities is useful as we examine the relationship between infrastructure and the communities that Marqueños create around religion and development enterprises. Marqueño communities share a physical presence in a way that Anderson's larger, national communities do not, but they have in common many of the same aspects of idealization around imagined histories and purpose which Anderson documents. Many of these imagined histories and purposes are focused on infrastructure. Water systems, mills for grinding grains, and agricultural buildings such as greenhouses are often the major focus of local religious and development communities; they are the very things around which some communities form. The Catholic congregation in Alta Pamba, a small community just outside of San Marcos, for example, spent most of the year I was in residence raising funds to renovate their aging church, which still lacked a bell tower.

In a similar manner, while Santa Anita activities were often centered in the completed cheese factory building, it was not uncommon for the group to continue to focus on infrastructure issues by entering into discussions about building maintenance or expansion. The association in Sinche also kept infrastructure at the center of their activities. Indeed, local farmers created the group for the specific purpose of obtaining infrastructure in the form of a nursery. All of their meetings centered on this goal as the municipal engineers and local association

members spent their time together petitioning for and then constructing the seedbeds for the nursery the municipio had pledged to install.
Infrastructure, then, is often at the center of projects undertaken in the
name of both religion and development. It is another place where development desire and its negotiation in daily life are on display.

Desire in Public Places: The "Primitive" Drive for Modern Structures

Certainly desire focused on infrastructure is a central component
of people's experiences with religion and development as ideological
movements centered in specific spaces. What I termed "development
desire" in the introduction and more fully explored in the previous
chapter is often manifested as a longing for visible "progress" in the
form of infrastructure such as roads and buildings. Development desire focused on infrastructure is a driving force behind many people's
willingness to become involved with development projects or organizations.[4] During my time in San Marcos, for example, the president of
a newly formed coffee cooperative approached me to ask if I knew of
any organization that might be willing to help the group construct a
building similar to the Santa Anita cheese factory. The coffee group did
indeed need space in which to sort, roast, and grind their product, tasks
that they had been undertaking in the lower part of a member's house,
but they also wanted the greater visibility and prestige a "real building"
would bring. In asking for my assistance, the president assured me that
the cooperative was a "real group" and "very organized," capable of living up to the responsibilities of permanent infrastructure.

The president's use of language linking the group's status as "real"
and "organized" to the possibility of infrastructure is not coincidental.
Development desire not only drives people to become involved with
projects, it also requires them to engage in certain kinds of language
games. The president of the coffee cooperative assured me that the
group was "organized" because this is a prerequisite for receiving funding from any development organization. By approaching me, she was
also signaling the other key component for development participation,

a "genuine" drive for improvement and change. Individuals and communities looking for assistance must *prove* their desire for development involvement, codifying it in the correct paperwork and language.

Ruth Bauer, for example, will only work in sites where she has been invited. It's difficult to sit and wait for people to come to her for help with projects, she commented when I asked her about how she chooses communities with which to work. "It's hard, it's hard to just sit and wait. It's hard for development agencies as well. But I would never have done the water project with [a local community] except that they came asking for it. They came with a letter." For Ruth, communities must consciously choose to seek out development aid if it is to be successful. They must take individual desire and make it communal desire, codifying their wishes in formal requests for assistance.

Ruth's emphasis on community as the basis for successful development is not unique. Communities must fill out official requests for assistance from organizations as varied as the Peace Corps and the Ministry of Agriculture. In these *solicitudes* (applications) they are making their wishes official, formalizing desire in paperwork and government language. At the same time, they are making this desire a public, communal entity.

In this manner, then, buildings and other "cement things" are often monuments to development desire as it comes into contact with institutional and more broadly cultural imaginations of community. They are places where desire turns public, where it is linked to community and people's imaginations of what community is and should be.

Thus buildings are places of communal imagination and enactment. When members of the Santa Anita cooperative, the Sinche association, and the parish in Alta Pamba get together to break ground and lay brick for the buildings they have decided to erect, they are not simply constructing workspaces. Rather, they are equally involved in constructing community itself. Building community, often tied by religious groups to building faith, is frequently just as important for members of the groups and their sponsors as completing the projects at hand.

In this manner, the bricks and cement of construction projects become yet another point of contact between the religious and development networks, another place where Ecuadorians negotiate, appropriate, and challenge the ideologies those networks bring. Bamboo beams and barbed wire become pieces of common ground, and common wants. They become the physical structures where religion and development may come together or be walled off, allowing people to form new and changing ideologies and imaginations that carry into everyday life, and particularly into people's conceptions of community as the necessary, often idealized basis for both spiritual and material progress.

Public Spaces, Public Lives: Infrastructure and Community in Development

One of the clearest examples of the linkage between infrastructure and a collective imagining of community in San Marcos came at the dedication of the Santa Anita cheese factory in October 2002. Workmen had finished the fence around the building just in time for the dedication, clearing away the last of the debris less than an hour before the Promoción Humana Land Rover pulled up to the building and spilled its cargo of two priests and personnel from the Guaranda office. The fence was twelve feet tall and constructed of imposing and expensive chain-link on a rock base, and was the last component of the factory to be completed. Its finalization meant that the entirety of the funds donated by the Italian organization Mani Tese had gone to its intended use, and that the factory was now not only fully operational, but also fully protected from thieves and wayward livestock capable of demolishing cooperative gardens.

The Salesian priests, Father Antonio Polo and Father Mateo Panteghini, cast approving glances at the fence and the freshly washed walls of the factory building as cooperative members ushered them inside for the dedication ceremony. The grounds and all of the building spaces were spotless, the *socias* (members) and I having labored in a communal work party (*minga*)[5] two days previously and on the morning of the dedication to prepare the factory for the arrival of distinguished guests. While half of the women toiled in the kitchen, preparing pork, *chicha* (corn beer), rice, and salad over and near the smoky fire pit, the rest of us worked at putting the public spaces in order. We washed down walls covered with mud from the recent rains and prepared the upstairs knitting room for its central place in the day's events.

It was in that upstairs room, the table covered with a white lace cloth to serve as an altar, that the priests, cooperative members, and guests gathered for the Mass and dedication ceremony. Under the watchful eye of a new image of Santa Anita that had been donated by a *socia* in honor of the event, Anamaría Carvajal, president of the cooperative, nervously welcomed the crowd of fifty people to the dedication. Reading from a sheet of notebook paper she had prepared for the occasion, she explained that the group had labored for many long years to be able to celebrate such an important accomplishment as the cheese factory. She was honored, she said, that so many guests had joined them to celebrate its opening.

She then turned the program over to Padre Antonio, who had just managed to get his robes in place when she invited him to begin the Mass. After an opening prayer, he invited a cooperative member to give a reading from one of Paul's letters in which he emphasizes the necessity of unity as groups work together. Padre Antonio then continued the theme in his homily, thumbing through his Bible until he found a passage from Mark that also treated the importance of cooperation within a group. True success, he intoned as he gestured around the newly finished room, comes from faith, dedication, group effort, and above all else, community. The success of the women's group was, and would be, directly tied to their ability to work together.

Padre Antonio again emphasized cooperation and community as he formally blessed the cheese factory by throwing holy water on the entrance gate and cutting a ribbon sporting the colors of the Ecuadorian flag. Just as good milk makes for good cheese, friendship and community make for success in any group, he quipped as he threw the holy water on the loading dock where milk deliveries come into the factory.

His sentiments were echoed yet again in the next part of the program. Regathering in the upstairs room after cutting the ribbon, and leaving most of the men outside to prepare fireworks, we sang the Ecuadorian national anthem, and then listened as Sofía Flores, a past president of the cooperative and its current technical adviser for knitting, read from the original charter. Founded by her and Magdalena

Figure 4. Santa Anita women's cooperative building, with cheese factory on the ground floor and other activities above. Photo by author.

Lopez fourteen years previously, the group was, from the beginning, intended as a cooperative "to benefit the community of San Marcos. Not for the good of one woman, but for all women, to capacitate and aid them to become better, more productive community members."[6] Pointing to a small side table on which cooperative members' handiwork was displayed, she smiled as she commented that they certainly had been productive and, for the most part, unified in their efforts. At the end of her speech, Magdalena and a few other *socias* served sweet muscatel wine and store-bought cookies to the crowd as the men released their bottle rockets to the sky. Before too long, the benches were cleared to let the dancing and celebration begin.

The dedication is a clear example of one way in which people link buildings, as public commodities, to community as an imagined and enacted ideal. Throughout the dedication ceremony, both in its overtly religious and more secular segments, the women's ability to work together was highlighted and reinforced as the key to their success. The dominant narrative of the day stated that without a unified community willing to work toward common development goals, there would be no building, and thus no foundation for the group's continued achievement as an entrepreneurial organization capable of improving the lives of its members.

While emphasized by the priests and the women in the course of the dedication ceremony, themes of community and cooperation were not unique to that day. Group members often referenced images of unity as they recalled the history of the group, speaking about the challenges of obtaining funding for the building and in continuing their many projects. "We started making cheese five years ago in a borrowed house," Anamaría Carvajal explained when I asked about the history of cooperative operations,

> and we worked there for three years. For three years we worked on fundraising and negotiations, primarily with the purchase of land. Three years went by, we were three years at the loaned house until we paid off the loan [on the land] and started to negotiate with Promoción Humana for the donation of the factory.
>
> The agreement for the donation of the factory was with . . . an Italian foundation that helped us, that supported us in the construction. We put in the labor. They gave us all the materials and we gave the labor . . . with the idea that the work that has to be done is always half, always half.
>
> As the group is a group, or that is, an organization, a group of women, we have to work, and it should be community work.

Anamaría's narration of the history of the cheese factory links the donation of building materials directly to the ability of the women's group to work together, both as they petitioned for help in obtaining the structure and as they executed its construction. She was quite proud that the group had made good on its "half" of the deal, providing all of the labor while the Italian organization donated the materials too expensive for the cooperative to buy.

Magdalena Lopez also attributed the success of the group to the women's ability to work together, especially as it related to the successful purchase of the land on which the cheese factory is located. Previously owned by a men's group sponsored by Promoción Humana, the land came up for purchase, Magdalena explained, because "they [the men] became disorganized. They started to fight among themselves and could not complete the project they started."

Several other cooperative members described the terms of the purchase in the same way, joining Magdalena in crediting their success to their gender and greater capacity for cooperation. "As women, we're more united [than men]," Sofía Flores explained when giving her account of the reason the cooperative has been successful where the now defunct men's group had not.

> If they [the men] get together, it's to talk about, I don't know, men's things. So even though there are various [development] groups in San Marcos, I think we're the most important because we know what we have to do. Men, on the other hand, they have a discussion and it ends and there they are, not having done anything, and there is discord or they even just get together and drink . . .
>
> What we want when we get together, whether in the cheese factory or in other activities, is to gain a space where women can develop themselves as human beings, where they can have ideas, where they can cultivate important roles in the community . . . We can do a lot of things. So this is the idea, that women feel a part of society.

For the women of the Santa Anita cooperative, the cheese factory is a symbol of the group's unique ability to work together, a monument to a cooperative spirit that they often link to their shared status as women struggling to gain a foothold in larger social contexts.

The women identify the building as more than just a monument to success, however, referring to it as a central component of the ongoing life of the organization. Their life as a community is centered in its spaces, and they frequently refer to it as a symbol of what they have accomplished as a group, and of what they feel they need to accomplish if they are to stay united, and successful, in their future endeavors. Their comments also reveal that they have come to think of the building, and of the cooperative, using development language. If they are to flourish as a group, to "develop themselves as human beings," they feel they need the building, the ultimate sign of development success. The language they use and the ideologies they profess tie together development, ideas of community, and infrastructure.

The members' connection between community and the group's ability to obtain, construct, and maintain their building is not unusual in San Marcos, or in development more broadly defined and enacted. Often, groups such as World Vision or Plan International will donate materials with the understanding that the recipient community, as a community, will provide most, if not all, of the labor required to complete the project. This is the "half" of capital construction projects that Anamaría described in the Santa Anita example.

For the donating organizations, this kind of partnership is designed to encourage a sense of ownership on the part of recipient communities, even as it is meant to mitigate failed projects placed in communities that have no vested interest in their existence or maintenance. In Sinche, for example, the municipio would not arrange for the donation of the money required to buy plastic, seeds, or chemical fertilizers for the nursery until the farmers' association had constructed nursery seedbeds with the assistance of the extensionists. The association had to prove its mettle as an organized community before receiving the bulk of the promised building materials.

The result of this kind of exchange—expensive building materials for proven community and cooperative ability—is an equation between community and development success which people reinforce as they imagine communities as the foundation of thriving development projects. Successful projects depend on successful communities, groups of people who can work together long enough to seek out and obtain materials from donor organizations. In a similar vein, lack of success in development is often equated, both by donors and recipients, to a lack of community cooperation, or to a lack of community at all.

Narrations describing this equivalency between successful community and successful infrastructure projects abound. In a completely spontaneous commentary, the carpenter Brian and I hired to fix our door one day responded to my description of the work I was doing by lamenting the end of San Marcos's Centro Agrícola, the farmers' cooperative. The cooperative had experienced its heyday in the late 1990s, having made contact through the Ecuadorian Ministry of Agriculture with the Chinese government, which had in turn donated two tractors and a thresher to the group. The cooperative had also managed to obtain the funds to build a meeting hall in the upper part of town.

When I asked why I had not seen the tractors or noticed any building dedicated to the group, the carpenter responded that the people in San Marcos were "*muy desgraciados,*" very ungrateful, hard to get along with. The cooperative members were too selfish (*egoista*) to learn how to share in their common properties, he said, and as a result the tractors sat on private land, unused by anyone. He went on to describe the vacant building as a "useless tons of bricks." He then related the failure of the project, and of the group, to a lack of community feeling and cooperation. According to the carpenter, individual self-interest trumped the loftier goals of the organization, leaving a pile of materials with no community spirit to make them utilitarian.

Such talk is common in development circles. The UMATA extensionists, Peace Corps volunteers, evangelical missionaries, and several Marqueños all cited "lack of cooperation" (*falta de comunicación*), "lack of community" (*falta de comunidad*), and "selfishness" (*egoismo*) as the primary reasons that development projects fail. Manuel Miguez, one of the UMATA extensionists, alluded to a lack of cooperation within communities, and between communities and development organizations, as he described what he sees as a stagnant development environment in the province: "Later [after initial meetings and the delivery of materials], what happened is there wasn't anything, there wasn't a sense of cooperation. So that's why a lot of the work was—what they sent in materials never resulted in anything like they said it would. People are poorer now than they were at the beginning."

Sam Martin, the Catholic Peace Corps volunteer who worked in San Marcos in the mid-1990s, cited similar concerns as he recalled that he refused to work on an irrigation project with an outlying township because he did not sense adequate cooperation within the community.

Well, you know, I would ask them, why don't you prepare this field, and next week we'll plant it. And then I'd tell them I'd get the seeds, all right, fine. I'll donate the seeds. You put in the work.

[The next week I'd] go back there, "Oh, no, sorry, didn't have time." I was just like, okay, they couldn't do their little part. And I said, I kind of wasted my day to come out here to try to help them do this.

And that would happen time after time, but they would always talk a good talk. They were like, "Oh yeah! Sounds like a great idea, we'll do that. Uh huh, uh huh, uh huh, uh huh." I felt like I was banging heads.

In hindsight, they did tend to be rather poor, and what I found later was if you work with the poorest people who need the help most, the problem is they usually can't put in enough time because they're too busy just trying to make ends meet. So to ask them to take a half day to clear that field, it doesn't sound like much, but for them, I mean, they had to go somewhere else and work for a day just to make enough money for the family. At the time I really didn't recognize that. But because of all those difficulties, and I felt that, it seemed like it was going to take way too much effort to come to the end result that I was seeking . . .

And then the other difficulty was they had to coordinate amongst themselves on the use of the irrigation system. And I could quickly see that really wasn't happening. So the whole community, it was kind of understood that they were going to have to organize, and coordinate to put the irrigation system in, which they finally did after a lot of nagging, but it looked like it was going to take way too much nagging from an outside person to get them to coordinate enough to actually use the irrigation system.

In both of these cases, the analysis of failure that Manuel and Sam provided focused on buildings and large infrastructure projects such as water systems which require some degree of community identity and cooperation in their construction, operation, and maintenance. Households that share a water line for irrigation, for example, must work out an equitable system of rotation in order to ensure that everyone on the system will benefit. And someone local needs to be in charge of collecting fees that the community will use for repairs when parts of the system begin to break down, usually within a year or two of installation. Any talk of infrastructure, then, must also involve some talk, and concept, of community: who the project will serve, who will benefit from it and be in charge of it once the parent/donor organization has pulled out, who will be working together, at some level, to ensure success. A lack of that cooperation at the most abstract, planning level guarantees failure, even as projects are in their infancy.

Infrastructure thus acts as a catalyst to create, maintain, and challenge ideas of community—their meaning, purpose, and flexibility. Ideas of communities—what they are and how they should operate—form around bricks, fences, hoses, and the walls of buildings that will house collective operations ranging from timber production to cheese manufacturing. Successful communities, particularly those that form around development goals, are those that manage to solicit, erect, and maintain infrastructure, especially buildings in which they may gather and perform the chosen activities of the group. Where things do not go well, where buildings end up as "useless tons of brick," the culprit is not bad planning or physical failure, but a "lack of cooperation," a lack of a community capable of working together to see the project through.

"Real" communities are thus envisioned by Marqueños and development officials as cooperative, like-minded groups of people pulling together to get the job done. Idealized as natural, homogeneous, and harmonious, community as it is imagined in the realm of development becomes as important as bricks, hoses, and roof tiles. It becomes a necessary, if idyllic, component of the infrastructure development organizations strive to build. It becomes another site where Ecuadorians negotiate development and modernity, a place where Ecuadorians imagine and enact progress in social terms over which they have some degree of control.

Building Faith: Infrastructure, Religion, and Foundational Community

The imagination of idealized community linked to infrastructure and progress is not limited to secular development discourses. As the example of the dedication of the Santa Anita building illustrates, conceptions of community, even as they relate to the nitty-gritty of construction projects and meters of fence, often form outside of the development world, drawing equally from the realm of religion. Religious organizations, both those involved in development work and those that are not, join development rhetoric as they connect buildings and material projects to idealized notions of community, making infrastructure another public space where Ecuadorians negotiate and reform ideas of modernity and progress.

In the Santa Anita cheese factory, for example, the building acts as a point of connection for the group's dual religious and development motivations. Father Antonio's homily and the cooperative members' description of their goals and history all pointed to the fact that those involved with the project do not separate their purpose as a development organization from that as a religiously based group. Both the priest and the women link their success to their ability to work as a group in the space of the community they have created. They are successful because they have heeded Catholic, specifically liberationist, teachings of solidarity and charity to come together into community, both in terms of their identity as a cooperative and as an integral part of greater Marqueño and Catholic life. The building, though a product of development enterprise, is thus a place where the women can and do define community in religious terms.

This does not mean, however, that the cheese factory is an overtly religious place. Indeed, explicitly Catholic activities were relatively rare in the year I attended functions in building spaces. Other than the dedication Mass and the image of Santa Anita on the wall, meetings did not begin or end with formal prayers, and the majority of the talk that treated religion during group sessions had to do with the local priest's strict new rules for catechism.

Still, their shared Catholic identity was important to cooperative members, both when they spoke about the cooperative's mission and when they reflected on the success of the organization. "When we get together as a group," Sofía explained when I asked about the Catholic nature of the cooperative and their activities in the factory, "we are with the word of God in each meeting. We are reflecting on what the word of God says."[7] For Sofía and for many of the women, this reflection translates into action as the group works to help individual members and also the larger community. "Of course we're Catholic!" one cooperative member exclaimed when I asked about the religious aspect of the organization. "We meet once in a while to pray and we are always trying to help those that need it the most. Because once in a while a group member has a sickness in the family, or needs economic help. Like that. And that's part of being religious because the person we see is a child of God. We help those that are needy."

Sometimes this help extends beyond the cooperative's immediate membership. During one particularly memorable meeting, the women engaged in a lively debate over a request from the San Marcos state-run assisted living center. Recently opened, the center had asked the group to donate six liters of milk a day. As the cooperative was buying milk from local farmers at the rate of twenty-five cents per liter, this added up to more than ten dollars a week, a sum many in the group protested not just for its economic impact on cooperative profits, but also because employees of the assisted living center outnumbered its occupants. Many in the group complained that the assisted living center was only asking them for the donation because the factory building made the cooperative appear rich.

After one *socia* reminded the group of its "Christian commitment" to the bettering of human welfare, however, the women decided to offer a compromise. The cooperative would donate three liters of milk once a week, preferably on a market day when the center gave government-mandated free meals to an itinerant clientele of elders coming into town from outlying communities. While the women were still fairly sure that the bulk of their donation would go to feed employees, they felt that at least some of the milk would find its way to the needy, thus fulfilling the group's (religiously based) charitable responsibility as a community organization.

Certainly the Santa Anita group is not unique in the way that they envision community commitment as a religious calling. Some of the emphasis on community within the group, and within Christianity more broadly, is doctrinal, and is linked to a long history emphasizing community as a necessary pillar of faith and religious praxis. Paul's letters, for example, describe ideal Christian communities as both in-clusive and unified. In his letter to the Galations, those united in a be-lief in Jesus as the Christ are famously "neither Jew nor Greek, neither slave nor free, neither male nor female," as all are "one in Christ Jesus." Paul continues this theme throughout his letters, writing in Ephesians 5:30 that "we are members of his [Christ's] body, and of his flesh, and of his bones."

This sense of community is enacted in the church in many ways, perhaps most significantly in Communion. Paul, again, describes Com-munion in 1 Corinthians 10:16 as a form of *koinonia,* or fellowship, asking, "The cup of blessing which we bless, is it not fellowship [*koino-nia*] in the blood of Christ? The bread which we break, is it not fellow-ship in the body of Christ?" For Paul, and for many modern Christians, the central ritual of church life engages the church as community: a uni-fied body of believers in Christ.

More recent histories are also at play. The Fondo Ecuatoriano Popu-lorum Progressio, the parent organization of Promoción Humana, which in turn oversees the Santa Anita cooperative, formed in Salinas, a poor and largely indigenous parish outside of Guaranda, in 1973 as a part of the Catholic liberation theology movement in Latin America.[8] Aside from calling on all clergy and church structures to embrace a "preferential option for the poor," liberation theologians also advo-cated for and enacted the establishment of "base communities" (CBEs), grassroots groups within churches that engaged in communal reading of Scripture and programs meant to raise consciousness of social prob-lems. Though no one in the Santa Anita cooperative, or anyone in the community, refers to the project as one stemming from "liberation the-ology," "solidarity," a central concept in liberation theology, is a term that the women use frequently when characterizing their mission and values as Catholics working in the cooperative. The women's (infre-quent) engagement in "reflection," where they would read a biblical pas-sage and then think about its lessons and applications to their conduct and mission as a group, as well as general democratic and communi-tarian governing principles, can also be traced to liberationist ideals and practice.

While church communities are formed around shared ideologies and practices that emphasize unity, then, they are also physical, embodied in the spaces that church buildings provide. Structures in which to enact religious ideals and practices, including those that explicitly build and reify community, are often a primary concern for religious organizations. Having a space in which to come together for worship and congregational activities is thus as important for Christian groups in San Marcos as it is for their development counterparts. The Jehovah's Witnesses, who currently rent a small building near the central town square, frequently commented on their hopes of building a "real Kingdom Hall" in which to house their growing congregation. Edgar Lorenzo, pastor to the Eternal Triumph Pentecostal Church, followed the narrative structure of the Santa Anita women as he began the history of his congregation by recalling their struggles to obtain funding for their new (1998) building, which includes a sanctuary and parsonage. As in development schema, new congregations must grow to a certain minimum size, and prove a certain basic stability and commitment as a community, in order to raise enough funding locally and/or to receive funding from their parent church organization.

Even where religious communities have made the leap to structural autonomy, the equivalency between infrastructure and community remains in play. The church in Alta Pamba, closest in location to the cheese factory and the home congregation of many Santa Anita members, was undergoing a major renovation during the time I was in residence. Church members had completed most of the work on the exterior by the time of the Epiphany Mass in early 2003, but interior work remained, including the purchase of enough cinder blocks to finish the project. In his homily, Padre Carlos, the parish priest for San Marcos and several surrounding communities, recounted the journey of the wise men to Bethlehem in Latin American terms. He compared their route to a similar trip from Argentina or Bolivia to Ecuador, and continued by saying that journeys of faith are always journeys of dedication. One can't quit halfway and expect results.

Looking to the back of the sanctuary where the gathered congregation stood among scaffolding and piles of building materials, the priest then linked his point to present circumstances: the renovation of the church was a journey of faith, one that the congregation had yet to complete. They needed to come together as a community to give enough and work enough to get the job done.

When the service ended and the collection plate came back with a scant fifteen dollars, an amount Padre Carlos calculated to be about ten cents per person in attendance at the Mass, he lamented a lack of community feeling and dedication in the congregation. People are not as dedicated to their faith as they used to be, he commented in a conversation we had after the service, continuing by saying that they do not rally around the church as the center of the community as in days past. In his opinion, the incomplete bell tower on the outside of the church was a perfect example of the disintegration of Alta Pamba as a community centered on faith. "Secularization!" he cried in response to my question about what had changed. He remembered when the entire community was involved with the Epiphany parade. Now, he claimed, they were too involved in work, school, and television, to the point where the 2003 Epiphany Mass was actually held on the day after Epiphany in order to accommodate other schedules. The trouble he and other church members had experienced in getting the work on the bell tower completed was only another sign of the problem, another symptom of the scattered, individual nature of a modern life ill fitted to the local good as he saw it.

The priest's linkage of community to (the still incomplete) infrastructure, then, closely resembles that of the carpenter and of the women commenting on the history of their experiences as members of the Santa Anita cooperative. Successful communities are reflected in successful building projects. Communities reside in and upon the buildings that they construct, but at the same time community is the foundation, the very pillars upon which buildings, religious or secular, rise or fall.

In this manner, then, the relationship between communities and the infrastructure they create is another point of contact where religious and development networks come together. Like development organizations that require proof of a cohesive community in order to fund and construct projects such as the seedbeds in Sinche, religious organizations also look for unity and cooperation as a prerequisite for creating permanent structures. For Marqueños, community idealized in the rhetoric of unity and cooperation is a common theme, and a common requirement, as they come into contact with, and negotiate, the processes and expectations religious and development infrastructure entail.[9]

This fusion between community and development success is particularly clear in projects conducted by organizations that are both religiously and developmentally oriented. HCJB employees often link religious ideas of community to the development work that they do, for example, tying success in projects and infrastructure to a communal acceptance and enactment of evangelical Christian values. Ruth would often make references to her success in health programs among evangelical communities. She credited her efficacy in establishing everything from functional water systems to universal vaccination to a sense of community that came from shared religious beliefs and practices. An executive staff member of HCJB's community development division also made a connection among evangelical beliefs, infrastructure, and community as an idealized entity capable of unified imagination and action. "You can't transform a community," she told me when I asked her how development work affected community life.

> People's lives become transformed by the power of God, and when you see God working in people's lives, communities become transformed . . . When the Gospel comes into the community, people change, and their values change. They start to think about things like health, education, security—a future for their kids. They're not involved in getting drunk and fighting and all that other stuff. And it's wonderful to see . . .
>
> We don't claim any credit because we haven't had a part in it. God has done all that. It's been a really mighty move of God, and it's refreshing to see people's whole goal system and value system have changed. That's real development.

It is this transformation, she went on to say, that allows for the most successful development projects that her division conducts. "Development works better in Christian [evangelical] communities; we've proven that," she said when I asked her to elaborate on the relationship among development projects, communities, and religious identity.

> From our experience, working with Christian communities is a
> lot easier than a community that's either divided or that has noth-
> ing to unite them. Again, going back to Chimborazo [where there
> are many evangelical communities with which HCJB has success-
> fully worked], the central focal point of the community, the life of
> the community, is now the evangelical church.
>
> Now, I'm not saying that if you go into a community, even
> if it's an evangelical community, that everybody you talk to has
> made—has certainly accepted Jesus Christ as their savior. It's al-
> most as if the community has decided to be evangelical and not
> Catholic . . . But when you get the church as the focal point of the
> community, people will work together for the good of the commu-
> nity. Everything is channeled through the church, everything is done
> through the church. And so yes, I think development works better
> through a church system, through an evangelical community.

For the staff member, unity in belief and in (specifically Protestant)
religious practice allows for the social foundations upon which successful development projects may be erected and maintained.

Like the priest in Alta Pamba, then, the HCJB staff member made
a connection linking religious belief and practice to successful development projects through the medium of community. Both she and
Padre Carlos join Ruth in imagining community as a unified group of
individuals who draw upon common beliefs, practices, and location
to work for the progress that development promises.

This is not a view limited to clergy or to laity working for development organizations. Recall that Vicente, the farmer who first asked if I
was in Ecuador to convert Catholics to Protestant Christianity as we
worked together with earthworms, said that he had become suspicious
of my motives due to the success of a local evangelical community in
obtaining a water system. While he assumed that the community had
converted in order to receive greater access to development aid, others in my Peace Corps site elaborated further on the cause of their
neighbor's good fortune, attributing their achievement to a sense of
unity that came with their new religious identity and practice. "They
know how to work together!" one woman told me. Several other people

weighed in with their own opinions, crediting the success of the evangelical community not so much to its new religion but to the prohibition of alcohol that came with it. Like the HCJB staffer and Ignacio Cayambe, the evangelical pastor in the Runa community outside of San Marcos, they figured time spent sober was time potentially used for communal, constructive activities.

People in San Marcos also equated a communal, evangelical identity with a greater capacity to solicit and maintain infrastructure projects. Lucía, all the while emphasizing that she would never leave the "true church," spoke with respect about evangelical towns. "They know how to get things done," she commented when I asked about the relationship between evangelicals and development aid. In a similar manner, Manuel Míguez, one of the UMATA extensionists, said that all else being equal, evangelicals have the advantage when it comes to development because of a greater sense of community identity and cooperation.

> *JD*: Is there a relationship between development and religion? Do you see a difference [between Protestants and Catholics]?
>
> *MM*: Well, for example, here in the canton there isn't any difference.
>
> *JD*: There isn't any difference between the two?
>
> *MM*: There aren't any differences. You see that the evangelicals are poor, and the Catholics don't have anything either. What you do note is communities that work better together. For example, the evangelical communities have more than the indigenous communities [that aren't evangelical]. Because they [the evangelical communities] had an extensionist to help them. The church helped with resources . . .
>
> Also, there is a relation between development and community. Because, for example, between community and religion there is a synergy. And this facilitates cooperation. It's that religion comes and makes people brothers. And they all walk together to plant the same things, to say what their intentions will be. They will all have the same mission, an integral mission. And so this helps with development . . .

In the imagination of Marqueños then, religion and development come together in communal spaces, especially those related to infrastructure and large development projects. Communities that convert to evangelical Christianity are presumed to convert to a more unified sense of togetherness and purpose, a sense that allows for development progress.

Where there are public buildings, then, be they the work of evangelical, Catholic, or secular organizations, people assume that there is a community behind them—that there is a minimum amount of cooperation and unity built into their foundations. In many cases, people assume that this unity is the result of a common, religious understanding. In other words, where there are cinder blocks and rebar, bricks and hoses, people are apt to look for signs of shared understandings of the divine as much as they are for signs of more quotidian processes. Always, they are looking at buildings with an understanding that mysteries of human cooperation and solidarity are as important a foundation as any blocks, bricks, or cement undergirding their construction.

In this sense, then, Ecuadorians, at least in religious and development contexts, have repudiated a progress marked by Western individuality and assumptions of easy or natural communitarianism among "developing" and/or "religious" groups, even as they recognize and have come to share in idealization of community and the power it wields in religious and development discourses. While they embrace the stamp of approval that large infrastructure projects give, they do so with an understanding that there must be a negotiated community, one that can come together, and stay together, long enough to get the job done. Modernity, which many people join Padre Carlos in associating with individualism and with (at least public) moves toward secularization, looks quite different in the rural Ecuadorian context. Where projects, especially infrastructure projects, succeed, it is because people have "come together" as a "community." Where they fail, it is because people were "selfish" or too concerned with individual return over the good of the group.[10]

Marqueños are negotiating religious and development discourses in such a way that while buildings retain what may be termed a classic status as a marker of progress, they do not represent a progress based on presumably isolated efforts that work to break down communities or religious activities. The modernity that Ecuadorians are in the process of reforming is not only open to community, it depends upon it as a literal, ideological, locally crafted, and informed foundation.

Cracked Foundations: When Community Fails

Of course, community as a foundation sometimes crumbles away, leaving no place for construction or visible signs of progress on the landscape. As the objects of development desire, buildings and other projects can engender envy and fighting that may tear relatively unified communities apart. Indeed, people in development organizations, religious groups, and larger communities often cite the careless introduction of infrastructure and materials by development agencies as the reason for divisions that appear along religious, ethnic, class, or other lines. Even as people may imagine new community formations around buildings, seedbeds, and bell towers, they may also imagine, and enact, discord that shatters communal objectives when these same objects are introduced, or when imagined and idealized communities fail to materialize along with the cement things meant to house them. There is a danger in desire.

This first became clear to me in 1994 when, as a part of my Peace Corps training, I visited an indigenous community close to Ambato which I'll call Santa Catalina. Six other volunteers and I were scheduled to assist the community in a terracing project and had arrived in town on the day usually set aside for communal work projects. Rather than being greeted by the usual work crew of men and women, shovels in hand and ready to get to work, we stepped out of our van into a divided humanity. Half of the town stood on one side of the central plaza in front of the church, and half stood on the other. A partially unloaded truck of cinder blocks was parked in the center.

The cinder blocks were the cause of the visible rift. Santa Catalina had petitioned World Vision for a latrine project, and the evangelical organization had agreed, in the usual manner, to provide the building materials if the community would supply the labor to dig pits and then erect the structures. The problem, and the cause of the heated debate we witnessed that morning, came in the timing of the delivery. World Vision saw the latrines as a community project, and had arranged to transport the materials so that they would arrive on Santa Catalina's community work (*minga*) day. For many in town, however, the latrines, which would be constructed by the individual families that would use them, were not community property, and therefore not something to which a community work day should be applied.

We watched as they argued the case, one man pointing to the truck full of building materials and saying that they would be fools to turn to the truck back, still loaded with the valuable supplies. World Vision would not return, he told the gathered crowd, and they would not have the chance either to complete the latrine project or to petition for other infrastructure that the organization was known to provide. And besides, the community had asked for the blocks *as a community*. They had filled out the forms as a group. It didn't matter that the beneficiaries would be private, at the household level.

Across the square, however, a second man made the case that as an indigenous community they had an obligation to keep their traditional ways, including the one day each week set aside for shared projects. They had already agreed to work with the Peace Corps on the terracing of community lands, a venture that would benefit everyone in town as crops planted on those lands went to a common fund. If they didn't work with the Peace Corps that day, he argued, they would not only lose the trust of the Peace Corps and the possibility of future collaboration, but also the community traditions that had allowed them to survive as indigenous people with a unique culture. One can buy cinder blocks in the city, he concluded, but one cannot simply shop for heritage.

In the end, the town decided to take the cinder blocks for the latrines, choosing to postpone construction on the terraces for another week despite the fact that they would then work without the aid of the Peace Corps. The man who had argued for heritage accompanied us back to our van, apologizing for our inconvenience in having traveled so far. What we had witnessed that morning, he told us, was becoming more common as the town was becoming more adept at soliciting development aid. Sometimes coming together to ask for and then build projects was good for them as a community, he commented as we took our leave, but sometimes it had just the opposite effect. Sometimes, he said, it was difficult to maintain unity and tradition in the face of progress.

For the people in Santa Catalina, the cinder blocks and building materials that development brought did not shore up community, even as people in town imagined and idealized community and structures such as the *minga* as a part of their indigenous heritage. Rather, the cinder blocks and cement that World Vision offered became points of division and negotiation, places where larger debates over identity and commitments to tradition came to light.

While I never witnessed such a stark example of division over building materials in San Marcos, debates about the use of group materials within the Santa Anita cooperative illustrate the importance and the difficulties the group members faced in enacting their own ideals of community as they solicited and received outside resources. Specifically, the cooperative was deeply divided over the use of the food they were awarded as a social group registered with the Ecuadorian Ministry of Social Welfare. Every two or three months, they received a shipment of rice, tuna, and cooking oil meant to be used to "support the group."

When the cooperative first received the food, they agreed to use it for "group purposes," specifically to make dinner for the women and their children after the Thursday afternoon knitting sessions. Because the women could not be home to cook dinner for their families on these days, the group rationalized, it made sense to use the food to ease the women's domestic burden, encouraging and enabling more of them to attend the meeting. Also, Anamaría added after the vote was taken to approve the plan, eating together would improve the "sense of unity" within the group.

To a certain extent, she was right. The women seemed genuinely to enjoy cooking together in the kitchen at the cheese factory, despite the painfully smoky conditions, and attendance at the Thursday meetings began to improve. The unity she desired was threatened, however, when she began to use the supplies to make lunch for the factory's three employees (every woman worked as a salaried employee at the factory for a term of three months). Magdalena, not currently at the factory full time, objected that such use of the ministry supplies did not fall under their intended use as "group resources." Further, she was upset that the food was going to the women who were receiving a salary for the work that they did. "They're already being paid!" she protested in the meeting where the women debated the correct use of the food. "This is pure selfishness!"

The issue came to a head at a meeting in which the group was scheduled to review its finances, looking at what the factory had brought in and at what they could reasonably budget for the small, intragroup loans that many women used to invest in livestock and minor home repairs. Magdalena, upset over what she saw as the injustice with the food distribution, asked for a cooperative-wide vote on the issue. She did so, appealing to the cooperation and unity within the group, cooperation and unity to which she attributed the group's successes over the years. "This use of the food," she said as she concluded her remarks, "it could lead to the end of everything we've accomplished. We can't afford to be selfish. We've got to work together as a group!"

For her part, Anamaría also used arguments about cooperation and community as she argued for the right to use the food. "It is group food," she explained as she laid out her reasoning for giving factory employees access to the supplies, "and this is a group project. Keeping the employees happy is good for us as a community."

Several other women weighed in with their opinions during the course of debate, which raged off and on for more than two weeks. Many of them saw it as a clash of egos between two powerful women, and several were worried that it could be the end of the success of the cooperative. They joined both Magdalena and Anamaría in their emphasis on the importance of unity and work. "Disorganization is always a danger to us," one woman commented. "If we don't all work, and can't agree, this will all fall apart. We need to work together better."

In the end, Anamaría continued to use the Ministry of Welfare supplies to feed the factory workers but agreed to limit the amount she would take every month. This led to an uneasy truce between her and Magdalena, and they shared a seat on the bus as the women went to Guayco to celebrate International Women's Day, the two of them reciting the Hail Mary together.

For the people of Santa Catalina, as for the women of the Santa Anita cooperative, the allocation of development resources called into question issues of community and cooperation. In both instances, the debate over resources became a debate over the future of community as an idealized form. What the people of Santa Catalina and the women of the Santa Anita cooperative imagined they were as a community became as important as, if not more so than, what they imagined they wanted to do with the resources they received as communities recognized by development donors. In this way, development infrastructure acted as a catalyst for discussions of what community is and should be, as a place where community was imagined, enacted, and sometimes, threatened with failure as a foundation for further progress.

These kinds of discussions and actions, brought about by development desire and what might equally be termed the will to progress, are well documented in literature evaluating the efficacy of traditional development that focuses on basic infrastructure resources such as latrines, bridges, shelter, and so forth. Writing about the disintegration of community that can come with the introduction of Western standards of prosperity, C. Douglas Lummis writes that Western-style infrastructure, designed to raise "poor" communities in the Third World to an "equal" status of "wealthier" Western communities, disregards other kinds of "commonwealth" that may serve to bind a community together.[11] In a similar manner, traditional development critics have chastised early development programs that revolved around handouts and large infrastructure projects with little or no community contribution. Their criticism stems from assertions that such "handout" programs fail to be efficacious over the long term, and also from concerns that fighting over the new resource may damage previously harmonious community relationships.[12]

This kind of criticism has had an effect. Peace Corps Ecuador discontinued its program in water and sanitation in 1995, partly in an effort to move the organization completely out of infrastructure projects. In San Marcos, both Plan International and the municipio have moved away from infrastructure as a primary concern, citing the detrimental effects that competition over large projects can bring about as reasons for the departure. "We used to only look at technology [in giving aid]," one Plan employee commented when I asked if the organization's approach to development had changed since they started working in Ecuador in the 1970s. "We forgot to see the human being . . .

Now we look at problems from their roots, from communities. We work in people. Now we work in the development of human beings instead of [the development of] cement things." She went on to say that this kind of development was more effective, in part because there could be "no fighting" over human development projects.

Questions of infrastructure are invariably questions of community and how people imagine it should be, even where that imagination leads to tensions between the need for infrastructure and the need for cohesive and cooperative community organizations. Infrastructure and its community-related debates are one place where Marqueños negotiate development as a global and changing paradigm.

Marqueños also tap into larger debates that center on infrastructure as it relates to debates about community and evangelical development aid. Though HCJB was the only evangelical development organization active in the region at the time of this study, Marqueños are keenly aware of the work that groups such as World Vision and Compassion International are doing in neighboring Chimborazo province, and frequently discuss the potential benefits and detriments of evangelical proselytizing and aid on community life.

This discussion is often repeated in academic circles, and it mirrors in many ways the debates in Santa Catalina and in the Santa Anita cooperative. In his insightful analysis of World Vision in Ecuador, for instance, David Stoll lauds the organization for attempting to stem community division brought about by the common practice of donating materials with no contribution from beneficiary communities.[13] While not always effective in its efforts, Stoll asserts, the organization does recognize the potentially divisive nature of development aid, especially as it is combined with World Vision's agenda as a Protestant agency encouraging people to "respond to the Gospel."[14] A more comprehensive study conducted by CEPLAES (Ecuadorian Center for Planning and Social Studies) supports Stoll's assertions, though more critically, citing community strife around donated infrastructure and money, especially in religiously diverse places where community members perceived a bias toward evangelical members.[15]

Stoll's work, in combination with the CEPLAES study, shows again that infrastructure is often a point where people negotiate the meaning of progress as it is embodied in contact between religion and development networks. Infrastructure acts as a point of contact where religious and development understandings of community are fused and formed, and where people use those understandings to coalesce and to express and enact views in the public realm.

As a focal point around which people imagine and idealize community, modernity, and progress, infrastructure is an engine, something that motivates secondary actions and worldviews. It is not always, however, the "engine for progress" that the Ecuadorian Ministry of Public Works claims it to be. The object of development desire, infrastructure may be the foundation upon which a community forms and grows, or the very combination of desire and conflict that causes it to break apart.

SPIRITUAL CARDIOLOGY

Wholeness, Becoming, and (Dis)Integration

"Do gringos believe in bad air [*mal aire*]?" Lucía asked me one evening as I stood in her living room. I had come over to borrow her phone in order to check on a friend who was ill. She posed the question in a casual, conversational tone, but she had stopped folding the pile of clothes in front of her. Her still hands were an indication that she was waiting with attention for my reply. Thinking it over, I answered that I was open to the idea of *mal aire,* a general name for a host of illnesses that Ecuadorians associate with ghosts and other spirits, especially as scientific medicine had failed me on more than one occasion.

Nodding in agreement, Lucía resumed her work as she remarked that she had once had a terrible case. For weeks after having inadvertently walked past a graveyard, she recalled, she had suffered odd swelling in her joints and extremities, a condition that local clinic doctors attributed to high blood pressure. Though she sought relief both at the hospital in San Marcos and at a larger clinic in San Miguel, the high-protein and low-salt diet the doctors recommended did no good, and her problem worsened. She began to see red and to bleed from her eyes. It was only when she visited a local healer (*curandera*) that she found some relief.

The healer quizzed Lucía about her activities, eventually naming the graveyard as the likely cause of her problems. She then mixed a

169

gallon of sugarcane alcohol with strong herbs from the mountains and told Lucía to consume it, as much as she could at a time, until it was gone. Though it made her sweat profusely, Lucía said the mixture cured her of the ailment inside of a week. Gringos and doctors did not believe in mal aire and the power of spirits, she commented, but it was clear to her that modern medicine ("*los doctores*") had its limitations.

Lucía's story and the way she chose to relate it to me is remarkable for several reasons. First, as a Catholic, she had no reservations about blaming "ghosts" (*fantasmas, espectros*) for her illness. When I asked about the spirits in relation to her faith, she explained that the church recognized the power of the dead over the living. She named All Saints' Day and All Souls' Day as times when "ghosts and spirits" made their way into church life, and then remarked that even Jesus acknowledged the existence of demons. Her religious commitments did not prevent her participation in traditional healing practices, or in talking about them with me.

Instead, her reservation in raising the topic had to do with my status as a gringa, as a North American she presumed to be fully incorporated into a modern worldview that places faith in scientific medicine. She was aware that her narrative, in which she gave up on "modern" medicine in favor of a more "traditional" approach, might make her appear backward or superstitious in my eyes. Indeed, she only proceeded to tell her story after I confirmed that I might be sympathetic by saying that I found scientific medicine to be lacking at times.

As much for its revelation of a particular religious worldview or as a marker of an awareness of a social hierarchy that divides the scientific from the traditional, however, Lucía's story is remarkable as a tale that shows the keen awareness Marqueños have for the discourses on modernity and tradition as they relate to healing, development, and religion. In telling me about her illness and subsequent cure, Lucía was reproducing, at least in part, development and religious discourses about healing and the body as they relate to the larger world. Her story included certain overlaps—she could easily place ghosts and spirits into a Catholic pantheon, she was willing to seek modern medical assistance as well as traditional remedies—but it was also a tale of resistance and separation. In declaring that scientific medicine did not cure her, she was making a statement that modernity and its accoutrements, at least as they relate to health and the body, may not always lead to progress, relief, or certain kinds of salvation.

We will now turn to the role of bodies and persons in religion and development discourses, looking at the many ways in which bodies and persons are imagined and reimagined by religious and development organizations and by the people they aim to serve. Exploring the use of "whole person" language and ideology at HCJB, within the Santa Anita group, and in secular settings including the municipio and Plan International, highlights imaginations of people as integrated entities consisting of body, mind, and spirit. Bodies and persons are significant points of contact where religious and development discourses come together, and where their integration and meaning are negotiated by those whom such discourses are meant to affect. "Whole people," I argue, are hybridized people, people imagined in a particular combination of religious and development discourses that highlight the possibility of their combination and bodies as sites of resistance as Ecuadorians embrace and reject the meanings such combinations draw from and produce.

"Becoming whole," becoming physically, spiritually, and psychologically developed, is one way that religious and secular development agencies express the paradigms of the "alternative" development explored in chapter 3. While those involved in administrating development work see themselves as reintroducing much-needed elements of tradition, authenticity, and environmental awareness as they aim to rectify and refit a development drive for progress, I suggest that recipients of development interventions are often impatient, concerned less with wholeness, becoming, and preserving tradition than with the nitty-gritty of roads and usable infrastructure. The result of this is a proliferation of discourses within discourses, the creation of new hybrids of language and ideology that deploy in the same spaces, but which talk over and around one another as donors and recipients work to imagine and reimagine religion and development in the twenty-first century. Such talking over and around, such slippage in the meanings and goals of development programs, allows the negotiation and reformation of modernity highlighted throughout this work.

Modernity in Tradition: Whole Person Discourses in Religious Development

As a Protestant organization with a large health care division, HCJB presents a good example of the ways that religious and development discourses come together in institutional imaginations of persons and bodies. North American missionary Clarence Jones founded HCJB as a radio station to spread the Protestant Gospel to Ecuadorians in 1931. HCJB began work in health care soon thereafter and built its first hospital in Quito in 1955. A second hospital, in the Amazonian oil town of Shell-Mera, followed in 1958. In both hospitals, as well as through medical caravans, HCJB began to integrate its operations, offering medical care alongside a religious message. Beginning in 1979, the organization further expanded the scope of its programs, offering water systems and other infrastructure projects as a part of the community development division.

The reasons are varied for HCJB's expansion from an organization that dealt almost exclusively with spiritual matters to one involved in large health care projects. When the organization began its work in health and basic community development, it was joining other Protestant groups that had, from their first days in the country, combined their spiritual messages with literacy programs and mission activities ranging from gardening to basic household construction. The Gospel Missionary Union, Seventh-Day Adventists, and Christian Missionary Alliance all organized schools, community centers, and education programs as a part of their work throughout Ecuador for doctrinal and practical reasons. Because Protestants believe that the ability to read Scripture is fundamental to faith and is a cornerstone of a personal relationship with Jesus Christ, most of the early Protestant missions in Ecuador engaged in literacy and education projects. Gardens, nutrition, and basic health care came quickly thereafter as mission personnel worked to keep their clientele healthy as they came to mission programs or began to live in mission compounds. The programs were also spiritually oriented, as most missions emphasized change in local cultures as a key element of conversion and Christian living.[1]

In this regard, Protestant missions in Ecuador, both those that began when the country opened to evangelization in 1895 and those such as HCJB that implemented programs later in the twentieth century, were places where Western ideas of progress and modernity were firmly entwined with the "traditional" aspects of religion, most notably an emphasis on doctrine, belief, and salvation. A 1951 pamphlet published by the New York–based United Andean Indian Mission, for example, bears the title "Soils and Souls in Ecuador." The front cover shows an Ecuadorian farmer plowing his field with oxen and presents a description of life before the mission came and acquired a hacienda in Picalquí, a community just north of Quito.

> . . . hungry sheep and goats roaming recently harvested stubble fields; a decrepit horse or two, three or four head of seedy cattle. Earth huts with roofs of straw; a wooden ox plow; the meager harvest reaped by a sickle, the beat and thread of threshing; the flutter of winnowing. Neglected souls, downtrodden, with a life expectancy under thirty years; withdrawn, distrusting, sometimes drunken; illiterate and enslaved by debt . . .
>
> That WAS Picalquí Farm, but NOW—five years have passed since the United Andean Mission brought desolate Picalquí Farm agriculture, education, medicine and evangelism.[2]

The pamphlet goes on to list reclaiming the soil and improving agriculture, bringing health to diseased bodies, training youth and adults for lives of service, reclaiming souls from oppression, and enabling "the Indian to enter upon his rightful inheritance as a child of God" as the "aims of the Mission." The "one compelling purpose" of the mission, however, "[was] to present the Gospel of Jesus Christ as relevant to the whole of life and as redeeming love and power."

The pamphlet shows that for the United Andean Indian Mission, as for most Christian aid organizations in the early and middle twentieth century, religious progress was tied to material and physical progress, to a certain view of modernity that required tiled roofs, tractors, and mechanical threshers alongside Bible study. Indeed, missions were often the institutions through which native populations encountered Western-style modernity and all of its trappings. "By virtue of its global reach," writes mission historian William Shenk, "the [mission] movement became a primary carrier of modernity, and the artifacts and institutions associated with modernity early became hallmarks of missions."[3] Where Christianity went, modernity was sure to follow, entangling religious teachings with technical change and expectations of progress in the mission field.

The result of this entanglement is a certain kind of imagination that links religious and development discourses together in bodies and persons. The United Andean Indian Mission pamphlet, for example, begins with a description of living conditions and livestock, and then goes on to inform its intended North American audience about the Indians. They are "withdrawn," "distrusting," and "illiterate." They are also ill and "eroded" by oppression. Only by taking care of the Indian's physical needs through programs of education, agriculture, and medicine, the pamphlet asserts, can the Indians fully "enter upon [their] rightful inheritance as children of God." Curing the ills of Indian souls required first saving Indian bodies; running the wheels of progress over the well-worn paths of religious tradition and beliefs to create a way out of perceived stagnation and backwardness.

In this manner, bodies and persons (often linked in religious discourses to souls) have shared a distinct place in religious and development schema. In the mission imaginary, people become objects to be saved physically through technical innovations, and spiritually through religious revelation and conversion. Modernity in the form of progress was thus tied to tradition in the form of religious doctrines and belief. In the missions, and especially in mission images of bodies and persons, God has not been crossed out with the advent of modern times. Rather, God has been and continues to be the purveyor and ultimate purpose of that modernity, the very foundation upon which it is built.

This hybrid imagining of bodies and persons persists in religiously based development efforts. HCJB, for example, founds much of its development work on a model of the "whole person." Sheila Leech, the director of the community development program at HCJB, described the institution's dedication to whole person theology and action as she explained its mission. The Gospel message must be accompanied by care and attention to the circumstances of the people to which it is delivered, she remarked when I asked why HCJB had expanded beyond its initial programs of preaching and religious teaching. "Jesus didn't just preach, he taught and he healed," she said. Their mandate as a Christian organization, therefore, is "taking care of the whole person . . . We show the love of God in practice and ways."

Indeed, the idea of the "whole person" as a spiritual, physical, and psychological entity is conscientiously practiced throughout HCJB's programs. Every patient at the Quito and Shell hospitals receives a daily visit from an HCJB chaplain, and administrative meetings always begin with a prayer. The medical caravan, a mobile clinic that makes rounds to rural communities offering basic medical and dental services, aims to meet the spiritual needs of its clientele by bringing a portable movie theater along with medical and dental equipment. Patients receive care and occasional referrals to the Quito hospital during the day, and are invited back in the evenings to watch the *Jesus* film, a 1979 Warner Brothers movie that presents the life Jesus based on the Gospel of Luke.[4] The film is accompanied by prayer and a brief sermon, and where possible, testimonial accounts from local evangelicals. When communities request medical services without the evening program, they are politely declined. If HCJB is not allowed to care for the "whole person" by offering spiritual as well as physical healing, the organization will not work with a community.

The guiding text for this integration of faith and physical aid is a book by Daniel E. Fountain, *Health, the Bible and the Church,* which HCJB distributes to every incoming employee. In the work, Fountain, a missionary doctor in the Congo/Zaire, draws a line between "secular thinking," which separates spirit and body, and what he terms a "Christian approach" to health care, which has as its goal "the restoration of the whole person."[5] Part of this restoration involves going beyond the individual as "health is not just an individual matter; it is . . . a community concern." "How we relate to one another," Fountain says, "and the customs and practices in which we engage together affect our health."[6] Good health care and good development start with a view of the patient as person, and specifically, the patient as person within a community. Whole people come from whole communities, where, in the HCJB model, physical and spiritual needs are met, where people become aware of themselves as beings that are a part of something bigger: community, ecological systems, God.

This image of bodies unified with spirit and community is not unique to Fountain. Rather, the history of whole person theology is rooted in a resistance to modern understandings that separate minds from bodies as distinct entities in scientific discourses, what Fountain terms "secular thinking." While Latour does not use the term, he does to some extent echo Fountain's description of a false and harmful disconnect between bodies and spirits. Recall that Latour and others writing about the foundational claims of modernity assert that one project of modernity is to keep minds, aligned in the modern constitution with culture, separate from bodies, which must be counted in the realm of nature.[7]

While Fountain credits theologians with reuniting bodies, minds, and spirits—keeping God in the picture and defying the aspect of modernity that requires keeping God one step away from both science and society—the first use of the term "whole person" came not from the church but from the laboratory. In 1932 Johns Hopkins psychiatrist Adolf Meyer used the term "whole person" when he proposed the study of psychobiology, an integrated investigation of human beings meant to do away with behaviorism and institute a way of knowing that "can do justice to all the facts, whether they be those of physics and chemistry or the growth and function of special organs or the functioning of the whole person." The advantage of this kind of integrated approach, according to Meyer, was that "it becomes possible to give consideration to the parts without losing sight of the unity of the person."[8] For Meyer, minds and bodies had to be imagined and studied together to get a complete picture of reality. Science of the mind must also be a science of the body, part of a new kind of modernity creating a hybrid that subsumes the culture of the mind into the natural, physical aspects of the body knowable through empirical investigation.

While the instigation of whole person discourses was secular and scientific, then, Christian theologians followed Meyer's basic approach, incorporating whole person language and science into theological discourses in the mid-1950s. These early references by theologians to the whole person were usually in the context of education. Dr. John Charles Schroeder, for example, gave a speech on liberal education in 1953 in which he claimed that Christianity is fundamental to any concept of learning that aims to train people as to what they are, especially in relationship to society: "Christianity at its best is a ferment—a creative force which brings men alive, which thrusts the whole person into a significant and redemptive relationship with his society and which in his redeeming comradeship with God in Christ makes man a new creature."[9]

Theologians were not the only ones drawing on whole person discourses to describe people and improved methods in education, and by the middle of the twentieth century the term was freely incorporated in secular, especially government rhetoric. The 1950 Ford Foundation Report, for example, lists "education of the whole person" as a fundamental component of human welfare and social well-being.[10] As international development aid was entering its grand period with the Marshall Plan and the "hearts and minds" programs of the Cold War era, whole person images became popular in development discourse, and were often invoked as the way to people's minds, hearts, and political allegiances.

This integrated imagining of the "whole person" continued into the 1960s, when "whole person" regained its status as a medical concept, all the while remaining encamped in theological and educational discourses. President Kennedy made use of the term in his 1962 address on health care, and an examination of a *New York Times* issue from 1965 reveals advertisements for radio shows on "how to be a whole person."[11] In moving from its initial home in psychological discourse to the theological and educational realms and back again, the idea of the "whole person" thus bridged the divide from the scientific to the cultural, creating an image of people affected as much by the workings of their bodies as by the workings of their souls and the communities in which they live.

In all of these contexts, whole people may or may not have been religious, but they were at once emotional and physical, and subject to the influences of traditional culture, modern science, and the communities of which they were a part. Points of contact for religious and development discourses, whole people were imagined in these discourses as hybrid people, equally composed of body, soul, and their physical environment.

This hybrid imagination and articulation of the "whole person" is very much alive in the work that HCJB performs today. Aside from Fountain's book and institutional rhetoric, such hybrid images of people and their right relationships to their environment, community, and God are clear in the way that organization employees conceive of and perform work both in the field and in HCJB's Quito headquarters. As an HCJB missionary, for example, Ruth Bauer was often critical of what she called "*patrón*-style" development work undertaken by Plan and other secular development organizations.[12] Rather than ask communities what they need, she said, too many development organizations impose their own ideas, recreating a *patrón* system where poor people turn to those in power in order to fulfill basic needs. Such development fails, she said, because it does not take into account community and personal growth as a fundamental part of the development process. "For development to really fly," she said when I asked what made for successful development projects, "it has to be from the inside-out. The community has to decide what they really want. Unfortunately, that's not how most of them [development programs] are. And that's why you see so many projects flop."

The root of the failure, she went on to explain, is that such top-down development focuses on developing things and areas without really looking at people as human beings capable of both spiritual and physical betterment. "For me," Ruth explained,

> a person is a whole. I can't look at them as just being physical. They're physical, they're mental, they're spiritual, they're social. All of this makes up the person, and you have to hit all of those areas. You have to take all of that, all of that person, if you will . . .
>
> I think people don't see their need, maybe, their spiritual need. I think it goes hand-in-hand with the physical. Because, when I work with a Christian community, a community that has a relationship with the Lord Jesus . . . you see change in their physical— in the physical self so much faster than when you are with a community that does not have that personal relationship. And they don't see, they may not see the correlation between the spiritual and the physical as being a healthy person . . .

I want to help people get better, be able to progress. Yes, I'm a missionary first, and I would love to see everybody in a personal relationship with the Lord Jesus. That's not going to happen, I know. That's not my only purpose in development. Because I want to see them progress, I'm going to help them physically.

For Ruth, successful development cannot be undertaken without approaching people as "whole persons" with physical, spiritual, social, and psychological needs. She links her success in evangelical communities to their awareness that health is as much spiritual as it is physical, and also to their willingness to take action to "progress" at the community level. Whole people are those capable of recognizing their hybrid status as spiritual, physical, and social beings; are those able to advance where religious and development understandings of progress come together in the space of a religiously unified and motivated community.

While Ruth linked religious understandings and identity to successful development, she was quick to separate development projects from the process of initial religious conversion.

JD: Do you think that development is a form of conversion?

RB: It can be, but it doesn't have to be . . . I don't see development as the only means to conversion.

JD: But conversion can sometimes result?

RB: It can be a result because people are interested in knowing, well, why are you here doing that? It gives me an opportunity to share. Or, why are you interested in us? These questions come up. What's different about you? You don't do things the way other people do, why not?

I'd love for everyone to know Jesus personally, but I can't push it down their throats. Everybody's got to make their own decision.

For Ruth, whole people were formed as the result of religious awareness and becoming, a process that has little to do with development itself. While her constituents may come to Christ through her work and her testimony, becoming involved in development projects was not enough, in and of itself, to begin the long road to wholeness and completion. Rather, development was one place where spirits, bodies, and minds might come together and initiate a platform for real advancement.

In her use of whole person rhetoric, then, Ruth portrays bodies as places where religious understandings and development progress come together. Healthy bodies will be joined by healthy minds and healthy souls, and will live as a part of healthy communities capable of working together for a better standard of living. Bodies, in this instance, act much like buildings, becoming the meeting grounds for religious and development discourses that imagine idealized people as a part of idealized, unified communities.

Ruth's construction of "whole people" as spiritually aware physical beings is replicated throughout HCJB's programs, as well as in its institutional and service cultures. Every Friday morning, for example, externs (fourth-year medical students) on rotation at Vozandes, HCJB's Quito hospital, gather for "Spiritual Cardiology," a Bible study meant to introduce them to the spiritual aspects of their vocation as healers. Though many of the externs are either Catholic or profess no religion, the Bible study is a mandatory part of their training at the hospital. The program was implemented in 1978, the same year that Vozandes began receiving students from the Ecuador's Catholic University at Cuenca.

The sessions open with a prayer, and then the leader, usually the extern director, leads the reading and discussion of Bible passages, which may or may not relate directly to medicine. During the May 2003 session I attended, for example, the text was Genesis 48, where the dying patriarch Israel bestowed his blessing upon the younger of Joseph's two sons. The leader of the session had the externs take turns reading the passage, and then opened the discussion, giving some historical background about the lineage of Abraham before asking what the externs concluded from the reading. Are some descendents of Abraham holier than others? What about Huaranis (an indigenous Ecuadorian group from the Amazon) and other native Ecuadorians who have no knowledge of the Bible? Can they become chosen people as well? What does the concept of a "chosen people" have to do with justice, either divine or human?

The discussion was animated and varied, and the externs approached the questions from a variety of religious and philosophical standpoints. While many echoed Christian doctrine about salvation only through the knowledge of the Bible and salvation through Christ, others took the conversation to biblical notions of justice, asking what it is to love one's neighbor, or whether an eye for an eye was really a fair policy. As healers, did they not have to obey both the laws of the land and of their hearts? Israel seems to have broken with tradition for a greater good. Should they not occasionally do the same?

In the Spiritual Cardiology session, then, the students were allowed and encouraged to think about their role as healers outside the usual confines of clinical discussions and close attention to physical pathologies. They freely combined the traditional world of wisdom literature and Scripture with the scientific world of medicine, forming a hybrid structure that encouraged them to view themselves and their patients as "whole people," both physical and spiritual, living in various social, historical, and religious contexts. Science and healing through modern medicine were always in the background of the discussion, though as aspects of modernity that had been carefully shelved and drawn upon in the course of an explicitly theological investigation of cultural and historical realities.

In the way missionaries and staffers describe what they do, and in the programs they instigate, HCJB employees are clearly committed to a vision of the "whole person" that uses a careful blend of tradition and modernity, science and religion. They have made a commitment to bridging the modern divide when it comes to bodies and persons, forming the hybrids Latour claims that the modern constitution prohibits. What is more, they have and continue to do this quite consciously, maintaining their agency as actors with feet firmly planted in both the traditional and the modern worlds. In their own bodies, and in the bodies of their clientele, HCJB staffers seek to reunite what modernity has ostensibly torn asunder, negotiating and spreading a religious message through the wonders of science and healing even as they integrate those wonders with religious understandings of reality.

HCJB is not alone in its use of whole person language and ideologies as it blends religious understandings with modern and development discourses. In San Marcos, members of the Santa Anita group also used whole person images and ideologies, though they tended to apply them to the group more than to individuals as they articulated their views about the purpose of the cooperative as a Catholic development organization working for the good of the larger community. Anamaría Carvajal, for example, cited "social development" as one of the major goals of the cooperative. "Social or personal development," she said when I asked her to describe development in San Marcos, "is our own formation. Because we [live with] the impact that we have made, that we have the idea that we are individuals and nobody else can influence us, the formation of organizations here [in San Marcos] is impossible. We don't have the mentality to be organized . . . Everyone is on his or her own side." Religion, she said, can help make people less selfish, giving them a more complete view of development as something more than simply an economic entity. "Here in the cooperative," she said, "we have spiritual development at the same time as economic development, but we could do more."

Unlike Ruth Bauer, who reserved the term "conversion" for a particularly religious change in worldview even as she later went on to link that change to successful development endeavors, Anamaría was content to use the religious metaphor in describing the transformations that development can bring. Good development, she said, *is* a form of conversion.

> Development is a conversion, that is, in a positive manner. For example if you have good development, positive development, what do you have to do? You have to try to excel more, to reach out more, with help. That is, to look for help, and to look to help other people. It isn't just "I developed, I converted myself, and that's it." That's the way it should be, that I am going to develop and I want to convert others. It's not just for me . . .
>
> You can have economic development, social development, moral development, or development in general. If I have a goal, it's that I feel that development will be better if I try to implement a development that is social, economic, and moral. And that includes religion, because the moral is also religious.

Becoming whole means integrating religious and moral views with economic advancement, creating an integrated approach that allows for morally positive, community-based actions.

While she did not join Anamaría in using the term "conversion" to describe positive and integrated development processes, cooperative member Sofía Flores also defined development as something that is better understood as both economic and social. Development has "something to do with human relations," she commented when I asked about development in the context of the cooperative. "We have to respect each other if we want to be successful. We give seminars in human relations: how to organize people, how to prepare them, how to give them more alternatives for work. And also how to lend a hand; how to make them feel like they are moving forward." For both women, development has come to be something that affects and is affected by social and cultural factors as much it is by the engines of economics or opportunity. Whole development must be enacted by whole people, people aware that they have the capacity to work within a community to help themselves.

In both HCJB and the Santa Anita cooperative, then, the modern language of development progress has been bolstered by an understanding of an ideal "whole person" made up of the physical, spiritual, and psychological self. "Whole people" are those who have progressed to an understanding of their multifaceted yet connected nature. In a strikingly similar manner, "good development" is also measured in such explicitly integrated terms. Both whole people and whole development must form through a process of recognition and conscious action that takes into account the social, economic, and psychological factors that make up complete human beings and complete communities, what Anamaría described as a process of "conversion." For both organizations, becoming developed begins by becoming whole, working consciously to achieve some level of transformation and completion.

Within HCJB, this attention to completion is most apparent in its direct adaptation of whole person language in both its institutional and its community work, while in Santa Anita rhetoric it has been transferred to development as a communal operation. Whole people— moral, social, and religious—are necessary for successful development, which depends upon an awareness of one's position as a part of the group. In both instances, actors in the organizations have consciously created a blend of religious language that favors images of the whole person within the modern discourse of development, allowing a carefully constructed hybrid of tradition and modernity to flourish in the spaces of bodies and persons.

Tradition in Modernity: Wholeness and Becoming in Secular Development

Religiously based development institutions are not the only organizations to have adopted "whole person" discourses, or to have focused on bodies and persons in the course of development work. As we saw in chapter 3, secular institutions have also adopted and employed whole person, integrative approaches to development, seeking, much like their religiously based counterparts, to redefine development as a process of personal and community growth that takes into account people's cultural, psychological, and social requirements as well as their physical needs.

In San Marcos the best example of such an adaptation of whole person discourse comes from Plan International. Reflecting trends in development theory, Plan has recently reinvented itself as an organization dedicated as much to "human development" as to infrastructure. Much as HCJB has been doing for decades, the organization has begun training community health coordinators, and their organizational approach to health care is, in their own terms, "integrated" as they study environmental and communal factors in disease. The new "integrated" approach includes coordinating education and health programs so that local educators are able to encourage greater knowledge of basic medical issues. It also includes a new program in human rights. "We're getting back to looking at the human being," commented Carmen García, coordinator of the health and education programs for Bolívar province, as she explained the integrated approach. "We're trying to make it so the person excels—develops internally and externally." She went on to explain that the organization had focused for too long on developing "technology," losing sight of "human development" along the way.

In this manner, Plan International has incorporated at least some of the whole person discourse and practice that HCJB and members of the Santa Anita group employ. Religious or secular, these major development organizations working in San Marcos come to town with strikingly similar messages: that complete development includes an element of human development; that "whole people" are those most likely to progress and contribute to their communities.

For the people whom religious and secular development agencies serve, then, the secular incarnation of whole person rhetoric is yet another place where religious and development networks are negotiated. To employ a whole person or integrated approach in a secular setting is necessarily to call up its religious implications, even where talk of conversion or morality are not directly addressed. When I asked Carmen if Plan acknowledged the religious aspects or overtones their new, integrated approach might have, however, she reiterated that Plan is a secular organization, and that this was something the organization's clientele clearly understood. "The institution is not affiliated with any religion," she said when I asked if people sometimes thought of the organization in religious terms. "We don't have an official religion here. We don't speak about any religion. Everyone can have our own personal religion, but in the institution we don't promote one."

An examination of Plan literature, however, shows that the organization's adoption of whole person understandings of development, especially as they relate to health and the environment, have not entirely escaped the religious realm. A poster designed for classroom and community center use in the province of Bolívar, for example, takes on overtly religious overtones as it mirrors the Catholic Credo. "I believe," it says, "in my nature [or nationality], in its great biodiversity. I believe in the human being as the artisan of its conservation. I believe in the sun, the rain, the air, the soil, and the winds."

Other Plan literature includes a pamphlet extolling the "Ten Commandments of Personal Hygiene." Whole person theology never quite leaves religious modes and mannerisms in becoming an integrated, new development philosophy that joins religious and development understandings of the person as an entity capable and deserving of physical, social, and psychological progress.

Plan is not the only secular institution to have adopted whole person rhetoric and ideologies into the programs it runs in San Marcos and in the surrounding communities, and is therefore not the only place where religious and development ideologies of integration and wholeness come together. The municipio, for example, began the meeting in Sinche by asking people in the organization, "What do you want to become?" Becoming—reaching development goals that included reforestation and cleaner water—began with an assessment of a social state. What the community wanted in terms of physical progress began with a larger ontological question.

Indeed, the UMATA extensionists in charge of the meeting viewed the project in Sinche as emblematic of a "new kind" of development that does a better job of reacting to people's real needs in a sustainable and integrated manner. Commenting on the municipio's previous development style, extensionist Manuel Miguez said,

> What happened was, there wasn't anything, there wasn't anything in the sense of cooperation [between the municipio and communities], and so things were hard and after a while nothing of the projects remained. And so it was like there was a lot of work and no results. People today are poorer than when we started. There's more poverty, more malnutrition, water sources are drying up . . . and there is a tremendous inequality in the marketplace. Farmers sell what they produce for nothing, and the prices of what they buy have only gone up. We never paid attention to those things in the past . . .
>
> Development in the past was really nothing. It dealt with passing things, very superficial things . . . But lately we've changed. We have the idea to work technical assistance to develop and to support campesinos . . . Now there is the idea that we should try to listen to people, that they also know what they need . . . we should listen to them identify their problems, and have them help us create solutions and programs. To do this we've identified several relevant areas in which to work, including health, education, infrastructure, and government.

Carlos Chiluizo, the extensionist directly in charge of the Sinche project, agreed with Manuel's assessment. While the Sinche project wasn't perfect, he said, blaming a lack of transportation and adequate funding for his frustrations in not being able to visit the site on a regular basis, he was pleased with the general approach to the project. "Now," he said, "we as extensionists are going to every community and helping them with technical assistance. Now it's not just based here in the middle of San Marcos. Now we're walking from community to community and asking what kind of development they want. Where it is they want to go and what it is they want to be. That's the kind of development that's happening here now. And it all depends on the support of the people . . . Development starts with them now."

For both extensionists, "old development" was ineffective or even destructive because it failed to take into account people's greater circumstances, be they social, economic, or agricultural. The "new development" they were trying to implement attempted to do so, and therefore keenly resembled the "social" and "personal" development members of the Santa Anita cooperative cited in its effort to integrate education, health, and agriculture together with infrastructure into a complete package, and the pedagogically based, "integrated" approach employed by the U.S. Peace Corps.

While the municipio did not bring any overtly religious references into their presentation, then, and focused less directly than Plan on human rights or the psychological aspects of whole person ideologies, their presentation and approach to development did echo some of the larger themes of whole person theology both as a religious and a development concept. Development, for the municipio as well as for Plan, HCJB, and the Catholic development organization, is not simply about physical needs and physical progress. It is also about realizing and expanding the potential of a community as an organization made up of individuals with psychological and social, as well as physical needs. It is about going beyond building cement things to building a moral, social, and communal infrastructure that will endure over time.

By adopting integrated, whole person imaginings of people as beings in need of social, physical, and moral development, secular development organizations have entered into a rhetoric and practice that brings tradition, in the form of religious understandings of the self and community, into the ostensibly modern world of development programs. By asking people what they "want to become" in the course of asking about their future developmentally, Plan and the municipio are, in some very real ways, asking for a version of people's cosmology. They are asking how recipients see themselves vis-à-vis their community, their environment, and their plan for the future as individuals capable of moral, even spiritual progress. These organizations are in many ways bringing the modern world of development back into the traditional realm of religion, citing human needs and desires as the starting point of progress and conversion to a new kind of life.

(Un)Becoming: The Limits of Integration

For all these efforts aimed at integrating the traditional and the modern, the social and the cultural, however, the construction of whole people in the context of hybridized discourses of religion and development is fragile. Sometimes, tradition impinges on modernity, or modernity holds sway over reinvented traditions in such a way as to separate them out again, creating a collision instead of an easy mixture.

In religious adaptations of whole person discourses, it is often the reintroduction of traditional things and ideas that threatens people's constructions of integrated wholes. Take, for instance, the example of Henry Palacios, the young American doctor asked to deliver the baby while on an HCJB caravan trip in Puyupamba. As a committed evangelical Christian and medical missionary at HCJB, Henry is dedicated to whole person ideologies as theological and vocational realities. When describing his decision to become a doctor and a missionary, he emphasizes that while he initially was interested in medicine for its prestige and a chance at wealth, he came to realize that he could use it to combine his spiritual and intellectual interests. "I came to see [medicine] as a calling," he explained during an interview, "as a way to serve the glory of God."

In his years of medical practice, he has also come to a definition of healing that relies on a blending of physical and spiritual health:

> Now, having said that, you know, physical healing, I do believe, and this goes outside of what I can measure, but I really do believe

that there is a conjunction between our spiritual state and our physical state. And I do believe that one's general health is stronger and better in the presence of a good spiritual relationship. Now, I'm not going to tell you that I understand the mechanism clearly, but I can tell you that I see the relationship, and I recognize it, and I believe it. And I also believe, and this is secondarily, even beyond that, I believe that following God's mandates and laws produces for us a healthier lifestyle. It's just easier, with more physical health. There was some data that said that people who attend church had some longer living or something like that. And you can say that it's just spiritual thing, or you can say that people who attend church have lifestyles that are less risky and destructive.

So, which is it? Maybe it's both. Quite frankly, both are equally as miraculous to me because they're both the hand of the Lord, the hand of the Lord's protection. One's [scientific medicine] the hand of the Lord's protection and a mechanism I feel I understand. And one's [divine mystery] the hand of the Lord's protection and a mechanism I yet do not understand. The only difference is my understanding.

For Henry, then, his work at the hospital and as a part of the medical caravans is a way of practicing the integrated approach he believes in. His work in medicine and as a missionary helps to create the circumstances in which people can become whole and healthy in a way that integrates modern, scientific approaches to the body with spiritual well-being, which he links to religious doctrine, belief, practice, and divine mystery. In this way, Henry's understanding of the whole person blends the "traditional" world of religious belief and doctrine with modern medicine, creating an alliance in which he feels people are most likely to flourish as complete human beings.

With the birth at Puyupamba, however, this complete, even divinely ordained integration of tradition and modernity showed signs of unraveling. While he was asked to perform in his scientific capacity as a doctor at the birth, the woman's culturally traditional position, squatting with her hands on her sister's lap in front of her, confounded his ability to handle the situation. He had been trained to assist at births in a scientific situation that left him no flexibility for cultural variation, or the woman's desire to combine her own physical traditions with his scientific expertise. By saying that he had "no training for this position," he was calling attention to the fact that tradition had broken in at an unexpected place and rendered him virtually helpless. The woman had managed to shatter the illusion of wholeness in the scene via the position of her body. Despite her wishes to combine her cultural traditions with modern science (and possibly with the religious authority the caravan doctors brought to the evangelical community of which she was a part), her position rendered her a stranger to the world of science, unreachable by any bridge Henry could easily construct.

In this instance, then, a body was the place where imaginings of whole people fell apart. In that room and nearing the end of her labor, the woman was living proof that there is a limit to hybridity and what negotiations can bring, even when that hybridity or the negotiations that form it are carefully constructed by actors who place great stake in its validity and utility.

In a similar manner, the discord in the Santa Anita group over the use of food donated by the Ministry of Social Welfare also presents an example of the limits of whole person discourse and its application to community. Though cooperative members were clearly committed to the notion of community and working together to become an institution where women could "develop as human beings," where "social" and "moral" development were as important as the group's economic goals, the rift between Anamaría and Magdalena exposed the fragility of such idealized aspirations. "Progress" was halted while the women worked out what to do about competing claims for group resources.

Indeed, it was only when the group retreated out of the integrated world of the cheese factory and into the religious world of the Hail Mary that further steps toward their mutual development as a group could be made. On the bus going to the Catholic shrine as a part of International Women's Day, they made peace as a group by consciously entering their shared religious world and asking for grace and mercy using the words of the prayer, momentarily leaving all talk of development—social, moral, or communal—behind. Successful negotiation in this case resulted in the untwining of religious and development discourses, into their very modern and conscious separation.

While Magdalena and Anamaría took several more weeks to work out a division of the Ministry of Social Welfare resources which everyone could live with, their conversations did not start until they found common ground in the religious environment of the bus ride. Thus, while they consciously worked to incorporate the world of religion into modern understandings of development and progress, the occasional separation of the two allowed them to back away from their immediate problems, and then to persist in achieving their goals. Where integration failed, separation achieved the desired result of unity and further progress toward their goals.

Where people consciously combine religious and development discourses that concern the whole person, then, they create hybrid and idealized images of people and communities that they believe are better able to handle the challenges of development as a form of personal and communal progress. Whole people—physical and overtly spiritual and religious—are imagined as the basis of whole communities, groups of people who recognize that they do not necessarily want modernity without tradition, nor economic progress without a solid social foundation. Though such hybrid and idealized visions of persons and bodies sometimes fail, causing a reseparation of the discourses that compose them, they nevertheless persist as an ideal that people use to link religion to development, tradition to modernity, and technological progress to social institutions. They persist as a way of keeping God from leaving modern scenes.

Clearly, not everyone involved in development is dedicated to the active fusion of modernity and tradition, new and old, offered by integrated, whole person development approaches. While secular development organizations have consciously worked to create "integrated" development programs that go beyond "cement things" and into the realm of personal and community advancement, not all aid recipients are convinced that they need to become "whole people" in order to reap the benefits of development aid. Indeed, many Marqueños and others who negotiate development assistance actively resist such integrated approaches. They reject the hybrid notions of "becoming" in favor of older, more stratified programs that focus on roads, buildings, infrastructure, and the transfer of technical knowledge without any but the barest references to "social" or "psychological" advancement.

Take, for example, the woman who stood up at the end of the municipio's initial presentation of the plan for the Sinche nursery. She sat through a series of speakers, ranging from the extensionist who asked the group "what they wanted to become" to two young men promoting helioculture (snail farming) as an environmentally sound means of creating community revenue. One of the poorest at the meeting that day, the woman wore indigenous clothing and did not have the advantage of shoes when she rose to her feet to address the crowd. While she said that all of the talk about community advancement and future environmental gains was well and good, the real need in the area was for a road. The municipio had been promising a graded dirt track for years. Where was it?

The mayor addressed her question, explaining that he had been working on rescuing a languishing bulldozer from Quito to begin construction, but also said that progress had been slow due to administrative difficulties. The woman listened intently to his reply, but it was clear that she came away unsatisfied. She had apparently heard the story before.

Despite all of this, the woman took an active part in project activities as nursery construction got under way in subsequent months, arriving to help clear the land and then to cut bamboo for the seedbeds. When I asked why she was helping with the nursery after her comments about the road being the real need in the area, she responded that she hadn't changed her mind. Indeed, she was working on the nursery project in order to facilitate a speedier implementation of the road. "If we can prove that we can be successful with this," she said, indicating the nursery, "then they will have to give us the road. They will know that we're organized, that we're ready."

The woman's sentiments were echoed by several others working on the project. While most claimed at least a passing interest in improving their long-term fortunes by planting hardwood tree species and moving into the cacao, citrus, and bamboo production the project offered, many also counted "experience" as a reason to spend two

Thursdays every month working away from their home farms and animals. Like the woman, they had decided that if they could impress the municipio with their diligence and apparent organization, they would be more likely to receive a road, electricity, and potable water when the government came across sufficient funds to enable such projects.

In this respect, the organization members in Sinche accepted some of the propositions of whole person ideologies in the development program the municipio offered and rejected others, adapting the larger ideological framework to their own devices. They would participate in the smaller project, proving their worthiness as an "organized" community capable of thinking about development in a holistic sense. But they would do so with the hopes of eventually gaining the trust of those capable of granting larger, more desirable, and concrete projects.

The association members in Sinche were aware of the tenets of integrated development, in other words, but they were not converted to it, and maintained a stronger desire for "cement things" than for becoming "whole people" capable of "integrated" development. They spoke the language of holistic development but in a way that resisted its larger message. Working within the system, they created their own, communally shared network of understanding and actions aimed at achieving the results they desired without the need to share in the beliefs of that system. They would build the seedbeds, attend the meetings, and answer questions about what they wanted to "become," but they did so not for the purpose of "social" or "personal" betterment. For most of the association members, the seedbed and nursery project were the first steps toward a road, electricity, and potable water, modern infrastructure meant to ease their lives in the modern world.

The association members' participation in the Sinche project, then, looks strikingly similar to the scenario that Vicente imagined when he asked me if I was an evangelical out to win his soul with earthworms during my time as a Peace Corps volunteer. He and several others in his community supposed that the community over the hill had converted to evangelical Christianity in order to receive the water system. They imagined that their neighbors had learned, in a sense, to talk an evangelical talk and walk an evangelical walk well enough to reap the rewards of evangelical money and technical assistance. While Vicente never accused evangelical community members of being duplicitous in their conversion, he did seem to think that they might have been motivated by material rather than spiritual desires.[13] Like the Sinche association members, they may have learned to create a constellation of understanding and action within the larger principles presented by the aid agency, one that worked to achieve physical ends despite ideological differences.

Such instances of talking over, of combining competing claims and motivation into a single conversation in the way of Bakhtin's hybrids, mark the creation of competing networks of language and ideologies within dominant whole person theologies and "alternative" development approaches.[14] Where people do not want to take part in the integration that aid agencies or religious officials offer, they create their own form of resistance, choosing a conscious separation of development and religion. Where they are more interested in roads than in becoming "complete" human beings or communities equally attuned to their physical and psychological makeup, they are rejecting the postmodern move toward reintegration and work to keep the modern constitution alive. In this respect, they ensure that development remains, or perhaps becomes, modern, ostensibly separated from the shackles of tradition. They create a workable negotiation of tradition and modernity, the social and the concrete, becoming along the way more modern than many of those who would modernize them.

In the deployment of and resistance to whole person discourses, religious and development imaginings of bodies and persons come together and fall apart, showing the limits of hybridity as people either accept or reject propositions that progress is as much about personal and community development as it is about roads and electric grids. Though religious and development ideologies and discourses freely combine in places such as HCJB's medical caravans, Spiritual Cardiology sessions, and Plan International posters replicating the "Ten Commandments of Personal Hygiene," Marqueños and other people who negotiate religious and secular development aid do not always allow such hybrids between the religious and the secular, the modern and the traditional, to go unquestioned. Rather, and as Lucía's rendering of her *mal aire* story at the beginning of this chapter shows, Marqueños build their own forms of modernity, sometimes blending religious and development ideologies together into integrated hybrids, and sometimes separating them out again. Always, they are creating varied, workable, and multiple discourses that work over and around one another. They are discourses that keep God either in close or crossed out, but which allow God to remain as a potential part of the greater development picture depending on the wishes of those who would invoke or reject such understandings of the world. The reformed modernity they create through these negotiations is not a fixed modernity but rather a flexible field, evocative of local histories, needs, and desires.

CONCLUSION

Truman's Earthworms

Two weeks before I was scheduled to leave Ecuador after my fieldwork in 2002–3, I found myself across the fence from Vicente's backyard, once again up to my elbows in earthworms. This time I was digging up the great-great-grandchildren of Viche's original bunch to take back to San Marcos, where Ruth had requested them for a gardening project she had started with a local evangelical community. Though my efforts in the compost pile outside of the health care clinic drew some attention from passersby and clinic patients, no one asked if these were Protestant earthworms, or if I was going to use them for religious purposes.

The irony, of course, is that this particular collection was destined to become directly involved in an evangelical aid project. Though I had assured Vicente seven years before that these earthworms were secular creatures, unaffiliated with any of the Protestant projects he had heard about, my actions were about to launch the worms on the road to conversion. I was giving them over to a development project that consciously combines development aid with attempts to lead people to a Protestant understanding of salvation through a personal relationship with Jesus Christ. Truman's earthworms—cycled through Kennedy's vision of secular service and more than half a decade of care by an Ecuadorian Catholic peasant farmer—were about to come full circle, realizing their roots in a Christian ethic that combines technological change with the idea that, as Truman put it, "all men are created in the image of God" and are therefore eligible for the "benefits of [Western] scientific advances and industrial progress available for . . . improvement and growth."

Throughout this book, I have attempted to explain how earthworms could be the objects of both religious and secular concern, and subsequently vehicles through which people negotiate the role of religion and development in their lives and worldviews. Beginning with an analysis of development discourse, we have seen that whereas most scholars locate development in a modernity characterized by a separation of "progress" from tradition, and especially from religion, development never moved entirely away from its home in religious discourses on salvation or in religious practices. When Columbus and other Spanish *conquistadores* came to the New World, they did so with the motivation of a double conversion. Seeking to turn New World wealth into material gain, they also looked to bring New World souls to Christianity for what they perceived to be a greater spiritual good. And they were not the first to do so. Before the Spanish conquest of the New World, intra-Andean conquest also linked technical and religious change to the state. The antecedents to modern development in the Andes were thus forged along Inca roads, and in Jesuit, Franciscan, Augustinian, and Dominican missions that combined religious education with Western agricultural and industrial techniques in an effort to bring spiritual and physical advancement to New World peoples as they brought material and spiritual gain to Europeans and the institutions of crown and church.

While development has been a state concern since before colonial times, then, I have also shown that it has never entirely made the leap into the secular realm, and remains entangled in religious discourses and practices as it deploys through the networks of everyday contemporary life. In San Marcos kitchens, bedrooms, gardens, buildings, and bodies, religious and development discourses come together, creating a situation in which Ecuadorians negotiate the terms of this confluence, sometimes combining them and sometimes breaking them apart, often in ways unintended by the people with whom such discourses originate and through whom they deploy. Recognizing the hybridity created by religious and development discourses where they come together, Marqueños use that hybridity and resist it in the process of negotiating the terms of progress, and thus the terms of modernity itself.

In bedrooms people combine religious doctrine with development rhetoric on cleanliness and family planning to create worldviews that either support or reject artificial birth control. In kitchens women keep open fires and propane stoves in order to cook both traditional and modern foodstuffs. For many, cleanliness is equated with godliness, as Jehovah's Witnesses and evangelical missionaries combine lessons on sanitation with a religious message of salvation. And guinea pigs, the subject of religious and development discourses, live both inside the kitchen and outside in cages, their location in the household a determining factor in the way that they may be used for healing or capital gain.

"Whole person" discourses in religious and development circles underscore that where religion and development come together in the intermediate space of bodies, people actively choose to resist the intentional blending of modernity and tradition that such discourses represent. For some people, cement things, be they offered the context of religion or secular development, remain more important than becoming "whole" or attaining a perfect mix of spiritual and physical fulfillment.

Amidst these physical spaces, three sites of negotiation—desire, community, and tensions between "cement things" and newer forms of "becoming" and social development—are important ideological territory where Marqueños work through and reform religion and development as discourses constituent of modernity. Where religious and development networks meet in public spaces, community is often idealized, becoming something people work to achieve and maintain in everything from formal applications for development projects to notions of community within religious organizations. The object of publicly expressed development desire, infrastructure is frequently at the heart of debate over community aspirations and images centered on notions of progress. Buildings and seedbeds act as places where private, unarticulated desire must turn public, becoming pronounceable and codified in formal applications for aid and in ceremonies such as the Santa Anita cheese factory dedication. The object of that desire, of development itself, is negotiated in planning meetings that pit infrastructure against social development; which open spaces of negotiation around the meaning of "progress."

While religion and development may reside and become hybridized in the same social spaces, then, this kind of hybridity is not automatic, invisible, or the inevitable result of entangled discourses. In some instances, the networks along which religion and development travel collide, causing people to separate the two discourses out again as they choose one mode of understanding over another. While Truman's earthworms have the ability to become religious in the context of evangelical development projects that emphasize spiritual as well as physical development, they may also remain largely secular. While they are the products of a history that includes religious motivations, they are not necessarily religious themselves. They may, in other words, be converted, moving from one world to the other depending on time, circumstance, and the predilections of those seeking to define their meaning and significance in daily life.

There are no easy answers, then, to the question Vicente posed to me more than a decade ago as we worked together on a rural Ecuadorian hillside. While I was right to tell him that my particular earthworms were not intended to convert him to a new understanding of Christianity, I too easily dismissed their longer, religiously significant genealogy. I failed, at that point, to read development religiously.

I also failed to understand Truman's earthworms as objects of negotiation. As agents aware of the long and tangled nature of religion and development in Ecuador, Marqueños and other Ecuadorians make conscious decisions about how they will choose and interact with religious and secular development organizations. Some, such as the Santa Anita women, do so in a way that freely combines religious understandings of people and community with economic and societal goals. Others, such as the woman lobbying for a road in Sinche, will keep things separated, consciously resisting hybridity and development discourses that favor integration in the hopes of attaining straight roads to progress and a brighter future just over the horizon.

By undertaking such negotiations, especially around issues of integration as it manifests in "alternative" development strategies, Marqueños demonstrate a keen awareness that development, be it targeted at households, infrastructure, or bodies, is at some level cosmological. They recognize that changing one's physical circumstances has sociological, psychological, and metaphysical consequences and implications. For this reason, when Marqueños and other Ecuadorians negotiate the terms and strategies of development, they read development religiously. They engage development's religious roots and contemporary deployments in a cosmologically aware manner, embracing religion or technological definitions of progress in some instances, and rejecting them in others, and often blending them in ways that baffle those with whom such discourses originate. In doing so, they reform the terms of the modernity in which they live, opening a space for a greater awareness and enactment of religious ideals in some instances, and rejecting them in others. They negotiate a cosmologically aware, localized development, one that helps to define and create a reformed modernity not bounded by the strict terms of either technological advancement or ideals of integration.

The reformation of modernity under way in San Marcos is thus a reform aimed at recognizing that progress, and development as a part of that progress, is never entirely secular and is always local. The recognition that development has cosmological significance is quite different from a full and uncritical embrace of integrated or alternative development strategies. Cosmologically aware development, such as the kind demonstrated by the Santa Anita cooperative, recognizes local histories, needs, and desires as it uses many of the facets of religion to enact progress on its own terms. At the same time, however, cosmologically aware development resists an overuse of "integrated" and "whole person" rhetoric and ideologies, as well as organic or naturalistic views of community. The woman who stood up at the end of the municipal meeting at Sinche to ask about the road and the Santa Anita *socias'* emphasis on the difficulty of maintaining a working community both embody this resistance, and the realities of the *lucha* with which Marqueños characterize daily life. The Sinche woman pointed to a tendency of integrated or whole person discourses to discount the immediacy of physical need, while the Santa Anita members remind us that functioning communities, even those rooted in shared religious histories and understandings, require sophisticated social work. Indeed, the Santa Anita emphasis on the difficulty of creating and maintaining community may be read as a critique of colonialist development that may view aid recipients as "primitive"—more naturally spiritual, communal, and somehow closer to or more dependent upon nature or the divine.

The possibility of such a cosmologically aware development, and the recognition of its roots in the negotiation of modernity under way in the Ecuadorian countryside, could have a significant impact on the practice and success of development programs. By opening up a space to consider how modernity is being negotiated at local levels—how people are combining, breaking apart, and creating discourses from local and global flows—personnel in development programs and those they seek to serve could avoid some of the dichotomies that have plagued successful development since its inception. Tradition or religion may no longer be imagined in opposition to modernity, and development itself may not always be modernity's ultimate marker. Where there is a recognition that modernity is being reformed, in other words, and is therefore flexible in its definitions and enactment, there exists a greater chance for the globally networked yet locally responsible development programs for which both developers and their critics have called.[1]

This book does not claim that religion is good for development, or that development is bad for religious understandings or values. These are important concerns, but they are not the primary concerns of the people with whom I spoke, worked, and lived in San Marcos. Rather, Marqueños and others in highland Ecuador are engaged in a process of negotiation that places religious and development discourses into the specific and concrete spaces of bedrooms, kitchens, buildings, and meeting halls. How they do this, and how this in turn affects Christianity and development as constituent parts of the modernity in which they live, affects the efficaciousness and relevance of both church and secular programs.

Finally, the reformation of modernity enacted at least in part through the mechanisms of religion and development in San Marcos demonstrates that the reality of development in San Marcos is one that directly challenges the colorful M.O.P. highway signs, even as the signs reveal a long and tangled history. Clearly, in San Marcos and in other communities in rural, highland Ecuador there is not simply one way to development, to progress, or to salvation, though all of these things come together in daily practices and spaces. Rather, there are many, the result of an active retooling of both traditional and alternative development in cosmologically aware terms, an active process of fusing physical and metaphysical discourses and breaking them apart. Not just along for the ride, Ecuadorians in the twenty-first century are negotiating the terms of their modernity and the struggle to fulfill its promises, work that will have profound and lasting consequences for Christianity and development in Latin America in the years and decades to come.

NOTES

Introduction

1. Following ethnographic tradition, this and all other names of Ecuadorian community members, local clergy, and local development workers are pseudonyms. Public figures, including those who hold management positions in national organizations, are identified by their actual names.

2. The translation from the Spanish *conquistar* (to conquer) to the English "to take over" is deliberate. When Ecuadorians use *conquistar* to refer to the events of the Conquest, and also to sexual exploits, it translates readily to the English "to conquer." When used in this and similar contexts, however, it has a less specific meaning, and "to take over" renders a more appropriate feeling.

3. Ecuador does not collect religious affiliation figures as a part of its national census. These figures are estimates and projections from the data collected in Barret, Kurian, and Johnson, *World Christian Encyclopedia*, 246.

4. U.S. Department of State, "Background Note: Ecuador."

5. In 2008, for example, USAID gave almost $448 million in prime contracts to faith-based organizations worldwide. U.S. Agency for International Development, *2008 VOLAG Report*, 126–53.

6. See Bergeron, "The Post-Washington Consensus"; Haidari and Wright, "Participation and Participatory Development"; Lomnitz, "Informal Exchange Networks in Formal Systems."

7. See Tyndale, "Faith and Economics in 'Development'"; Alkire and Braham, "Supporting the MDGs"; Hula, Jackson-Elmore, and Reese, "Mixing God's Work and the Public Business."

8. Orsi, "Everyday Miracles," 7.

9. Escobar, *Encountering Development*; Rist, *The History of Development*; Sachs, *The Development Dictionary*.

10. Rist, *The History of Development*, 23.

11. J. Z. Smith, *Imagining Religion*, xi.

12. Appadurai, *Modernity at Large*, 9.

13. Hume, *The Natural History of Religion*, 75.

14. Weber, *The Protestant Ethic*, 121.

15. See Foucault, *The Archaeology of Knowledge*; and Appadurai, *Modernity at Large*, 3.

16. Latour, *We Have Never Been Modern*, 13.

17. Ibid., 33.

18. Further blurring these lines, article 71 of the 2008 Ecuadorian constitution includes language granting "nature" (*la naturaleza/Pacha Mama*) "the right to integral respect for its existence and for the maintenance and regeneration of its life cycles, structure, functions and evolutionary processes."

19. Cox, *Fire From Heaven*, 81–92; Martin, *Tongues of Fire*, 9–26, 163–84.

20. See Barber, *Jihad vs. McWorld*.

21. Heralding Christ Jesus' Blessings, or *Hoy Christo Jesus Bendice*. The name comes from the call letters of the organization's mission venture, a large Quito radio station.

21. There are more than two dozen political parties in Ecuador, all of which are on ballots in "lists," so that one may vote for "the list," casting a ballot for party candidates in every position for which they stand. "Lista X" in this case is a pseudonym for a political party that held office in San Marcos from 2000 until 2004.

22. A Marqueño is someone from San Marcos. "Marqueños" is the plural. I use both terms throughout the book.

23. Castells, *The Rise of the Network Society*, 407–9.

24. Clifford, *Routes*, 21–30.

Chapter 1. "Things Both Good and Bad"

1. See Geertz, "Religion as a Cultural System"; Tweed, *Crossing and Dwelling*; and M. Taylor, *After God*.

2. Wittgenstein, *Philosophical Investigations*, §66.

3. For a more complete discussion of discourses and their dispersion through time, see Foucault, *The Archaeology of Knowledge*.

4. Truman, *Inaugural Address*.

5. See Esteva, "Development," 6–25; and Escobar, *Encountering Development*, 4. While other scholars, most notably Michael Cowen and Robert Shenton, have traced "development" as a distinct rhetoric before Truman's 1949 speech, they, like Escobar and Esteva, assume that development leaves its religious roots to become an entirely secular pursuit. See Cowen and Shenton, "The Invention of Development," 27–43.

6. Shanin, "The Idea of Progress," 65.

7. Herbert, *Culture and Anomie*, 30–33.

8. For more on the nineteenth-century foreign mission movement in North America, see Carpenter and Shenk, *Earthen Vessels*; and Hutchison, *Errand to the World*. Both works profile nineteenth-century American Protestant Arthur Tappan Pierson, one of several premillennialists attempting to convert the world in order to bring about a second coming of Jesus. Indeed, Pierson singled out Latin America as a region ripe for Protestant evangelization, which he linked explicitly to material progress. Despite the frequent interruption of Protestant mission work by civil war, he wrote, ". . . it is plain that God is 'overturning' as He has seldom overturned anywhere, in preparation for his reign whose right it is.

"Material progress is visible. Better dwellings, farming implements, roads, bridges, factories and mills, railroads, steam-boats, telegraphs—in fact, all the marked features of a higher civilization are rapidly impressing themselves on this great country. The people may not love Protestantism for its spiritual religion, but they see that it is everywhere linked with civil and religious freedom, with aggressive enterprise, good government and national prosperity; and as they look at their own condition—no intelligence or intellectual progress, low moral standards and lower moral practices, in bondage to a Jesuitical priesthood, and living the lives of slaves rather than free men—they naturally turn to Protestantism as a help to political and national progress" (Pierson, *Crisis in Missions*, 150–51).

9. Sbert, "Progress," 192–205; See also Pagden, *European Encounters with the New World*; and Todorov, *The Conquest of America*.

10. The Bahamian island where Columbus first made landfall remains a point of debate among scholars. Columbus never made an accurate navigational reading of his position, believing he was indeed in the extremities of the Orient. I use here the Taino word for the island as transcribed by Columbus.

11. Lardicci, *A Synoptic Edition of the Log of Columbus's First Voyage*, 48.

12. Ibid.

13. Ibid.

14. Native American groups working under the auspices of the Indigenous Law Institute presented a petition demanding the revocation of *Inter Caetera* to Pope John Paul II in 1992, a move that received little public attention and no official response from the Vatican, though annual "bull burning" protests continued until at least the late 1990s.

15. Rusconi, *The Book of Prophecies*, 1–2.

16. Deck, "Jesuit Contributions," 169. See also Cushner, *Farm and Factory*.

17. Kant, "What Is Enlightenment?" 58.

18. Hegel, *Introduction to the Philosophy of History*, 59.

19. Escobar, *Encountering Development*, 125–30.

20. Some of this blindness that Rist criticizes seems to be wearing off. International economic development has undergone many changes since the

1980s, most notably in emphases on locality, gender, and sustainability. The United Nations Millennium Development Goals published in 2000, for example, highlight access to education for women and girls, as well as environmental sustainability. In addition, protests such as those at IMF meetings in Seattle and Cancún give ample evidence for a broader rethinking about many of the assumptions behind international assistance programs. See Broad, *Global Backlash,* for a particularly comprehensive view of the protests and the multiplicity of economic views behind development strategies and those of the protesters.

21. Truman, *Inaugural Address.*

22. Dulles quoted by Black in *The Good Neighbor,* title page. See also Inboden, *Religion and American Foreign Policy,* 226–56.

23. See Sen, *Development as Freedom;* and Nussbaum, *Women and Human Development.*

24. Malloc, "Social, Human and Spiritual Capital in Human Development."

25. Murra, "El 'Control Vertical,' " 427–76.

26. For a detailed study of pre-Inca Ecuador, see Salomon, *Native Lords of Quito in the Age of the Incas.*

27. Ibid., 126.

28. Newson, *Life and Death in Early Colonial Ecuador,* 208.

29. A new paved road to the coast, which will shorten the travel time to Guayaquil to as little as two hours, is scheduled for completion in 2012. The ease of travel and access to coastal areas may make San Marcos a much more "coastal" community in cultural ties and norms in the years to come.

Chapter 2. La Lucha

1. "Él es buena gente. Muy Católico, pues." There are many distinct accents and idioms that make up Ecuadorian Spanish, many of them the result of a long coexistence and interdependence with Kichwa. Where possible, I translate colloquial expressions directly, seeking to render a reproduction of local speech that best captures some of its distinct tone and flavor.

2. Latour, *We Have Never Been Modern,* 12.

3. FLACSO, Ecuador, *Las Cifras,* 9.

4. This kind of trafficking was highlighted in August of 2010 when an Ecuadorian was one of two survivors after a massacre of migrants in Tamaulipas, Mexico, which killed seventy-two men and women from several Latin American countries. The migrants were allegedly killed by members of the Zeta drug cartel, which survivors claimed had attempted to extort money from them, shooting when they resisted. "Victims of Massacre in Mexico Said to Be Migrants," *New York Times,* August 25, 2010.

For a detailed account of Ecuadorian migration and its effect on gender roles and families, see Pribilsky, *La Chulla Vida*.

5. In 2008 there were 45,000 registered Colombian refugees in Ecuador, with the estimate of unregistered refugees and migrants between 150,000 and 250,000. Source: "Colombian Refugees in Ecuador," United Nations News Centre.

Because they do not generally file for refugee status, it is more difficult to estimate the number of Peruvians in Ecuador. The 2001 census counted 5,682 Peruvians with legal permission to reside in Ecuador, but most sources estimate the Peruvian population to be between 60,000 and 120,000. Source: Migration Policy Institute.

6. For an excellent analysis of decisions to migrate, as well as the effects of migration on families, see Pribilsky, *La Chulla Vida*.

7. Stutzman, "El Mestizaje," 46.

8. See Weismantel, *Food, Gender, and Poverty in the Ecuadorian Andes*; Colloredo-Mansfeld, *The Native Leisure Class*; Meisch, *Andean Entrepreneurs*; Wogan, *Magical Writing in Salasaca*; Lyons, *Remembering the Hacienda*; and Corr, *Ritual and Remembrance in the Ecuadorian Andes*.

9. The issue came to the fore in popular culture when Miss Bolivia, Gabriela Oviedo, echoed many *blanquista* sentiments in the interview competition of the 2004 Miss Universe pageant in Quito. When asked what she wanted people to know about her country, she replied, "Unfortunately, people that don't know Bolivia very much think that we are all just Indian people from the west side of the country, it's La Paz all the image that we reflect [*sic*], is that poor people and very short people and Indian people . . . I'm from the other side of the country, the east side and it's not cold, it's very hot and we are tall and we are white people and we know English so all that misconception that Bolivia is only an 'Andean' country, it's wrong" (*El Comercio* [Quito], May 23, 2004). The pan–Latin American indigenous movement, of which the 1992 indigenous uprising in Ecuador is a part, is also changing some of the ways in which people perceive and negotiate categories of race and class. In Ecuador, CONAIE and Pachakutik, two indigenous political parties, have become powerful political actors, assisting in the 2000 coup that overthrew President Jaime Mahuad, and the election in 2008 of Rafael Correa (though in a police uprising in October 2010, characterized by the Correa administration as a coup attempt, Pachakutik issued a statement condemning Correa's "totalitarian practices"). The groups have applied continual pressure on the Correa administration to keep election promises, and have also highlighted the diversity within indigenous groups. As Rudi Colloredo-Mansfeld writes, "Internal pluralism—not the sharing of core values—has driven the politics, uprisings and electoral victories of Latin America's most comprehensive indigenous movement" (*Fighting Like a Community*, xiii).

10. See the discussion in Yúdice, *The Expediency of Culture*, where a Peruvian suggested that rather than celebrate the Mexican-American Día de la Raza

(Day of the Race—a Mexican and Chicano term used to denote a celebration of Chicano history and heritage), Latinos should instead celebrate "*el día del campesinado*" (103).

11. Though I have identified the *lucha* as primarily campesino in its usage, small business owners, government employees, and others living in San Marcos also use lucha language to characterize their position and struggles in society. Identifying with the struggle of daily life is one way people may enter into common dialogue about the realities of modern existence, though they may contest the validity of another's struggle or use of lucha language when the speaker appears to have a more urban lifestyle.

12. *Luchar* may be translated as either "to struggle," "to fight," "to wrestle," or "to dispute" (Canfield, *University of Chicago Spanish Dictionary*). In Ecuadorian Spanish, the most common meaning is "to struggle," as I have most often rendered it here, though the reader should read it with the sense of fighting against or breaking out of a confining or oppressive situation.

For a detailed account of la lucha and sharecropping among campesinos in rural Ecuador, see Lyons, Aranda, and Guevera, "Simple People," 403–14. Also, Pribilsky, *La Chulla Vida*.

13. What I have translated here as "fell off the wagon" is on my tapes as "*emburré*," an adaptation of the Spanish "*emborrachar*," "to get drunk." I use it here in its full English sense, meaning either to get drunk after a period of abstinence or to fall away from any goal or ideal activity. Ignacio, like many people in his community, speaks Spanish as a second language.

14. For more on the indigenous resurgence in Ecuador, see Becker, *Pachakutik*, and *Indians and Leftists in the Making of Ecuador's Modern Indigenous Movements*; Becker and Clark, *Highland Indians*; and Colloredo-Mansfeld, *Fighting Like a Community*.

15. Population figures are from the 2010 national census, which counted more than 15,000 people in the canton of San Marcos. Of these, roughly 6,000 live in the town of San Marcos. Source: Instituto National Estadistico y Censos del Ecuador.

16. Carmen García, personal communication, February 13, 2003.

17. For more on Plan International and its changes in development philosophies and strategies in the international context, see J. H. Smith, *Bewitching Development*, 179–214.

18. For a thoughtful essay on the ways networks are channeled through existing viaducts rather than invented out of whole cloth, see Tsing, "The Global Situation."

19. Geographer Anthony Bebbington notes that religious institutions are often a conduit for global linkages. "The global entanglements in which Andean localities are enmeshed are, and have long been, multi-stranded: beyond market relationships, the webs linking Andean places and the wider world pass

through globalized religious institutions, civil society networks, intergovern-mental relationships, migrant streams and more." Bebbington, "Globalized Andes?," 415.

20. There is a vast literature on the effects of particular religions on quo-tidian life and various incarnations of "progress." From the Western canon, Weber's *The Protestant Ethic and the Spirit of Capitalism* is an early example of an effort to link religious belief and practice to capitalist success. In the Latin American context, Burdick, *Looking for God in Brazil*; Brusco, *The Reformation of Machismo*; Berryman, *Religion in the Megacity*; Chesnut, "A Preferential Op-tion for the Spirit"; and others have explored the liberationist Catholic Church and conversion to Pentecostalism in the context of poverty. In the particular case of Ecuador, former president of the republic Osvaldo Hurtado credits Protestant concern for the here and now, as well as a greater permissiveness to-ward wealth, with economic and social progress in the country. Speaking of the colonial church in his book *Portrait of a Nation* he comments, "Catholicism made selective social hierarchies legitimate, praised poverty, numbed initia-tives and accumulation of wealth" (43). See also Andrade's *Visión Mundial* for an examination of evangelical organization World Vision in the Ecuadorian highlands.

21. See Cahill, "Popular Religion and Appropriation."

22. Wogan's *Magical Writing in Salasaca* is an excellent account of the power that this linkage, and its embodiment in writing, came to have in the Salasaca region.

23. Jones, *Radio: The New Missionary*, 72.

24. Stoll, *Is Latin America Turning Protestant?*, 337.

25. *Connections*, church newsletter.

Chapter 3. Pedagogies of Power

1. For other critiques of "alternative" development, see Parpart, Rai, and Staudt, *Rethinking Empowerment*; and Deneulin and Shahani, *An Introduction to the Human Development and Capability Approach*. For an overview of the re-lationship between "alternative" development and "empowerment" approaches, see Friedmann, *Empowerment*.

2. Truman, *Inaugural Address*.

3. Kennedy, "Staffing a Foreign Policy for Peace," 1237–41.

4. Kelly, *New Rules for the New Economy*, 5.

5. Hoadley, "The Rise and Fall of the Basic Needs Approach," 149. Mit-lin, Hickey, and Bebbington link alternative development to increasing num-bers of NGOs beginning in the 1960s, peaking in the 1980s, and becoming linked to neoliberalism in the 1990s. In many ways, they argue, NGOs became

synonymous with alternative approaches to development, even as they were funded by state agencies. See Mitlin, Hickey, and Bebbington, "Reclaiming Development?"

6. For specific approaches to WID programs and empowerment approaches, see Boserup, *The Conditions of Agricultural Growth*; Nussbaum, *Women and Human Development*; and Tinker, *Persistent Inequalities*.

7. See Scott, *Seeing Like a State*, for an analysis of the ways in which states use development schema to control populations. See also Broad, *Global Backlash*, for an overview of some local forms of resistance to this control.

8. May, "Passing the Torch," 5.

9. Rice, *The Bold Experiment*, 15.

10. These principles, touted as "well conceived" in the initial report (7), continue to inform official Peace Corps policy.

11. U.S. Peace Corps, *First Annual Report to Congress*, 8.

12. Ibid., 35.

13. "Community development" became popular as an effort to harness the energy of intellectual, artistic, and technological leaders for urban renewal in the United States in the 1960s, though some trace the movement back to the nineteenth century, and also describe Mohandas Gandhi's work in India as a form of "community development." The most visible form of community development, especially in its North American mode, is community organizing— efforts to organize community members to work together for social, political, and/or economic change. See Clay and Jones, "A Brief History of Community Economic Development."

14. U.S. Peace Corps, *First Annual Report to Congress*, 36.

15. Fischer, *Making Them Like Us*, 145–47.

16. Cowan, *The Making of an Un-American*, 99.

17. U.S. Peace Corps, *Annual Report to Congress 1973*, 12.

18. U.S. Peace Corps, *Annual Report to Congress 1973*.

19. Ibid., 15.

20. Cowan, *The Making of an Un-American*, 92.

21. Ibid.

22. Cowan's concerns were, as it turns out, well founded. When Bruce Murray, a volunteer in Chile, signed a petition opposing U.S. involvement in Vietnam as antithetical to the world peace for which he ostensibly worked in 1967, Peace Corps Washington asked him not to make this position public. When he responded by writing to the *New York Times* to publicize the event, he was removed from Peace Corps service. This event, especially, compelled Cowan and his wife, Rachel, to reexamine the political nature of the Peace Corps and eventually to tender their resignations. Fischer, *Making Them Like Us*, 86.

23. Reeves, *The Politics of the Peace Corps & Vista*, 97.

24. U.S. Peace Corps, "What Is the Peace Corps?"

25. U.S. Peace Corps, *Annual Report to Congress 2006,* 44.

26. Indeed, a consistent criticism of the Peace Corps, both from conservatives who see the program as a waste of government money and from liberals who worry about neocolonialism and the persistence of Western empire, has been the role of nonspecialists as volunteers in development work. See Strauss, "Too Many Innocents Abroad."

27. From 2003 until 2009, 33 percent of PEPFAR (President's Emergency Plan for AIDS Relief) funds were earmarked for abstinence and monogamy training, and all PEPFAR associated programs followed an "ABC" rule that privileged abstinence, "being faithful," and then "condoms" for AIDS prevention. The President's Emergency Plan for AIDS Relief Office of the U.S. Global AIDS Coordinator, "ABC Guidance #1."

28. Foucault, *Discipline and Punish,* 222.

29. Peace Corps Ecuador, *Training Plan: Rural Public Health/Youth and Families,* 5.

30. This kind of approach is generally classified as an "empowerment" approach to development. Many credit Paulo Freire with pioneering empowerment approaches to development and community organizing, especially as he emphasized a "pedagogy of the oppressed," which he characterized as necessary to prevent "dehumanization." For Freire, pedagogy is a central social and political act and the only reliable practice for change. See Freire, *Pedagogy of the Oppressed.* It is important to note, however, that no one in the Peace Corps training sessions I observed mentioned Freire's name or attributed "Positive Community Development" to him.

31. Peace Corps Ecuador, *Training Handbook for Rural and Community Health,* 13.

32. World Bank, *World Development Report* (1990), 131.

33. World Bank, *World Development Report* (2005), 54, 164, 174.

34. Peace Corps Ecuador, *Training Handbook for Rural and Community Health,* 10.

35. A pseudonym. See DeTemple, Eidenshink, and Josephson, "How Is Your Life Since Then?," 119–32.

36. Indigenous development models also follow the participatory approach outlined in the PACA manual. The Federation of Indigenous Organizations from the Foothills of Chimborazo (FOCIFCH) produced a guide to rural development entitled "Development, Knowledge and Participation in the Andean Community" under the auspices of PRODEPINE, the indigenous development agency in Ecuador. The booklet emphasizes that "in the first place, local development should not be defined and executed by technicians or university students with the help of the community. Rather, it should be defined and executed by the community with the help of technicians. The major responsibility for the results obtained should rest in the community, although the problems may be

of a technical nature." Campana, *Desarrollo, Coinocimiento y Participación en la Comunidad Andina*, 9.

37. U.S. Peace Corps, *Booklet 5: PACA Tools*.

38. Peace Corps Ecuador, *Training Handbook for Rural and Community Health*, 10.

39. *El Hoy*, July 10, 2006.

40. "USAID Contracts with Faith-Based Organizations," *Boston Globe*, October 8, 2006.

41. There is also a substantial corpus of literature dedicated to the ways religious views may change development goals and measures of success. See Bornstein, *The Spirit of Development*; DeTemple, Eidenshink, and Josephson, "How Is Your Life Since Then?"; and Hoksbergen, "Approaches to Evaluation of Development Interventions." For an insightful analysis of interpretation in measuring success and failure in development projects, see Mosse, "Is Good Policy Unimplementable?"

42. J. H. Smith also identifies pedagogy as a place where religious and development discourses intertwine. "Pedagogy," he writes, "once directed at Wataita by institutions like the state and NGOs, is now generalized and 'reasonable' people feel the imperative to use reason to convince other people . . . While this interest in teaching is not exactly new, and dates back at least to the early days of mission Christianity, what is new is the direction that pedagogy takes: in particular, toward creativity and intervention in response to the perceived inadequacy of structures" (*Bewitching Development*, 90).

Chapter 4. Good Housekeeping

1. See Scott, *Seeing Like a State*, for an excellent analysis of state control of populations via methods such as census taking and mapping.

2. Households are not an uncontested category. Though they have been a privileged locus of anthropological and economic study (see Hamilton, *The Two-Headed Household*; Weismantel, *Food, Gender, and Poverty in the Ecuadorian Andes*; and Wilk, *The Household Economy*), feminist, Marxist, and other scholars have highlighted problems that come from Western assumptions about the composition of households and those who make decisions within them. See Guyer, "Dynamic Approaches to Household Budgeting"; Pigg, "Inventing Social Categories through Place"; and Pribilsky, *La Chulla Vida*.

3. For an analysis of the way development discourses favor Western-style nuclear families and presume heteronormativity, see Bedford, "Loving to Straighten out Development," 295–322.

4. See Brusco, *The Reformation of Machismo*; Gutmann, *The Meanings of Macho*; and Weismantel, *Food, Gender, and Poverty in the Ecuadorian Andes*.

5. *Visión Mundial: Evaluación y Segurimiento en Algunas Comunidades Indígenas de la Sierra Ecuatoriana,* CEPLAES (Centro de Planificación y Estudios Sociales), 1984.

6. For an analysis of the ways that such immigration affects family units, see Pribilsky, *La Chulla Vida.*

7. Indeed, the gap between Catholic recorded parishioners and attendance at Mass, along with a declining rate for those taking major sacraments, has become such a concern in San Marcos that in 2007 the priest began a "mission" program to "re-Catholicize" communities where Catholic participation had dropped off or become nonexistent, or where many people in the community had joined other Christian traditions.

8. Mayer, *The Articulated Peasant,* 4.

9. Ibid., 245.

10. Murra, "El 'Control Vertical.'"

11. Mayer, *The Articulated Peasant,* 241.

12. Latour, *We Have Never Been Modern,* 41.

13. Bakhtin, *The Dialogic Imagination,* 358.

14. Weismantel, *Food, Gender, and Poverty in the Ecuadorian Andes,* 87–113.

15. There is also an overt racial overtone in the scenes the pamphlets portray. The woman holding the egg toward the lightbulb wears a dress and has her hair in a European style most Ecuadorians would associate with a white urbanite, and the man washing vegetables also has distinctly European features and wears urban clothes. No one in the pamphlets appears to be indigenous or Afro-Ecuadorian, nor particularly mestizo, thus furthering the elision of a "developed" Ecuador with a "white" Ecuador. For more on race and development, see Stutzman, "Mestizaje."

16. *Alimentación Escolar,* 1.

17. More commonly referred to as a *cuy mejorado* (improved) or *de raza* (purebred).

18. Watchtower Bible and Tract Society of New York, Inc., "Una Tragedia de Gran Magnitud," 3–12.

19. This particular incident, while popular in local hagiographic lore, appears to be absent from official accounts of the saint's life.

20. Duden, "Population," 149.

21. As quoted in ibid.

22. As quoted in ibid., 150.

23. PEPFAR, "Community and Faith-Based Organizations. Report to Congress."

24. *Mejorando mi Familia.*

25. More than half of twenty-five entering volunteers in the youth and families program were assigned to sites or agencies where they would be directly involved in sex education or HIV/AIDS prevention.

26. This is not, of course, to imply that religion and development are the only discourses or realities which influence sexuality and reproduction. In 2008 two-thirds of all births in San Marcos were to unwed mothers, and several were to couples in marital relationships with other people. There is also a significant disparity between civil marriages, recognized by the state, and marriages performed within the Catholic Church. In 2008 there were forty-five marriages recorded at the Registro Civil (civil records office) in San Marcos but only fourteen performed in the church. Some of this disparity reflects an increasingly diverse population, so that not all marriages are Catholic, and it also reflects a certain conservatism on the part of couples who want legal recognition of their union but do not commit "to God" until they are sure the marriage will last. Finances are also a consideration, as church weddings, which often require sponsors and the completion of premarital counseling at the church, are more often accompanied by large celebrations and are thus substantially more costly and time consuming. There is also evidence of "trial marriages" in Andean contexts. For more on this see Price, "Trial Marriage in the Andes"; Borque and Warren, *Women of the Andes*, 99; and Pribilsky, *La Chulla Vida*, 140.

27. Like many Ecuadorians, Miguel calls all Protestants, regardless of theology or affiliation, "evangelicals" (*evangélicos*). Thus, Methodists, Pentecostals, Baptists, and Seventh-Day Adventists may all be referred to as "evangelicals."

28. Herbert, *Culture and Anomie*, 29.

29. Shepherd, "Agricultural Hybridity and the 'Pathology' of Traditional Ways."

30. Stutzman, "El Mestizaje."

31. There is a long history of this practice within Christianity. Paul frequently referred to fellow believers in the divinity of Christ as "brothers" and "sisters," terms derived from Jesus' frequent references to God as "father" and the subsequent Christian construction of Jesus as God's son. See especially Luke 14:26, Mark 3:35, and Romans 16:1.

32. Magdalena Lopez, interview, May 6, 2003.

33. See Davis, *Victims of the Miracle.*

Chapter 5. Cement Things

1. Source: Ecuadorian Ministry of Public Works website. Accessed at http://www.mop.gov.ec/historia.asp, February 10, 2005.

2. Specifically, Anderson notes that maps often include religious sites and natural features as a part of state holdings and national heritage, serving to tie God and nature into state imaginations. See *Imagined Communities*, 163–86.

3. Anderson, *Imagined Communities*, 37–46.

4. For more on development desire, and also roads as a particular object of that desire, see Vries, "Don't Compromise Your Desire for Development!"; and Wilson, "Toward a Political Economy of Roads."

5. "*Minga*" is a Kichwa word for a communal work party which has found common currency in Ecuadorian Spanish. While it tends to refer to community-wide events such as canal cleanings in indigenous communities, in largely mestizo settings such as San Marcos people use it to refer to any group effort.

6. The "Libro de Actas," a book of minutes the group has kept since its formation in 1989 (and which is legally required for recognition as a group by the state), supports this description of the cooperative's purpose. The first recorded act, titled "History of the Santa Anita Group," begins by describing the purpose of the group as "providing support and motivating the campesina woman to overcome marginalization by utilizing her own will." The first act ends with a list of goals, saying, "We will try to unify ourselves as people, to learn to participate in community, in actuality" ("Libro de Actas," 4).

7. Here, Sofía is using language that comes directly from liberation theology teachings that emphasize such active reflection on "God's Word" in social contexts. Such reflection, liberation theologians teach, will lead to social action meant to benefit the local community, especially the poor. See Gutierrez, *A Theology of Liberation*; Boff and Boff, *Introducing Liberation Theology*; and Freire, *Pedagogy of the Oppressed*, especially chap. 4. It should be noted, however, that I never heard the term "liberation theology" (*Teología de la Liberación*) used in reference to the Santa Anita cooperative or to its parent organization. Indeed, the term is relatively rare in Bolívar, though the movement has had an influence in the province, and in Ecuador more broadly, particularly in neighboring Chimborazo province, which was home to liberationist and activist bishop Leonidas Proaño.

8. The name "Populorum Progressio" (On the Development of the Peoples) is taken from the 1967 papal encyclical of that title, in which Pope Paul VI expressed concerns over capitalism and living conditions for the world's poor, and called for human development in a "spirit of solidarity." Such development, said the pope, "cannot be restricted to economic growth alone. To be authentic, it must be well rounded; it must foster the development of each man and of the whole man." For more on the Salinas project, see North and Cameron, *Rural Progress, Rural Decay*.

For more on liberation theology and the ways it has and has not affected life and endeavors such as the Santa Anita group in Latin America, see Burdick, *Looking for God in Brazil*, as well as *Legacies of Liberation*; and Drogus, *Women, Religion and Social Change in Brazil's Popular Church*.

9. There is an impressive literature on community—its meanings, structures, efficacy, and particularity—in the Andean context. Studies that combine questions about community with development (usually in the indigenous

context) include Gelles, *Water and Power in Highland Peru*; Allen, *The Hold Life Has*; Guerrero Cazar and Ospina Peralta, *El Poder de la Comunidad*; Colloredo-Mansfeld, *Fighting Like a Community.*

10. One way of describing such a "coming together" in communal contexts is with reciprocity, a concept many scholars have drawn upon to characterize Andean societies. Enrique Mayer, in the same studies in which he described "production zones," characterized Andean economies as "reciprocal," made up of exchange networks in which individuals contribute resources from personal and familial activities, a form of resource pooling that takes place at every level of society, from households to communal organizations. See Mayer, *The Articulated Peasant.*

Though he does not use the term "reciprocity" explicitly, economic anthropologist Rudi Colloredo-Mansfeld uses the notions of exchange within communities as he explores community and political change in contemporary Otavalo. In *Fighting Like a Community,* he explores networks of relationships among members of indigenous communities as they struggle to come together for development projects and for political power at local and national levels, making the case that indigenous communities are pluralistic, a diversity that requires reciprocity and work if something like community is to be effective.

While the majority of Marqueños do not identify as indigenous, reciprocity—in which individual contributions and exchange work together to create a functioning community—does play an important part in local life, and people consciously exchange labor and resources in everything from agricultural *mingas* to systems of *compadrazgo.*

11. Lummis, "Equality," 39.

12. See Gupta, *Postcolonial Developments*; Rueschemeyer, *Capitalist Development and Democracy*; Schech and Haggis, *Culture and Development*; and O'Gorman, *Charity and Change.*

13. Stoll, *Is Latin America Turning Protestant?*, 268.

14. World Vision International, "Our Mission." See also Andrade, *Visión Mundial.*

15. CEPLAES, *Visión Mundial: Evaluación y Seguimiento,* 29.

Chapter 6. Spiritual Cardiology

1. The extent of required cultural change is still hotly debated, both in ecclesiastical and academic circles. For a history of Protestant missions and their programs in Ecuador, see Goffin, *The Rise of Protestant Evangelism in Ecuador.* For a more critical view of missions and their cultural impact in Latin America, see Hvalkof and Aaby, *Is God an American?*; Stoll, *Is Latin America Turning Protestant?*; and Brouwer, *Exporting the American Gospel.* For primary

missionary accounts of the need for cultural change, see Kingsland, *A Saint among Savages.*

2. United Andean Indian Mission, *Soil and Souls in Ecuador.*

3. Shenk, "General Introduction," xii.

4. For a more complete history of the film, the ministries that have grown up around it, and a free viewing, see the *Jesus* film website at http://www.jesusfilm.org.

5. Fountain, *Health, the Bible and the Church,* 49.

6. Ibid., 43.

7. See C. Taylor, *Modern Social Imaginaries*; Casanova, *Public Religions in the Modern World.*

8. "New Science Views Entire Man," *New York Times,* April 9, 1932, 16.

9. "Education Parley Ends," *New York Times,* March 16, 1953, 21.

10. *Trustees Report,* Ford Foundation, 4.

11. *New York Times,* January 26, 1965, 75.

12. When Ruth critiques development as "*patrón*-style," she is referring to the colonial system of haciendas in which European "*patróns*," usually hacienda landlords and overseers, used Indians as labor on large agricultural holdings. Each Indian family was granted a small plot of land to farm for personal use, but they generally became so indebted to the patrón for seed money and food that their earnings kept them tied to the haciendas indefinitely. The *huasipun-guero* and *concertaje* systems, widely criticized for cultivating dependent relationships between wealthy landowners and indigenous peasants, was formally abolished with the 1964 land reform. However, *patrón* relationships have persisted to the present day.

13. For more on these kinds of negotiations, especially in the context of the institutional church in Ecuador, see Lyons, *Remembering the Hacienda*; and Corr, *Ritual and Remembrance in the Ecuadorian Andes.*

14. Geographer Anthony Bebbington speaks about these processes as influencing the local impact of global discourses, and the discourses themselves, through the "pull" exerted by local actors, a pull that can build up local capacities. Bebbington, "Globalized Andes?," 416.

Conclusion

1. See especially Escobar, *Territories of Difference,* in which he investigates assemblages of and the use of networks and discourses, including development, by local communities in Colombia.

BIBLIOGRAPHY

Alkire, Sabina. *Valuing Freedom.* New York: Oxford University Press, 2002.

Alkire, Sabina, and Ann Braham. "Supporting the MDGs: A Faith-Based Movement's Story." *Development* 48, no. 1 (2005): 122–25.

Allen, Catherine. *The Hold Life Has: Coca and Cultural Identity in an Andean Community.* Washington, DC: Smithsonian, 1988.

Anderson, Benedict. *Imagined Communities: Reflections on the Origin and Spread of Nationalism.* Austin: University of Texas Press, 1986.

Andolina, Robert, Nina Laurie, and Sarah Radcliffe. *Indigenous Development in the Andes.* Durham, NC: Duke University Press, 2009.

Andrade, Susana. *Visión Mundial: Entre el Cielo y la Tierra—Religión y Desarrollo en la Sierra Ecuatoriana.* Quito: Abya Yala, 1990.

Appadurai, Arjun. *Modernity at Large: Cultural Dimensions of Globalization.* Minneapolis: University of Minnesota Press, 1996.

Archetti, Eduardo P. *Guinea-Pigs: Food, Symbol and Conflict of Knowledge in Ecuador.* Oxford: Berg, 1997.

Asad, Talal. *Anthropology and the Colonial Encounter.* Atlantic Highlands, NJ: Humanities Press, 1973.

Ayala, Felipe Guaman Poma de. *Nueva Crónica y Buen Gobierno.* Edited by John Murra, Rolena Adorno, and Jorge Urioste. Mexico City: Siglo XXI, 1987.

Bakhtin, Mikhail. *The Dialogic Imagination.* Austin: University of Texas Press, 1981.

Barber, Benjamin. *Jihad vs. McWorld: Terrorism's Challenge to Democracy.* New York: Ballantine Books, 1995.

Barret, George, Thomas Kurian, and Todd Johnson, eds. *World Christian Encyclopedia: A Comparative Survey of Churches and Religions in the Modern World.* 2nd ed. New York: Oxford University Press, 2001.

Barriga, Franklin. *Las Culturas Indigenas y el Instituto Lingüistico de Verano.* Quito: Ediciones Amauata, 1992.

Bebbington, Anthony. "Globalized Andes? Livelihoods, Landscapes and Development." *Ecumene* 8, no. 4 (2001): 414–36.

———. "New States, New NGOs? Crisis and Transition among Rural Development NGOs in the Andean Region." *World Development* 25, no. 11 (1997): 1755–65.

———. "Reencountering Development: Livelihood Transitions and Place Transformations in the Andes." *Annals of the Association of American Geographers* 90, no. 3 (2000): 495–520.

———. "Reinventing NGOs and Rethinking Alternatives in the Andes." *Annals of the American Academy of Political and Social Science* 554 (2007): 117–35.

Bebbington, Anthony, and Thomas Perrault. "Social Capital, Development and Access to Resources in Highland Ecuador." *Economic Geography* 75, no. 4 (October 1999): 395–418.

Becker, Marc. *Indians and Leftists in the Making of Ecuador's Modern Indigenous Movements.* Durham, NC: Duke University Press, 2008.

———. *Pachakutik: Indigenous Movements and Electoral Politics in Ecuador.* Lanham, MD: Rowman & Littlefield, 2011.

Becker, Marc, and Kim Clark, eds. *Highland Indians and the State in Modern Ecuador.* Pittsburgh: University of Pittsburgh Press, 2007.

Bedford, Kate. "Loving to Straighten out Development: Sexuality and 'Ethnodevelopment' in the World Bank's Ecuadorian Lending." *Feminist Legal Studies* 13 (2005): 295–322.

Belote, Jim, and Linda Belote. "Drain from the Bottom: Individual Ethnic Identity Change in Southern Ecuador." *Social Forces* 63, no. 1 (1984): 24–50.

———. "Suffer the Little Children: Death, Autonomy and Responsibility in a Changing 'Low Technology' Society." *Science, Technology & Human Values* 9, no. 4 (1984): 35–48.

Bending, Tim, and Sergio Rosendo. "Rethinking the Mechanics of the 'Anti-Politics Machine.'" In *Development Brokers and Translators: The Ethnography of Aid and Agencies,* edited by David Lewis and David Mosse, 217–38. West Hartford, CT: Kumarian Press, 2005.

Benediktsson, Karl. *Harvesting Development: The Construction of Fresh Food Markets in Papua New Guinea.* Ann Arbor: University of Michigan Press, 2002.

Bergeron, Suzanne. *Fragments of Development: Nation, Gender and the Space of Modernity.* Ann Arbor: University of Michigan Press, 2004.

———. "The Post-Washington Consensus and Economic Representations of Women in Development at the World Bank." *International Feminist Journal of Politics* 5, no. 3 (November 2000): 397–419.

Berryman, Phillip. *Religion in the Megacity: Catholic and Protestant Portraits from Latin America.* Maryknoll, NY: Orbis, 1996.

Bhabha, Homi. *The Location of Culture.* London: Routledge, 1994.

Bhatta, Gambir. "Of Geese and Ganders: Mainstreaming Gender in the Context of Sustainable Human Development." *Journal of Gender Studies* 10, no. 1 (2001): 17–32.

Black, George. *The Good Neighbor: How the United States Wrote the Story of Central America and the Caribbean.* New York: Pantheon, 1988.

Boff, Clodovis, and Leonardo Boff. *Introducing Liberation Theology.* Maryknoll, NY: Orbis Books, 2001.

Bolívar, Simón. "Letter from Jamaica." Available online at http://www.college .emory.edu/culpeper/BAKEWELL/texts/jamaica-letter.html (last accessed June 25, 2011).

Bolton, Ralph, and Enrique Mayer, eds. *Andean Kinship and Marriage.* Washington, DC: American Anthropological Association, 1977.

Borges, Pedro. *Misión y Civilización en América.* Madrid: Editorial Alhambra, 1987.

Bornstein, Erica. *The Spirit of Development: Protestants, NGOs, and Economics in Zimbabwe.* New York: Routledge, 2005.

Borque, Susan C., and Kay Warren. *Women of the Andes: Patriarchy and Social Change in Two Peruvian Towns.* Ann Arbor: University of Michigan Press, 1981.

Boserup, Ester. *The Conditions of Agricultural Growth.* London: Earthscan, 1998.

Bourdieu, Pierre. *The Logic of Practice.* Stanford, CA: Stanford University Press, 1977.

———. *Outline of a Theory of Practice.* Cambridge: Cambridge University Press, 1977.

Broad, Robin, ed. *Global Backlash: Citizen Initiatives for a Just World Economy.* Lanham, MD: Rowman & Littlefield, 2002.

Bromley, R. J. *Development Planning in Ecuador.* Sussex: Hove Printing Co., 1977.

Brouwer, Steve, Paul Gifford, and Susan Rose. *Exporting the American Gospel: Global Christian Fundamentalism.* New York: Routledge, 1996.

Brusco, Elizabeth. *The Reformation of Machismo: Evangelical Conversion and Gender in Colombia.* Austin: University of Texas Press, 1995.

Burdick, John. *Blessed Anastacia: Women, Race and Popular Christianity in Brazil.* New York: Routledge, 1998.

———. *Legacies of Liberation: The Progressive Catholic Church in Brazil at the Start of a New Millennium.* Hampshire, England, and Burlington, VT: Ashgate, 2004.

———. *Looking for God in Brazil: The Progressive Catholic Church in Urban Brazil's Religious Arena.* Berkeley: University of California Press, 1993.

Cahill, David. "Popular Religion and Appropriation: The Example of Corpus Christi in Eighteenth Century Cuzco." *Latin American Research Review* 31, no. 2 (2006): 67–110.

Campana, Victor Alejandro. *Desarrollo, Conocimiento y Participación en la Co-munidad Andina.* Riobamba: Federación de Organizaciones Indígenas de las Faldas del Chimborazo, 2001.

Canclini, Arnold. *La Fe del Descubridor: Aspectos Religiosos de Cristobal Colón.* Buenos Aires: Editorial Plus Ultra, 1992.

Canfield, D. Lincoln, ed. *The University of Chicago Spanish Dictionary.* 4th ed. Chicago: University of Chicago Press, 1987.

Cano, Ginnette, et al. *Los Nuevos Conquistidores: El Instituto Linguistico de Ver-ano en América Latina.* Quito: CEDIS & FENOC, 1979.

Carey, Robert G. *The Peace Corps.* New York: Praeger, 1970.

Carpenter, Joel A., and Wilbert R. Shenk, eds. *Earthen Vessels: American Evangeli-cals and Foreign Missions, 1880–1980.* Grand Rapids, MI: Eerdmans, 1990.

Casanova, José. *Public Religions in the Modern World.* Chicago: University of Chicago Press, 1994.

Castells, Manuel. *The Rise of the Network Society.* 2nd ed. Vol. 1 of *The Informa-tion Age: Economy, Society, and Culture.* London: Blackwell, 2000.

Catholic Relief Services. *Ecuador Program: Annual Public Summary, 1998.* Catho-lic Relief Services, 1998.

———. *Strategic Planning in Ecuador.* Catholic Relief Services Ecuador-Colombia, 2000.

CEPLAES (Centro de Planificación y Estudios Sociales). *Visión Mundial: Eval-uación y Seguimiento en Algunas Comunidades Indígenas de la Sierra Ecua-toriana.* CEPLAES, 1984.

Certeau, Michel de. *The Practice of Everyday Life.* Berkeley: University of Cali-fornia Press, 1984.

Chapple, Christopher, ed. *The Jesuit Tradition in Education and Mission: A 450-Year Perspective.* Scranton, PA: University of Scranton Press, 1993.

Chaquín, Carmen, and Frank Salomon. *Runa Shimi: A Pedagogical Grammar of Ecuadorian Quechua.* Madison: Latin American and Iberian Studies Pro-gram, University of Wisconsin, 1992.

Chatterjee, Nilanjana, and Nancy Riley. "Planning an Indian Modernity: The Gendered Politics of Fertility Control." *Signs* 26, no. 3 (2001): 811–45.

Chesnut, Andrew. "Pragmatic Consumers and Practical Products: The Success of Pneumacentric Religion among Women in Latin America's New Reli-gious Economy." *Review of Religious Research* 45, no. 1 (2003): 20–31.

———. "A Preferential Option for the Spirit: The Catholic Charismatic Re-newal in Latin America's New Religious Economy." *Latin American Politics and Society* 45, no. 1 (2003): 55–85.

Chevalier, François, ed. *Instrucciones a los Hermanos Jesuitas Administraciones de Haciendas.* Mexico City: Universidad Nacional Autónoma de México, 1950.

Chiriboga, Manuel. *Cambiar se Peude: Experiencias del FEPP en el Desarrollo Rural del Ecuador.* Quito: Abya Yala, 1999.

Clark, Kim, and Marc Becker, eds. *Highland Indians and the State in Modern Ecuador.* Pittsburgh: University of Pittsburgh Press, 2007.

Clay, Roger, and Susan R. Jones. "A Brief History of Community Economic Development." In *Building Healthy Communities: A Guide to Community Economic Development for Advocates, Lawyers, and Policymakers,* edited by Roger Clay and Susan R. Jones, 3–13. Chicago: American Bar Association, 2009.

Cleary, Edward L., and Hannah W. Stewart-Gambino, eds. *Power, Politics, and Pentecostals in Latin America.* Boulder, CO: Westview Press, 1997.

Clifford, James. *The Predicament of Culture: Twentieth-Century Ethnography, Literature, and Art.* Cambridge: Harvard University Press, 1988.

———. *Routes: Travel and Translation in the Late Twentieth Century.* Cambridge: Harvard University Press, 1997.

Cobo, Bernabe. *Inca Religion and Customs.* Translated by Roland Hamilton. Austin: University of Texas Press, 1990.

Colloredo-Mansfeld, Rudi. *Fighting Like a Community: Andean Civil Society in an Era of Indian Uprisings.* Chicago: University of Chicago Press, 2009.

———. *The Native Leisure Class: Consumption and Cultural Creativity in the Andes.* Chicago: University of Chicago Press, 1999.

"Colombian Refugees in Ecuador." United Nations News Centre. Available online at http://www.un.org/apps/news/story.asp?NewsID=25321&Cr=ecuador&Cr1=refugee (last accessed May 27, 2010).

Comisión Ecuatoriana de Justicia y Paz. *La Deuda Externa Ecuatoriana, un Obstaculo al Desarrollo Humano Sostenible.* Comisión Ecuatoriana de Justicia y Paz, 1999.

Compasión International, Ecuador. *De la Adversidad a la Oportunidad.* Compasión International, Ecuador, 1998.

Compassion International. *Nunca Hemos Comenzado un Proyecto de Ayuda a Niños.* Compassion International, 1999.

———. *Sponsor a Child: Let God Use You in a Very Special Way!* Compassion International, 1996.

Comunidec. *Un Nuevo Paradigma Para el Desarrollo: La Empresa Comunitaria Andina. Entrevista con el Padre Antonio Polo sobre la Experiencia Autogestionaria de Salinas.* Quito: Comunidec, 1993.

"Connections." Church newsletter. Missouri. April 2002.

Cornwall, Andrea, Elizabeth Harrison, and Ann Whitehead. "Gender Myths and Feminist Fables: The Struggle for Interpretive Power in Gender and Development." *Development and Change* 38, no. 1 (2007): 1–2.

Corr, Rachel. *Ritual and Remembrance in the Ecuadorian Andes.* Tucson: University of Arizona Press, 2009.

Cortés, Hernando. *5 Letters to the Emperor.* Edited and translated by J. Bayard Morris. New York: W. W. Norton, 1960.

Cowen, Michael P., and Robert W. Shenton. "The Invention of Development." In *The Power of Development,* edited by Jonathan Cush, 27–43. New York: Routledge, 1995.

Cowen, Paul. *The Making of an Un-American: A Dialogue with Experience.* New York: Viking, 1967.

Cox, Harvey. *Fire from Heaven: The Rise of Pentecostal Spirituality and the Reshaping of Religion in the Twenty-first Century.* Reading, MA: Addison-Wesley, 1995.

Crewe, Emma, and Elizabeth Harrison. *Whose Development? An Ethnography of Aid.* London: Zed Books, 1998.

Cush, Jonathan, ed. *The Power of Development.* New York: Routledge, 1995.

Cushner, Nicholas P. *Farm and Factory: The Jesuits and Development of Agrarian Capitalism in Colonial Quito, 1600–1767.* Albany: SUNY Press, 1982.

Davis, Shelton. *Victims of the Miracle: Development and the Indians of Brazil.* New York: Cambridge University Press, 1977.

Deck, Alan Figueroa. "Jesuit Contributions to a Culture of Modernity in Latin America: An Essay towards Critical Understanding." In *The Jesuit Tradition in Education and Missions: A 450-Year Perspective,* edited by Christopher Chapple, 169–81. Scranton, PA: University of Scranton Press, 1993.

DeLanda, Manuel. *A New Philosophy of Society: Assemblage Theory and Social Complexity.* London: Continuum, 2006.

Deneulin, Séverine, and Masooda Bano. *Religion in Development: Rewriting the Secular Script.* London: Zed Books, 2009.

Deneulin, Séverine, and Lila Shahani. *An Introduction to the Human Development and Capability Approach: Freedom and Agency.* Sterling, VA: Earthscan, 2009.

"La Desnutrición: Emergencia Silenciosa." *¡Despertad!* February 22, 2003.

DeTemple, Jill. "'Haiti Appeared at My Church': Faith-Based Organizations, Transnational Activism and Tourism in Sustainable Development." *Urban Anthropology and Studies of Cultural Systems and World Economic Development* 35, no. 2–3 (Spring–Summer 2006): 155–81.

———. "(Re)Production Zones: Mixing Religion, Development and Desire in Rural Ecuadorian Households." *Journal of Latin American and Caribbean Anthropology* 13, no. 1 (April 2008): 115–40.

DeTemple, Jill, Erin Eidenshink, and Katrina Josephson. "How Is Your Life Since Then? Gender Doctrine and Development in Bolivia." In Hefferan, Adkins, and Occhipinti, *Bridging the Gaps.*

Diaz, Bernal. *The Conquest of New Spain.* London: Penguin Books, 1963.

Dijkstra, A. Geske, and Lucia C. Hanmer. "Measuring Socio-Economic Gender Inequality: Toward an Alternative to the UNDP Gender-Related Development Index." *Feminist Economics* 6, no. 2 (2000): 41–75.

Dirlik, Arif. "Reconfiguring Modernity: From Modernization to Globalization." Unpublished manuscript. 2000.

Dobyns, Henry F., Paul Doughty, and Allan R. Holmberg. *Peace Corps: Measurement of Peace Corps Program Impact in the Peruvian Andes, Final Report.* Ithaca, NY: Cornell Peru Project, Department of Anthropology, Cornell University, 1966.

Drogus, Carol Ann. *Women, Religion and Social Change in Brazil's Popular Church.* Notre Dame, IN: University of Notre Dame Press, 1997.

Duden, Barbara. "Population." In Sachs, *The Development Dictionary,* 146–57.

Dupré, Louis. *Passage to Modernity: An Essay in the Hermeneutics of Nature and Culture.* New Haven: Yale University Press, 1993.

———. *Religion and the Rise of Modern Culture.* Notre Dame, IN: University of Notre Dame Press, 2008.

Eade, Deborah. *Development and Culture.* Oxford: Oxfam Publishing, 2002.

"Ecuador and the United States: Friends, Partners." *El Hoy* (Guayaquil, Ecuador), July 10, 2006.

Ecuadorian Ministry of Public Works. "Historia." Available online at http://www.mop.gov.ec/historia.asp (last accessed February 10, 2005).

"Education Parley Ends." *New York Times,* March 16, 1953, 21.

Egas, José María. *Ecuador y el Gobierno de la Junta Militar.* Buenos Aires: Tierra Nueva, 1975.

Engelke, Matthew, and Matt Tomlinson. *The Limits of Meaning: Case Studies in the Anthropology of Christianity.* New York: Berghahn Books, 2006.

Escobar, Arturo. "Culture Sits in Places: Reflections on Globalism and Subaltern Strategies of Localization." *Political Geography* 20, no. 2 (2001): 139–74.

———. *Encountering Development: The Making and Unmaking of the Third World.* Princeton: Princeton University Press, 1995.

———. *Territories of Difference: Place, Movement, Life, Redes.* Durham, NC: Duke University Press, 2008.

Esteva, Gustavo. "Development." In Sachs, *The Development Dictionary,* 27–43.

Fabian, Johannes. *Time and the Other.* New York: Columbia University Press, 1983.

Ferris, Elizabeth. "Faith-Based and Secular Human Organizations." *International Review of the Red Cross* 87, no. 1 (June 2005): 311–25.

Figueroa, Adolfo. "La Agricultura Campesina en América Latina: Desafios para los 90." *Estudios Rurales Latinoamericanos* 13 (1990): 85–102.

Fine, Ben. "The Development State Is Dead—Long Live Social Capital?" *Development and Change* 30 (1999): 1–19.

Fischer, Fritz. *Making Them Like Us: Peace Corps Volunteers in the 1960s.* Washington, DC: Smithsonian Institution Press, 1998.

FLACSO, Ecuador. *Las Cifras de la Migración International.* Quito, 2006.

Foucault, Michel. *The Archaeology of Knowledge.* 1969. Reprint, Oxon: Routledge, 1989.

———. *Discipline and Punish: The Birth of the Prison.* New York: Pantheon Books, 1977.

———. *The Order of Things.* New York: Vintage Books, 1970.

———. "What Is Enlightenment?" In *The Foucault Reader,* edited by Paul Rabinow, translated by Jose V. Harari, 32–50. New York: Pantheon Books, 1972.

Fountain, Daniel E. *Health, the Bible and the Church.* Wheaton, IL: Evangelism and Missions Information Service, 1989.

Fraser, Arvonne, and Irene Tinker. *Developing Power: How Women Transformed International Development.* New York: The Feminist Press at the City University of New York, 2004.

Freire, Paulo. *Pedagogy of the Oppressed.* 1970. Reprint, New York: Continuum, 2006.

Friedmann, John. *The Politics of Alternative Development.* Oxford: Blackwell, 1992.

Friedmann, John, Rebecca Abers, and Lilian Autler, eds. *Emergences: Women's Struggles for Livelihood in Latin America.* Los Angeles: UCLA Latin American Center Publications, 1996.

Gardner, Kay, and David Lewis. *Anthropology, Development and the Post-Modern Challenge.* London: Pluto Press, 1996.

Geertz, Clifford. "Religion as a Cultural System." In *The Interpretation of Cultures: Selected Essays,* 87–125. New York: Basic Books, 1977.

Gelles, Paul. *Water and Power in Highland Peru: The Cultural Politics of Irrigation.* Piscataway, NJ: Rutgers University Press, 2000.

Gibson-Graham, J. K. *Postcapitalist Politics.* Minneapolis: University of Minnesota Press, 2006.

Goffin, Alvin M. *The Rise of Protestant Evangelism in Ecuador, 1895–1900.* Gainesville: University Press of Florida, 1994.

Gonzalez, José Marín. "Las Misiones Indígenas del Protestantismo en América Latina: El Caso de la Amazonia Peruana." *Arinsana,* no. 10 (1989): 37–56.

Gramsci, Antonio. *Selections from the Prison Notebooks.* 1971. Reprint, New York: International Publishers, 1999.

Griffin, Nigel. *Las Casas on Columbus: Background and the Second and Fourth Voyages.* Turnhout, Belgium: Brepols, 2001.

Grillo, R. D., and R. L. Sirrat. *Discourses of Development.* New York: Berg, 1997.

Gudeman, Stephen. *Economics as Culture: Models and Metaphors of Livelihood.* London: Routledge & Kegan Paul, 1986.

———. *Relationships, Residence and the Individual.* London: Routledge & Kegan Paul, 1976.

Gudeman, Stephen, and Alberto Rivera. *Conversations in Colombia.* Cambridge: Cambridge University Press, 1990.

Guerrero Cazar, Fernando, and Pablo Ospina Peralta. *El Poder de la Comunidad: Ajuste Estructural y Movimiento Indígena en los Andes Ecuatorianos.* Buenos Aires: Consejo Latinoamericano de Ciencias Sociales (CLACSO), 2003.

Gupta, Akhil. *Postcolonial Developments.* Durham, NC: Duke University Press, 1998.

Gutierrez, Gustavo. *A Theology of Liberation: History, Politics, and Salvation.* Maryknoll, NY: Orbis, 1973.

Gutmann, Matthew. *The Meanings of Macho: Being a Man in México City.* Berkeley: University of California Press, 1996.

Guyer, Jane. "Dynamic Approaches to Domestic Budgeting: Cases and Methods from Africa." In *A Home Divided: Women and Income in the Third World,* edited by Daisy Dwyer and Judith Bruce, 155–72. Stanford: Stanford University Press, 1988.

Habermas, Jürgen. *The Philosophical Discourse of Modernity.* Translated by Frederick G. Lawrence. Cambridge: MIT Press, 1992.

Haidari, Shokrullah Hamd, and Susan Wright. "Participation and Participatory Development among the Kahlor Nomads of Iran." *Community Development Journal* 36, no. 1 (January 2001): 53–62.

Hallum, Anne Motley. *Beyond Missionaries.* London: Rowman & Littlefield, 1996.

Hamilton, Sarah. *The Two-Headed Household: Gender and Rural Development in the Ecuadorian Andes.* Pittsburgh: Pittsburgh University Press, 1998.

Hanke, Lewis. *The Spanish Struggle for Justice in the Conquest of America.* 1949. Reprint, Dallas: SMU Press, 2002.

Harrison, Regina. *Signs, Songs and Memory in the Andes: Translating Quechua Language and Culture.* Austin: University of Texas Press, 1989.

Haynes, Jeffrey. *Religion and Development: Conflict or Cooperation?* New York: Palgrave, 2007.

Hefferan, Tara, Julie Adkins, and Laurie Occhipinti, eds. *Bridging the Gaps: Faith-Based Organizations, Neoliberalism, and Development in Latin America and the Caribbean.* Lanham, MD: Lexington Books, 2009.

Hegel, Georg. *Introduction to the Philosophy of History.* 1831. Reprint, Indianapolis: Hackett, 1988.

Helping Hands: HCJB's Community Development Newsletter 2, no. 3 (Summer 1993).

Helping Hands: HCJB's Community Development Newsletter 2, no. 4 (Autumn 1993).

Herbert, Christopher. *Culture and Anomie.* Chicago: University of Chicago Press, 1991.

Hippert, Christine. "The Politics and Practices of Constructing Development Identities in Rural Bolivia." *Journal of Latin American and Caribbean Anthropology* 16, no. 1 (April 2011): 90–111.

Hirschman, Albert O. *A Bias for Hope: Essays on Development in Latin America.* Boulder, CO: Westview Press, 1985.

———. *Development Projects Observed.* Washington, DC: Brookings Institution, 1967.

———. *Getting Ahead Collectively: Grassroots Experiences in Latin America.* New York: Pergamon Press, 1984.

———. *Rival Views of Market Society.* New York: Viking, 1986.

Hoadley, J. Stephen. "The Rise and Fall of the Basic Needs Approach." *Cooperation and Conflict* 16, no. 3 (1981): 149–64.

Hoksbergen, Roland. "Approaches to Evaluation of Development Interventions: The Importance of World and Life Views." *World Development,* February 1986, 283–300.

Holland, Dorothy, William Lachiotte, Jr., Debra Skinner, and Carole Cain. *Identity and Agency in Cultural Worlds.* Cambridge: Harvard University Press, 1998.

Hula, Richard, Cynthia Jackson-Elmore, and Laura Reese. "Mixing God's Work and the Public Business: A Framework for the Analysis of Faith-Based Service Delivery." *Review of Policy Research* 24, no. 1 (2007): 67–89.

Hume, David. *The Natural History of Religion.* Edited by H. E. Root. Stanford: Stanford University Press, 1956.

Hurtado, Osvaldo. *Dos Mundos Superpuestos: Ensayo de Diagnóstico de la Realidad Ecuatoriana.* Quito: Instituto de Planificación para el Desarrollo Social, 1969.

———. *Portrait of a Nation: Culture and Progress in Ecuador.* Translated by Barbara Sipe. Lanham, MD: Madison Books, 2010.

Hutchison, William. *Errand to the World.* Chicago: University of Chicago Press, 1987.

Hvalkof, Søren, and Peter Aaby, eds. *Is God an American? An Anthropological Perspective on the Summer Institute of Linguistics.* Copenhagen: International Work Group for Indigenous Affairs and Cultural Survival, 1981.

Illich, Ivan. *Shadow Work.* Boston: Marion Boyars, 1981.

———. *Toward a History of Needs.* New York: Pantheon, 1977.

Inboden, William. *Religion and American Foreign Policy, 1945–1960: The Soul of Containment.* New York: Cambridge University Press, 2008.

Instituto Nacional Estadistico y Censos del Ecuador.

Jaquette, Jane S., and Gale Summerfield, eds. *Women and Gender Equity in Development Theory and Practice.* Durham, NC: Duke University Press, 2007.

Jara J., Fausto, ed. *Taruca: Ecuador Quichuacunapac Rimashca Rimaicuna.* Quito: Consejo Provincial de Pichincha, 1982.

Jenkinson, William, and Helene O'Sullivan, eds. *Trends in Mission: Toward the 3rd Millennium.* Maryknoll, NY: Orbis Books, 1991.

Jesus. Warner Brothers, 1979. Available online at http://www.jesusfilm.org (last accessed June 6, 2011).

Jones, Clarence. *Radio: The New Missionary.* Chicago: Moody Press, 1949.

Kabeer, Naila. "Gender Equality and Women's Empowerment: A Critical Analysis of the Third Millennium Development Goal." *Gender and Development* 13, no. 1 (March 2005): 13–24.

Kant, Immanuel. *Critique of Judgment.* 1790. Reprint, Indianapolis: Hackett Publishing, 1987.

———. "What Is Enlightenment?" In *What Is Enlightenment?*, edited by James Schmidt, 58–64. Berkeley: University of California Press, 1996.

Kelly, Kevin. *New Rules for the New Economy: 10 Radical Strategies for a Connected World.* New York: Penguin Books, 1998.

Kennedy, John F. "Staffing a Foreign Policy for Peace." November 2, 1960. U.S. Subcommittee on Freedom of Communications, part 1, *The Speeches of Senator John F. Kennedy, Presidential Campaign, 1960,* 1237–41 (Washington, DC: U.S. Government Printing Office, 1961).

Kiely, Ray. "The Last Refuge of the Noble Savage? A Critical Assessment of Post-Development Theory." *European Journal of Development Research* 11, no. 1 (June 1999): 30–55.

Kingsland, Rosemary. *A Saint among Savages.* London: William Collins & Sons, 1980.

Lardicci, Francesca, ed. *A Synoptic Edition of the Log of Columbus's First Voyage.* Turnhout, Belgium: Brepols, 1999.

Las Casas, Bartolomé de. *In Defense of the Indians.* Dekalb: Northern Illinois University Press, 1974.

Latour, Bruno. *The Pasteurization of France.* Translated by Alan Sheridan and John Law. Cambridge: Harvard University Press, 1988.

———. *We Have Never Been Modern.* Translated by Catherine Porter. Cambridge: Harvard University Press, 1991.

Lefebrvre, Henri. *Everyday Life in the Modern World.* New Brunswick, NJ: Transaction Books, 1984.

Léry, Jean de. *History of a Voyage to the Land of Brazil, Otherwise Called America.* Translated by Janet Whatley. Berkeley: University of California Press, 1990.

Lévi-Strauss, Claude. *Tristes Tropiques.* New York: Atheneum, 1973.

Lin, Nan. *Social Capital: A Theory of Social Structure and Action.* New York: Cambridge University Press, 2001.

Lind, Amy. *Gendered Paradoxes: Women's Movements, State Restructuring and Global Development in Ecuador.* University Park: Pennsylvania State University Press, 2005.

Lomnitz, Larissa Adler. "Informal Exchange Networks in Formal Systems: A Theoretical Model." *American Anthropologist,* n.s., 90, no. 1 (1988): 42–55.

———. "Mecanismos de Articulación entre el Sector Informal y el Sector Formal Urbano." *Revista Mexicana de Sociología* 40, no. 1 (1978): 131–53.

Lummis, C. Douglas. "Equality." In Sachs, *The Development Dictionary,* 38–52.

Lyons, Barry. *Remembering the Hacienda: Religion, Authority and Social Change in Highland Ecuador.* Austin: University of Texas Press, 2006.

Lyons, Barry, with Angel Aranda and Dina Guevera. "Simple People." In Torre and Striffler, *The Ecuador Reader,* 403–14.

Malloch, Theodore Roosevelt. "Social, Human and Spiritual Capital in Human Development." Templeton Foundation, Working Group of the Spiritual Capital Project, Harvard University, 2003. Available online at http://www.spiritualcapitalresearchprogram.com/pdf/malloch.pdf (last accessed March 5, 2011).

Marsden, George. *Religion and American Culture.* Orlando, FL: Harcourt Brace College Publishers, 1990.

Martin, David. *Tongues of Fire: The Explosion of Protestantism in Latin America.* Oxford: Blackwell, 1990.

May, Gary. "Passing the Torch and Lighting Fires: The Peace Corps." In *Kennedy's Quest for Victory,* edited by Thomas G. Paterson, 284–316. Lexington, MA: D. C. Heath, 1988.

Mayer, Enrique. *The Articulated Peasant: Household Economics in the Andes.* Boulder, CO: Westview Press, 2002.

Meisch, Lynn. *Andean Entrepreneurs: Otavalo Merchants & Musicians in the Global Arena.* Austin: University of Texas Press, 2002.

Migration Policy Institute. "Ecuador: Diversity in Migration." Available online at http://www.migrationinformation.org/USfocus/display.cfm?ID=575 (last accessed November 11, 2008).

Ministerio de Agicultura y Ganadería. *Proyecto Bolivar II: Informe de la Ejecución y Desarrollo del Primer Año de Actividades.* Ministerio de Agicultura y Ganadería, 1995.

Ministerio de Salud Pública del Ecuador. *Manual de Capacitación de la Partera Tradicional.* Ministerio de Salud Pública del Ecuador et al., 2001.

Mitlin, Diana, Sam Hickey, and Anthony Bebbington. "Reclaiming Development? NGOs and the Challenge of Alternatives." *World Development* 35, no. 10 (2007): 1699–1720.

Moore, Donald. "The Crucible of Cultural Politics: Reworking 'Development' in Zimbabwe's Eastern Highlands." *American Ethnologist* 26, no. 3 (2000): 654–89.

Mörner, Magnus. *The Andean Past: Land, Societies, and Conflicts.* New York: Columbia University Press, 1985.

Moser, Carolyn. *Gender Planning and Development: Theory, Practice & Training.* London and New York: Routledge, 1993.

Mosse, David. "Is Good Policy Unimplementable? Reflections on the Ethnography of Aid Policy and Practice." *Development and Change* 35, no. 4 (2004): 639–71.

Munck, Thomas, and Denis O'Hearn. *Critical Development Theory: Contributions to a New Paradigm.* London: Zed Books, 1999.

Mundo Shuar, ed. *Los Shuar y el Cristianismo.* Sucua, Ecuador: Mundo Shuar, 1978.

Murra, John. "El 'Control Vertical' de un Máximo de Pisos Ecológicos en la Economía de Sociedades Andinas." In *Vista de la Provincia de León de*

Huanuco en 1562, edited by J.V. Murra, 427–76. Huanuco, Peru: Universidad Nacional Hermilio Valdizán, 1972.

Nader, Helen, ed. and trans., and Luciano Formisano. *The Book of Privileges Issued to Christopher Columbus by King Ferdinand and Queen Isabel 1492–1502.* Berkeley: University of California Press, 1996.

Nagle, Robin. *Claiming the Virgin: The Broken Promises of Liberation Theology.* New York and London: Routledge, 1997.

Napolitano, Valentina. "Between 'Traditional' and 'New' Catholic Church Religious Discourses in Urban, Western Mexico." *Bulletin of Latin American Research* 17, no. 3 (1998): 323–39.

"New Science Views Entire Man." *New York Times,* April 9, 1932, 16.

Newson, Linda. *Life and Death in Early Colonial Ecuador.* Norman: University of Oklahoma Press, 1995.

Niebuhr, H. Richard. *Christ and Culture.* New York: Harper, 1951.

Nietzsche, Friedrich. "On the Advantages and Disadvantages of History in Life." In *Thoughts Out of Season,* translated by Adrian Collins. London: T. N. Foulis, 1910.

North, Liisa, and John Cameron, eds. *Rural Progress, Rural Decay: Neoliberal Adjustment Policies and Local Initiatives.* Bloomfield, CT: Kumarian Press, 2003.

Nussbaum, Martha C. *Women and Human Development: The Capabilities Approach.* Cambridge: Cambridge University Press, 2000.

O'Gorman, Edmundo. *The Invention of America: An Inquiry into the Historical Nature of the New World and the Meaning of Its History.* Bloomington: Indiana University Press, 1961.

O'Gorman, Francis. *Charity and Change: From Bandaid to Beacon.* Melbourne: World Vision, Australia, 1992.

Orsi, Robert. "Everyday Miracles: The Study of Lived Religion." In *Lived Religion in America: Toward a History of Practice,* edited by David D. Hall, 3–21. Princeton: Princeton University Press, 1997.

Pagden, Anthony. *European Encounters with the New World: From Renaissance to Romanticism.* New Haven: Yale University Press, 1993.

Pallares, Amalia. *From Peasant Struggle to Indian Resistance: The Ecuadorian Andes in the Late Twentieth Century.* Norman: University of Oklahoma Press, 2002.

Parpart, Jane L., Shirin M. Rai, and Kathleen Staudt. *Rethinking Empowerment: Gender and Development in a Global/Local World.* London and New York: Routledge, 2002.

Parra, Cesar. "Propuesto de Desarrollo de Líderes Estratégicos en la Iglesia Evangélica Ecuatoriana." Unpublished manuscript. Quito, Ecuador, 2000.

Peace Corps Ecuador. *Training Handbook for Rural and Community Health.* Quito, Ecuador, 2006.

———. *Training Plan: Rural Public Health/Youth and Families.* Quito, Ecuador, 2006.

Peet, Richard, and Elaine Hartwick. *Theories of Development.* New York: Guilford Press, 1999.

PEPFAR. "Community and Faith-Based Organizations. Report to Congress." Available online at http://www.pepfar.gov/progress/76864.htm (last accessed February 13, 2007).

Pierson, Arthur T. *Crisis in Missions; or, The Voice out of the Cloud.* New York: Robert Carter and Bros., 1886.

Pigg, Stacy Leigh. "Inventing Social Categories through Place: Social Representations and Development in Nepal." *Comparative Studies in Society and History* 34, no. 3 (1992): 491–513.

Plan International. *Atención Integrada a las Enfermedades Prevalentes de la Infancia: Cuadra de Procedimientos.* Plan International et al., 1997.

———. *Paises Patrocinadores.* Plan International, 1999.

Plan International Bolívar. *Guía Práctica del Manejo en la Crianza del Cuy.* Plan International Bolívar, 2002.

Plan International Ecuador. *Folletos Técnicos Agropecuarios.* Plan International Ecuador–Oficina de Programas Bolívar, 2000.

Plan International, Sud America. *Informe General.* Plan International, Sud America, 1997.

Polo F., Padre Antonio. *La Puerta Abierta: 30 Años de Aventura Misionera y Social en Salinas de Bolívar Ecuador.* Quito: Abya Yala, 2002.

Populorum Progressio. Encyclical Letter of Pope Paul VI, March 26, 1967.

Pottier, Johan, Alan Bicker, and Paul Sillitoe. *Negotiating Local Knowledge: Power and Identity in Development.* London: Pluto Press, 2003.

Pratt, Mary Louise. *Imperial Eyes: Travel Writing and Transculturation.* London: Routledge, 1992.

The President's Emergency Plan for AIDS Relief Office of the U.S. Global AIDS Coordinator. "ABC Guidance #1 for United States Government In-Country Staff and Implementing Partners Applying the ABC Approach to Preventing Sexually-Transmitted HIV Infections within the President's Emergency Plan for AIDS Relief." Washington, DC: U.S. Government Printing Office, 2003. Available online at http://www.state.gov/documents/organization/57241.pdf (last accessed May 26, 2011).

Pribilsky, Jason. *La Chulla Vida: Gender, Migration and the Family in Andean Ecuador and New York City.* Syracuse, NY: Syracuse University Press, 2007.

Price, Richard. "Trial Marriage in the Andes." *Ethnology* 4, no. 3 (1965): 310–22.

Pritchard, Elizabeth. "The Way out West: Development and the Rhetoric of Mobility in Postmodern Feminist Theory." *Hypatia* 15, no. 3 (2000): 45–72.

Programa de Desarrollo Infantil PDI-INNFA. *Mejorando mi Familia.* Programa de Desarrollo Infantil PDI-INNFA, 1998.

Programa de Educación Alimentaria Nutricional. *Alimentación del Adolescente.* Programa de Educación Alimentaria Nutricional, 2000.

———. *Alimentación del Niño Menor de Cinco Años.* Programa de Educación Alimentaria Nutricional, 2000.

———. *Alimentación Durante el Embarazo y la Lactancia.* Programa de Educación Alimentaria Nutricional, 2000.

———. *Alimentación en la Tercera Edad.* Programa de Educación Alimentaria Nutricional, 2000.

———. *Alimentación Escolar.* Programa de Educación Alimentaria Nutricional, 2000.

———. *Higiene, Conservación, Almacenamiento y Preparación de los Alimentos.* Programa de Educación Alimentaria Nutricional, 2000.

———. *Mezclas Alimentarias.* Programa de Educación Alimentaria Nutricional, 2000.

Radcliffe, Sarah A., Nina Laurie, and Robert Andolina. "The Transnationalization of Gender and Reimagining Andean Indigenous Development." *Signs: Journal of Women in Culture and Society* 29, no. 2 (2003): 387–415.

Rahnema, Majid, and Victoria Bawtree, eds. *The Post-Development Reader.* London: Zed Books, 1997.

Reeves, T. Zane. *The Politics of the Peace Corps & Vista.* Tuscaloosa: University of Alabama Press, 1988.

Research Institute for the Study of Man. *Peace Corps Training Program for Jamaica: April 2–May 31, 1962.* Research Institute for the Study of Man, 1962.

Rice, Gerald T. *The Bold Experiment: JFK's Peace Corps.* Notre Dame, IN: University of Notre Dame Press, 1985.

Riley, James Denson. *Hacendados Jesuitas en México: El Colegio Máximo de San Pedro y San Pablo, 1685–1767.* Mexico City: SepSentas, 1976.

Rist, Gilbert. *The History of Development: From Western Origins to Global Faith.* London: Zed Books, 1997.

Rittich, Kerry. "Engendering Development/Marketing Equality." *Albany Law Review* 67 (2003): 575–93.

Robalino Gonzaga, César Raúl. *El Desarrollo Económico del Ecuador.* Quito: Junta Nacional de Planificación y Coordinación, 1969.

Rostworowski, María de Diez Canseco. *History of the Inca Realm.* Cambridge: Cambridge University Press, 1999.

Rousseau, Jean-Jacques. *A Discourse on Inequality.* London: Penguin Books, 1984.

Rowe, Ann Pollard, ed. *Costume and Identity in Highland Ecuador.* Seattle: University of Washington Press, 1998.

Rubio, Marcelo Valdospinos. *Puesto de Guardia.* Otavalo, Ecuador: Editorial Gallocapitán, 1982.

Rueschemeyer, Dietrich, Evelyne Huber Stephens, and John D. Stephens. *Capitalist Development and Democracy.* Chicago: University of Chicago Press, 1992.

Rusconi, Roberto, ed. *The Book of Prophecies.* Berkeley: University of California Press, 1997.

Sachs, Jeffrey D. *The End of Poverty: Economic Possibilities for Our Time.* New York: Penguin, 2005.

Sachs, Wolfgang, ed. *The Development Dictionary.* London: Zed Books, 1992.

Sahagún. Bernardo de. *Historia General de las Cosas de Nueva España.* Madrid: HIPASAT, 1990.

Salomon, Frank. *Native Lords of Quito in the Age of the Incas.* Cambridge: Cambridge University Press, 1986.

Santa Anita Women's Cooperative. "Libro de Actas." Santa Anita Women's Cooperative, San Marcos, Ecuador, 1989–2009.

Sbert, José Maria. "Progress." In Sachs, *The Development Dictionary,* 192–205.

Schech, Susanne, and Jane Haggis. *Culture and Development.* Malden, MA: Blackwell Publishers, 2000.

Schech, Susanne, and Sanjugta Vas Dev. "Gender Justice: The World Bank's New Approach to the Poor?" *Development in Practice* 17, no. 1 (February 2007): 14–26.

Schiller, Friedrich. *On the Aesthetic Education of Man.* Translated by Elizabeth Wilkinson and L. A. Willoughby. Oxford: Clarendon Press, 1982.

Schleiermacher, Friedrich. *Hermeneutics and Criticism.* 1833. Reprint, Cambridge: Cambridge University Press, 1998.

Schwarz, Karen. *What You Can Do for Your Country.* New York: Morrow, 1991.

Scott, James. *Seeing Like a State: How Certain Schemes to Improve the Human Condition Have Failed.* New Haven: Yale University Press, 1998.

Seligson, Mitchell, and John T. Passé-Smith. *Development and Underdevelopment: The Political Economy of Global Inequality.* Boulder, CO: Lynne Rienner, 1998.

Sen, Amartya. *Development as Freedom.* New York: Knopf, 1999.

Shanin, Teodor. "The Idea of Progress." In Rahnema and Bawtree, *The Post-Development Reader,* 65–71.

Shaull, Richard, and Waldo Cesar. *Pentecostalism and the Future of the Christian Churches: Promises, Limitations, Challenges.* Grand Rapids, MI: Eerdmans, 2000.

Shenk, William. "General Introduction." In Taber, *The World Is Too Much with Us,* vii–xiii.

Shepherd, Chris. "Agricultural Hybridity and the 'Pathology' of Traditional Ways: The Translation of Desire and Need in Postcolonial Development." *Journal of Latin American Anthropology* 9, no. 2 (2004): 235–66.

Shils, Edward. *Tradition.* Chicago: University of Chicago Press, 1981.

Silberman, Todd. "Program Brings World to NC Pupils." *News and Observer* (Raleigh, NC), September 1, 2004.

Silverblatt, Irene. *Moon, Sun and Witches: Gender Ideologies and Class in Inca and Colonial Peru.* Princeton: Princeton University Press, 1987.

Smith, Adam. *The Theory of Moral Sentiments.* Oxford, 1976. Reprint, New York: Liberty Fund, 1984.

Smith, James Howard. *Bewitching Development: Witchcraft and the Reinvention of Development in Neoliberal Kenya*. Chicago: University of Chicago Press, 2008.

Smith, Jonathan Z. "Introduction." *Imagining Religion: From Babylon to Jonestown*. Chicago: Chicago University Press, 1982.

Sobrino, John, and Ignacio Ellacuría. *Systematic Theology: Perspectives from Liberation Theology*. Maryknoll, NY: Orbis Books, 1993.

Stiles, Thomas. "Almost Heaven: The Fiesta Cargo System among the Saraguro Quichuas in Ecuador and Implications for Contextualization in the Evangelical Church." PhD diss., Trinity International University, 1996.

Stoll, David. *Is Latin America Turning Protestant?* Berkeley: University of California Press, 1990.

Strauss, Robert L. "Too Many Innocents Abroad." *New York Times*, January 9, 2008.

Stutzman, Ronald. "El Mestizaje." In Whitten, *Cultural Transformations and Ethnicity in Modern Ecuador*, 41–94.

Sung, Jung Mo. *Desire, Market and Religion (Reclaiming Liberation Theology)*. London: SCM Press, 2005.

Swanson, Jeffrey. *Echoes of the Call: Identity and Ideology among American Missionaries in Ecuador*. New York: Oxford University Press, 1995.

Sylvester, Christine. "Development Studies and Postcolonial Studies: Disparate Tales of the 'Third World.'" *Third World Quarterly* 20, no. 4 (1999): 703–21.

Symcox, Geoffrey, ed. *Las Casas on Columbus: The Third Voyage*. Turnhout, Belgium: Brepols, 2001.

Taber, Charles R. *The World Is Too Much with Us: "Culture" in Modern Protestant Missions*. Macon, GA: Mercer University Press, 2000.

Taylor, Charles. *Modern Social Imaginaries*. Durham, NC: Duke University Press, 2004.

Taylor, Mark C. *After God*. Chicago: University of Chicago Press, 2007.

Thompson, Charles D., Jr. "Borders Bleed: Refugees, Repatriates, Religion and the Jacalteco Maya." PhD diss., University of North Carolina, 1997.

———. *Maya Identities and the Violence of Place: Borders Bleed*. Burlington, VT: Ashgate, 2001.

Thomsen, Moritz. *Living Poor: A Peace Corps Chronicle*. Seattle: University of Washington Press, 1969.

Tinker, Irene, ed. *Persistent Inequalities: Women and World Development*. New York: Oxford University Press, 1990.

Todorov, Tzvetan. *The Conquest of America: The Question of the Other*. New York: HarperCollins, 1984.

Tolen, Rebecca. "'Receiving the Authorities' in Chimborazo, Ecuador: Ethnic Performance in an Evangelical Andean Community." *Journal of Latin American Anthropology* 3, no. 2 (1999): 20–54.

Tomlinson, John. *Globalization and Culture*. Chicago: University of Chicago Press, 1999.

Torre, Carlos de la, and Steve Striffler, eds. *The Ecuador Reader.* Durham, NC: Duke University Press, 2008.

Traboulay, David M. *Columbus and Las Casas: The Conquest and Christianization of America, 1492–1566.* Lanham, MD: University Press of America, 1994.

Truman, Harry S. *Inaugural Address* (January 20, 1949). Available online at http:www.trumanlibrary.org/calendar/viewpapers.php?pid=1030 (last accessed June 14, 2004).

Trustees Report. Ford Foundation, 1950, 4.

Tsing, Anna. "The Global Situation." *Cultural Anthropology* 15, no. 3 (2000): 327–60.

Tweed, Thomas A. *Crossing and Dwelling: A Theory of Religion.* Cambridge: Harvard University Press, 2006.

Tyndale, Wendy. "Faith and Economics in 'Development': A Bridge across the Chasm?" *Development in Practice* 10, no. 9–18 (2000).

———. *Visions of Development: Faith Based Initiatives.* Burlington, VT: Ashgate, 2006.

United Andean Indian Mission. *Soil and Souls in Ecuador.* New York, 1951.

U.S. Agency for International Development. *2008 VOLAG Report.* Washington, DC: USAID, 2008.

U.S. Department of State. "Background Note: Ecuador." Available online at http://www.state.gov/r/pa/ei/bgn/35761.htm (last accessed April 26, 2011).

U.S. Peace Corps. *Annual Report to Congress.* Washington, DC: U.S. Peace Corps, 1973.

———. *Annual Report to Congress.* Washington, DC: U.S. Peace Corps, 2006.

———. *Booklet 5: PACA Tools.* Washington, DC: U.S. Peace Corps, 2000.

———. *First Annual Report to Congress.* Washington, DC: U.S. Peace Corps, 1962.

———. *Training Handbook for Rural and Community Health.* Quito, 2006.

———. "What Is the Peace Corps?" Available online at http://www.peacecorps.gov/index.cfm?shell=learn.whatispc.fastfacts (last accessed January 15, 2008).

"USAID Contracts with Faith-Based Organizations." *Boston Globe,* October 8, 2006.

Vásquez, Manuel A., and Phillip J. Williams. "Introduction: The Power of Religious Identities in the Americas." *Latin American Perspectives* 32, no. 1 (2005): 15–26.

Vega, Garcilaso de la. *Comentarios Reales de los Incas.* Lima: Librería Internacional del Peru, 1959.

"Victims of Massacre in Mexico Said to Be Migrants." *New York Times,* August 25, 2010.

Vicuña Izquierdo, Leonardo. *Política Económica del Ecuador: Dos Décadas Pérdidas, los Años 80–90.* Quito: ESPOL, 2000.

Vries, Pieter de. "Don't Compromise Your Desire for Development! A Lacanian/ Deleuzian Rethinking of the Anti-Politics Machine." *Third World Quarterly* 28, no. 1 (2007): 25–43.

Watchtower Bible and Tract Society of New York, Inc. "Una Tragedia de Gran Magnitud." *¡Despertad!* February 22, 2003.

Weber, Max. *The Protestant Ethic and the Spirit of Capitalism.* Translated by Talcott Parsons. London: Unwin, 1985.

Weismantel, Mary. *Food, Gender, and Poverty in the Ecuadorian Andes.* Philadelphia: University of Pennsylvania Press, 1988.

Whitaker, Morris D., and Dale Colyer. *Agriculture and Economic Survival: The Role of Agriculture in Ecuador's Development.* Boulder, CO: Westview Press, 1990.

Whitten, Norman, ed. *Cultural Transformations and Ethnicity in Modern Ecuador.* Urbana: University of Illinois Press, 1981.

———. "Ecuador in the New Millennium: 25 Years of Democracy." *Journal of Latin American Anthropology* 9, no. 2 (Fall 2004): 450.

———, ed. *Millennial Ecuador.* Iowa City: University of Iowa Press, 2003.

Wilk, R. R., ed. *The Household Economy: Reconsidering Domestic Modes of Production.* Boulder, CO: Westview Press, 1989.

Wilson, Fiona. "Toward a Political Economy of Roads: Experiences in Peru." *Development and Change* 35, no. 3 (2004): 535–46.

Wittgenstein, Ludwig. *Blue and Brown Books.* Oxford: Blackwell, 1958.

———. *Culture and Value.* Edited by Peter Winch. Chicago: University of Chicago Press, 1980.

———. *On Certainty.* Edited by G. E. M. Anscombe and G. H. von Wright. 1969. Reprint, New York: Harper & Row, 1972.

———. *Philosophical Investigations.* Translated by G. E. M. Anscombe. 1953. Reprint, Oxford: Blackwell, 1997.

———. *Remarks on Frazer's Golden Bough.* Edited by Rush Rhees. Cross Hill Cottage Gringly-on-the-Hill, England: Brynmill Press, 1979.

Wogan, Peter. *Magical Writing in Salasaca.* Boulder, CO: Westview Press, 2004.

Wolf, Eric. *Europe and the People without History.* Berkeley: University of California Press, 1982.

World Bank. *World Development Report.* New York: Oxford University Press, 1990.

———. *World Development Report.* New York: Oxford University Press, 2005.

World Vision International. "Our Mission." Available online at www.worldvision .org (last accessed January 12, 1997).

Xerez, Francisco de. *Verdadera Relación de la Conquista del Perú.* Edited by Concepción Bravo. Crónicas de América. Madrid: Historia 16, 1985.

Yamamori, Tetsunao, et al., eds. *Serving with the Poor in Latin America.* Monrovia, CA: World Vision International, 1997.

Young, Robert J. C. *Colonial Desire: Hybridity in Theory, Culture and Race.* London: Routledge, 1995.

Yúdice, George. *The Expediency of Culture: Uses of Culture in the Global Era.* Durham, NC: Duke University Press, 2003.

INDEX

Alfaro, Eloy, 61
Appadurai, Arjun, 7, 42

Bakhtin, Mikhail, 110–11
Bauer, Ruth, 3, 11, 62–63, 70, 97, 118,
    122, 142, 157, 178–80, 182, 197
bedrooms, 119–26, 198–99
bodies, 174, 176–77, 181, 190, 194,
    198–200
buildings, 137–39, 141–42, 144–48,
    160–61, 192, 199

Castells, Manuel, 15
Catholicism
    colonial history, 26–28, 57–61
    in development, 137, 181–82,
        211n20, 217nn7–8
    missions, 27–28, 215n7
    See also Salesians; Santa Anita
        women's cooperative
"cement things"/*cosas de cemento*, 10,
    12, 14, 50–52, 53, 137–38, 142,
    187, 191, 193, 199
charla (educational talk), 67, 80, 87,
    120. *See also* knowledge
cheese factory, 140–41, 143–48, 152,
    163–64
cheese production, 55, 64
child sponsorship, 131–32

class, 43–45, 209n9
Columbus, 19, 24–26, 207n10
community
    and infrastructure, 138–40,
        142–52
    limits of, 161–65, 190–93
    and *la lucha*/struggle, 201
    reproduction of, 129–34
    —through development, 130–34
    —through religion, 65, 129–30,
        154–61
    as site of negotiation, 10, 14, 45
    theories of, 105–11, 217n9,
        218n10
    types of, 52–57
    in whole person discourse, 175,
        180, 183, 190–93
conversion, religious, 1–2, 4, 9,
    26–27, 47, 100, 106, 179, 182,
    194, 197, 200

Davis, Joyce, 3, 62–63, 108, 122, 123
desire
    and infrastructure, 141–42, 161,
        165
    and progress, 65, 134–35, 141–42
    as site of negotiation, 10, 14, 45,
        65, 199
    theories of, 23, 96, 126–29, 195

development
  alternative, 14, 67–71, 85, 95–97,
    171, 194, 200–203, 211n5
  community, 67, 73, 75, 85, 212n13
  cosmological aspects of, 188,
    200–202
  desire for, 96, 134–35, 141–42,
    165. *See also* desire
  as discipline, 81–86
  as discourse, 20–21
  history of, 2, 22–32
  participatory, 14, 31, 85, 213n36
  positive community, 87, 89,
    93–94
  "reading religiously," 16–17, 200
  sustainable, 52, 90, 94–97, 186

earthworms, 1, 18, 193, 197, 200
education, 27–29, 34
Enlightenment, 23–24, 28, 68
Escobar, Arturo, 5, 29, 81

faith-based organizations (FBOs), 2,
    4, 70, 96–100
Fondo Ecuatoriano Populorum
    Progressio (FEPP), 154, 217n8
Foucault, Michel, 82
Freire, Paulo, 213n30

gender
  in development, 13, 31, 147
  GAD (Gender and Development),
    31, 93–94
  men's roles, 115
  WID (Women in Development),
    31, 69, 77
  women's roles, 46, 112–13, 115,
    122
globalization, 9, 14, 17, 41, 48, 51, 68,
    71
guinea pigs, 53, 64, 116–17, 119, 199,
    215n17

HCJB (missionary organization)
  health education and
    contraception, 124–25
  history of, 62–63
  medical missions, 11, 63
  whole person discourse in, 92,
    171–75, 181, 183–84
healing, 84, 116–17, 169–70, 172,
    188–89
health education, 79–80, 87, 113,
    117, 120–22, 124–26, 175,
    184–85
  and contraception, 79, 82, 123–25,
    199, 213n27
HIV/AIDS, 82, 121–22, 213n27,
    215n25. *See also* PEPFAR
households, 103–35
  theories of, 105–11, 209n9
hybridity, 8, 15, 53, 56–57, 64, 86,
    171, 181, 184, 191, 195, 198, 200

identity, 43–46. *See also* class;
    conversion, religious; gender;
    race/ethnicity
illness, 169–70. *See also* healing;
    health education
Inca Empire, 32–34
infrastructure
  and alternative development, 10,
    68, 91, 165–67, 171, 192–93,
    199–200
  and community, 130–31, 138–41,
    143–44, 148–52, 155–58,
    199–200
  and desire, 141–43, 199–200
  as visible development, 50–52,
    137–38
integrated rural development, 90–91
integration, 10, 67, 86–93, 184–88,
    201
International Monetary Fund (IMF),
    22, 41, 49, 82

Jehovah's Witnesses, 64, 117, 122, 130, 139, 155, 199

kitchens, 63, 111–19, 198–99
knitting, 49, 54, 94–95, 97, 163
knowledge, 67–68
    transfer of, 67–68, 74, 192

land reform, 35, 62, 219n12
Lara, Guillermo Rodriguez, 44, 127
Latour, Bruno, 8, 13, 39, 110, 140, 176, 181
liberation theology, 31, 54, 152, 154, 217n7
limited action, 86, 93–101
la lucha/struggle, 5, 46–50, 64, 201, 210nn11–12

mal aire, 169
market
    capitalist, 53, 140. *See also* neoliberalism
    in San Marcos, 3, 39–46
Martin, Sam, 38, 57, 149–50
Mayer, Enrique, 108, 218n10
mestizaje, 43–44. *See also* race/ethnicity
microfinance, 49, 54. *See also* Santa Anita women's cooperative
missions
    Catholic, 27–28, 215n7
    Protestant, 61–64, 172–74, 207n8, 218n1
Moreno, Gabriel Garcia, 61
municipio, 12, 49, 53–54, 56, 133, 140, 148, 165, 171, 186–88, 192–93. *See also* UMATA
Murra, John, 32–33, 108

neoliberalism, 6, 39, 69, 82, 91, 92, 213n30, 214n42

nongovernmental organizations (NGOs)
    in development, 2, 70, 122, 137, 211n5
    in San Marcos, 50–51

Peace Corps, U.S.
    and community, 149–50, 161–63
    and globalization, 41
    health education and contraception, 79, 122–24
    history of, 70–97, 165, 212n22, 213n26, 215n25
    and PACA (Participatory Analysis for Community Action), 93–94
    in San Marcos, 53–54, 149–50. *See also* Martin, Sam
    training, 67, 71–97
Pentecostalism, 1, 9, 64, 137, 139, 155
PEPFAR (President's Emergency Plan for AIDS Relief), 77, 82, 121, 213n27. *See also* HIV/AIDS
Plan International
    child sponsorship programs, 51, 130–32
    health education and contraception, 79, 121
    infrastructure projects, 49, 113–14, 130–32
    whole person discourse in, 49, 165, 184–85, 194
production zones, 108–9, 218n10
progress
    definition of, 23
    as element of modernity, 7, 14, 23, 64
    infrastructure as sign of, 141, 160
    negotiating meaning of, 198–99, 201
    as Western ideal, 5, 27, 29
    and whole person discourse, 183

Promoción Humana, 13, 49, 54, 55, 56, 143, 147
Protestantism
  in development, 157–60, 175–76, 178–81, 188, 197, 200, 211n20
  history in Ecuador, 61–64
  missions, 61–64, 172–74, 207n8, 218n1

race/ethnicity
  blanqueamiento, 43–44, 128, 215n15
  mestizaje, 44, 209n7, 215n15
  mestizo, 36, 43–45, 112, 128
  Runa/indigenous groups, 36, 43–45, 209n9
religion
  theories of, 4, 17, 20, 59

Salesians, 13, 55, 143–44, 146, 152, 217n8
San Marcos
  history of, 32–36, 57–64
Santa Anita women's cooperative
  Catholic identity of, 13, 152–54, 181
  community in, 13, 54–55, 131–34, 139–48, 163–64, 190–91
  history of, 53–56, 217n6
  and liberation theology, 217n7
  use of Ecuadorian Ministry of Social Welfare food, 161–64, 190–91
  and whole person discourse, 181–84
science, 23, 28, 68, 115, 118, 126, 170, 181, 189–90
sex/sexuality, 80, 82, 120–26, 215n25, 216n26
  Catholic teachings on, 122–25
  contraception, 79, 82, 121, 122, 123–25, 199, 213n27

Spanish conquest, 1, 24–28, 34, 198, 205n2
state
  and development, 28–31, 70–71, 73, 75, 82, 92, 96, 121, 139–40
  and religion, 26, 29–31, 34–35, 61
struggle. *See la lucha*/struggle

tradition
  as condition of native peoples, 28–31, 173–74
  in indigenous communities, 162–63
  as opposite of modernity/progress, 7, 9, 23, 28–31, 170, 181, 198
  as religious, 9, 187–91

UMATA (Unidad Municipal de Asistencia Técnica Agropecuaria)
  and alternative development, 53–54, 186–87, 192–93
  Sinche project, 3, 12, 49, 132–35, 139–40, 148, 186–87, 192–94
Unevangelized Field Missions International (UFMI), 62
United Andean Mission, 173–74
United Nations Millennium Development Goals (MDGs), 83, 87, 207n20
United States Agency for International Development (USAID), 63, 97–98, 205n5

verticality, 32–33, 109

Weber, Max, 7, 20
whole person discourse, 92, 172, 176–91, 199, 201
women. *See* gender
World Bank, 22, 90, 92
World Vision International (WVI), 106, 148, 161–62, 166

JILL DeTEMPLE

is associate professor of religious studies

at Southern Methodist University.